THE COPYRIGHT DIRECTIVE

UK IMPLEMENTATION

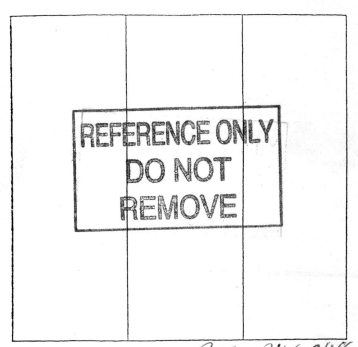

THE COPYRIGHT DIRECTIVE
UK IMPLEMENTATION

Trevor Cook
Lorna Brazell
Simon Chalton
Calum Smyth

BIRD & BIRD

JORDANS
2004

Published by
Jordan Publishing Limited
21 St Thomas Street
Bristol BS1 6JS

British Library Cataloguing-in-Publication Data
A catalogue record for this book is available from the British Library.

ISBN 0 85308 881 0

Typeset by MFK-Mendip, Frome, Somerset
Printed in Great Britain by MPG Books Ltd, Bodmin, Cornwall

PREFACE

On 31 October 2003 the Copyright and Related Rights Regulations 2003 came into effect, to implement in the United Kingdom EC Directive 2001/29/EC on the Harmonisation of Certain Aspects of Copyright and Related Rights in the Information Society. National implementation was due to have taken place by 22 December 2002, but the United Kingdom was not alone in delaying implementation. This was hardly surprising given the scope of the Directive and the difficulties in applying its provisions as to reservations and exceptions to national laws, which differ considerably in this respect.

The amendments introduced are likely to have a major impact upon users of copyright materials both in the physical and the electronic worlds. In the physical world, the removal of the exception permitting use of copyright materials in the course of commercial research will affect practically every organisation which carries out research. Where formerly the copying of extracts from materials was permitted, in future a licence is required and unlicensed use will be actionable as an infringement. In the elctronic world, the amendments grant new rights to copyright owners who protect their works through technological access controls. Both civil and criminal remedies are introduced to discourage the circumvention of such control mechanisms, in some cases exercisable not only by the copyright owner but also by the owner of intellectual property rights in the access control mechanisms.

Given the importance of these and other changes, we are very pleased to have had the opporutnity with our colleagues Simon Chalton and Calum Smyth to review in-depth the Directive, its origins in various international instrument and the eventual effects in the United Kingdom. We hope that the analysis which follows will prove useful to all those trying to make sense of the law in both its national and international contexts.

Lorna Brazell
Trevor Cook
March 2004

CONTENTS

TABLE OF CASES

References are to paragraph numbers.

TABLE OF STATUTES

TABLE OF STATUTORY INSTRUMENTS

References are to paragraph and Appendix numbers. Bold references indicate where material is set out in part or in full.

TABLE OF EUROPEAN AND INTERNATIONAL LEGISLATION

References are to paragraph and Appendix numbers. Bold references indicate where material is set out in part or in full.

Chapter 1

THE BACKGROUND TO THE COPYRIGHT DIRECTIVE AND AN HISTORICAL PERSPECTIVE

THE COPYRIGHT DIRECTIVE AND THE INFORMATION SOCIETY

1.1   Directive 2001/29/EC of 22 May 2001 ('the Directive') is titled 'on the harmonisation of certain aspects of copyright and related rights in the Information Society'. Its Recitals refer to a harmonised legal framework on copyright and related rights as fostering increased competitiveness in the areas of content provision and information technology and more generally across a wide range of industrial and cultural sectors.[1] The tenor of these and other Recitals reflects the growing use and importance of communications and information technology in the context of access to and use of content, including use of information contained in or derived from content.

1.2   This raises issues about the nature of information and the information society, the extent of the public domain in relation to information and the extent to which information in the public domain should be treated as freely accessible.

1.3   Although the Directive's reference in its title to harmonisation of copyright and related rights in the information society recognises the significance of information in today's world, the Directive does not distinguish between the protectable and unprotectable elements of information. It is generally accepted that ideas and principles, although they may be protectable by contract or under the laws of confidence and unfair trading, should not be protected by copyright. It is arguable that the Directive's harmonised reproduction right, right of communication and right of making available to the public and its obligations as to technical measures may have the indirect effect of protecting information as such, as well as directly protecting the works and productions with which the Directive is primarily concerned. This is because such works and productions carry, include and disclose such information which may not otherwise be accessible.

1.4   The term 'information' is defined by the *Concise Oxford English Dictionary* (10th edition, revised) as, first, 'facts or knowledge provided or learned as a result of research or study' and, secondly, as 'what is conveyed or represented by a particular sequence of symbols, impulses etc'. An example of this second core meaning is given as 'genetically transmitted information'. Such information, although transmitted genetically, may not yet be known: some such information, latent in the transmission,

---

1   See Recitals (2) and (4).

may never be known. Other information, not yet known, may be capable of being derived from, for example, a particular DNA sample or from a copyright database.

Information may thus alternatively be defined as 'that which is known or capable of being known', and so distinct from knowledge. All knowledge will include information, but not all information is knowledge.

1.5   As the Directive recognises in its title and its recitals, content is of growing importance in the information society. Content in this context may be taken to include information, both known and unknown although capable of being known, as well as copyright works, databases whether or not protected by copyright and information-related productions whether or not protected by related rights. Content is increasingly presented and processed in digital form and so is capable of extraction, manipulation, modification and further processing. Such processing may enable the extraction, extrapolation and derivation of underlying information from the original, even though such information may not be expressly identified in or disclosed by the original. At some point, legal protection of such information by copyright and related rights may be excessive, but the point at which the limits of such protection should be fixed is unclear. Even if such limits were clear under any rule of national law, a harmonised EU law is likely to be needed before a generally accepted rule on the limits of legal protection of information can be set within the European Union.

1.6   At present, the nearest we have to an international consensus on the legal protection of information as such is contained in Art 39(2) of the TRIPs Agreement[2] which provides:

> 'Natural and legal persons shall have the possibility of preventing information lawfully within their control from being disclosed to, acquired by, or used by others without their consent in a manner contrary to honest commercial practices so long as such information:
>
> (a)   is secret in the sense that it is not, as a body or in the precise configuration and assembly of its components, generally known among or readily accessible to persons within the circles that normally deal with the kind of information in question;
> (b)   has commercial value because it is secret; and
> (c)   has been subject to reasonable steps under the circumstances, by the person lawfully in control of the information, to keep it secret.'

The requirement that such protection should be available only to information 'lawfully within [a natural or legal person's] control' begs the question as to how and when such control may be secured and exercised.

1.7   The preamble to the World Intellectual Property Organization's Copyright Treaty 1996 (WCT)[3] recognises the need to maintain a balance between the rights of authors and the larger public interest, particularly in relation to education, research and access to information, as reflected in the Berne Convention.[4]

---

2   Agreement on Trade-Related Aspects of Intellectual Property, part of the suite of agreements concluded under the auspices of the General Agreement on Tariffs and Trade when the World Trade Organization was established.

3   See Appendix 6.

4   See **1.10**.

1.8   The public interest requires recognition and protection of the rights of authors and other rightholders in order to encourage the exercise of creativity and productivity by authors and others, which will in turn enable and protect learning, productivity and culture with their associated public and economic benefits. There is thus a public interest in protecting the works and productions of authors and others, provided that the protection given is in balance with the public interest in disclosure and use of information and in economic development and competition.

1.9   As between competition and protection, it may be said that protection should defer to competition at the point at which protection prevents or discourages competition in relation to content which is not directly or indirectly copied from protected works or productions. This is also in the interests of copyright itself, which can only thrive if there are effective markets for works and productions which are the subject of copyright and related rights.

THE BERNE CONVENTION

1.10   First established in 1886 and most recently revised in 1971, with amendments last made in 1979, the Berne Convention for the protection of literary and artistic works remains the foremost multilateral copyright treaty. It is based on the principle of national treatment, so that each country which is a Member of the Berne Union is required to give other Union Member nationals the same protection as that country gives to its own nationals. The Berne Convention also requires Members of the Union to recognise and protect certain minimum rights of authors: these rights include the rights to authorise copying, translation, public performance and broadcasting of literary and artistic works.

1.11   The term 'literary and artistic works' includes every production in the literary and artistic domain, whatever may be the mode or form of its expression.[5] Collections of literary and artistic works which, by reason of selection or arrangement of their contents, constitute intellectual creations are required to be protected as such, without prejudice to the copyright in each of the works forming part of such collections.[6]

1.12   The object of protection under the Berne Convention is the author's creative expression in literary or artistic work, not the work's underlying ideas or principles.

1.13   It is a requirement of the Berne Convention that the enjoyment and exercise of an author's rights under the Convention shall not be subject to any formality.[7] This requirement prevented the United States from joining the Berne Union until certain copyright marking requirements under US law had been removed. Formalities apart, it is a matter for national legislation in the countries of the Berne Union to prescribe that works in general, or any specific category of works, shall not be protected unless they have been fixed in some material form.[8]

---

5   Berne Convention, Art 2(1).

6   Article 2(5).

7   Article 5(2).

8   Article 2(2).

1.14   Broadly, civil law jurisdictions based on author's right (*droit d'auteur*) do not require fixation. Common law jurisdictions generally require some form of fixation as a prerequisite to copyright protection, although this is not required in the United Kingdom for artistic works. Since the principle of national treatment is required by the Berne Convention, a civil law author of a literary work seeking protection of that author's work under the Convention in a common law jurisdiction will need to show that the work in question has been fixed as required by that jurisdiction. In the United Kingdom, copyright does not subsist in a literary, dramatic or musical work unless and until it is recorded, in writing or otherwise, but it is immaterial whether the recording is by or with the permission of the author.[9] Recording in electronic form will usually be sufficient to show fixation and may be so even when the recording is of a transient copy in machine memory in the course of use of the work. It is less clear whether transient copying of a work in the course of electronic transmission through the United Kingdom (for example, by means of a communications system), will be sufficient to show that the work has been 'recorded, in writing or otherwise', for UK copyright qualification purposes. Since the Berne Convention leaves the issue of fixation to national law, a claim for copyright infringement in these circumstances may fail in the United Kingdom where it might succeed in a civil law jurisdiction. Widening use of the internet and other modern communications technology has made the point more significant since multiple and repetitive fixation and reproduction of copyright works has become an integral part of the communications process.

1.15   Although the Berne Convention remains the most widely established and authoritative multilateral treaty in the field of copyright and author's rights, its terms are broad and leave substantial freedom to Union Members to set their own laws. These laws may not make adequate provision for new technologies which are not explicitly covered by the Convention and which were not available when the Convention was last amended in 1979. It has been left to later international instruments, building on the foundation of Berne, to extrapolate and develop its principles to meet the world's evolving requirements.

OTHER MULTILATERAL INTERNATIONAL TREATIES

1.16   Despite the success of the Berne Convention, its prohibition on formalities deterred a substantial number of countries, including the United States and the Soviet Union, from adhering to it. For many years these countries were not covered by any international harmonising copyright treaty. In 1953 UNESCO promoted establishment of the Universal Copyright Convention (UCC), which avoided the Berne prohibition on formalities and so provided an alternative treaty which was joined by the United States in 1955 and by the Soviet Union in 1973. In many respects, the UCC followed Berne, notably in adopting the principle of national treatment. Many countries, including the United Kingdom, became members both of the Berne Convention and of the UCC.

1.17   When the United States joined the Berne Union in 1989 the urgent need for maintaining the UCC was largely removed. The Russian Federation joined Berne in

---

9   Copyright, Designs and Patents Act 1988, s 3(2) and (3).

1995. Accordingly, many of the UCC's Contracting States are now also members of the Berne Union, which provides a wider level of protection than does the UCC. The significance of the UCC has in consequence reduced, as have the prospects for its further development.

1.18   As the Berne Convention did not provide adequate protection for performers, for makers of instruments reproducing works mechanically, or for broadcasters, a diplomatic conference held in Rome led to the establishment in 1961 of the Rome Convention for the protection of performers, producers of phonograms and broadcasting organisations. Like the Berne Convention, the Rome Convention is based on the principle of national treatment which is for this purpose specifically defined but with special limitations. It provides mandatory exclusive rights for phonogram producers and broadcasting organisations but allows Contracting States to develop their own optional rights for performers, laying down no minimum standard of protection once the performer has consented to fixation of their performance. However, it has few members outside Europe.

1.19   The Rome Convention recognises related rights, so called because they are not strictly limited to the creative contributions of human authors. These related rights go further than the copyright and author's right concepts of protecting intellectual creativity, which are at the heart of Berne. The extension of protection to these related rights had become necessary because of technological developments made in the first half of the twentieth century and providing cheap and readily available means of reproducing and distributing records of works and of performances.

1.20   The term 'performers' is defined by the Rome Convention as meaning actors, singers, musicians, dancers and other persons who act, sing, deliver, declare, play in or otherwise perform literary or artistic works. 'Performance' is defined as the activity of a performer as such, and a 'phonogram' as an exclusively aural fixation of sounds of a performance or of other sounds. A 'producer of phonograms' means the person who, or the legal entity which, first fixes the sounds of a performance or other sounds, thus including sounds which are not sounds forming part of or related to a performance. A phonogram producer enjoys the right to authorise or prohibit the direct or indirect reproduction of his or her phonograms.

1.21   Under the Rome Convention broadcasting organisations enjoy the right to authorise or prohibit the fixation or rebroadcasting of their broadcasts, or the communication to the public of a television broadcast if made in a place accessible to the public against payment of a fee. 'Broadcasting' is defined as 'the transmission by wireless means for public reception of sounds or of images and sounds' and 'rebroadcasting' is defined as the simultaneous broadcasting by one broadcasting organisation of the broadcast of another broadcasting organisation.

1.22   In 1971 the Convention for the protection of producers of phonograms against unauthorised duplication of their phonograms (the Phonograms Convention) was established at Geneva. Unlike the Berne, UCC and Rome Conventions, the Phonograms Convention does not adopt the principle of national treatment but leaves each Contracting State free to establish, under its domestic law, protection of phonograms by copyright, by other specific rights, by unfair competition law or by criminal law. A Contracting State is free to use more than one of these means of protection: a national of a Contracting State is free to claim in any other Contracting

State the protection guaranteed by the Convention, but not free to claim other rights which may be available to nationals of that State but which go beyond the protection guaranteed by the Convention. The Convention adopts the definitions of 'phonogram' and 'producer of phonograms' contained in the Rome Convention, but contains new definitions of 'duplicate' and 'distribution to the public': the latter means 'any act by which duplicates of a phonogram are offered, directly or indirectly, to the general public or any section thereof'.

1.23   In 1994 the World Trade Organization Agreement ('the WTO Agreement') was concluded at the end of the Uruguay round of negotiations for revision of the General Agreement on Tariffs and Trade (GATT). The TRIPs Agreement formed part of the WTO Agreement and establishes high level standards for harmonisation of intellectual property rights to be adopted by Members of the WTO.

1.24   TRIPs is of wider application than are the earlier Conventions. It is a special agreement within the meaning of Article 20 of the Berne Convention: this Article provides that Governments of countries of the Berne Union may enter into agreements among themselves which grant to authors more extensive rights than those granted by Berne or which contain provisions not contrary to Berne. In addition to copyright, TRIPs deals with anti-competition practices in contractual licences relating to intellectual property rights and enforcement of intellectual property rights. It includes provisions dealing separately with trade marks, geographical indications, industrial designs, patents, topographies of integrated circuits, undisclosed information and unfair competition. Like Berne, TRIPs adopts the principle of national treatment but, unlike Berne and its successor Conventions, TRIPs includes provisions dealing with remedies and penalties for intellectual property rights infringement, for their enforcement, for resolution of disputes and for co-operation between Member countries. TRIPs may broadly be said to extrapolate but not restrict or replace Berne, bringing in provisions from the Rome and Phonogram Conventions and extending to other forms of intellectual property rights.

1.25   Most recently, two new treaties were proposed by the World Intellectual Property Organization (WIPO) at a diplomatic conference held in Geneva in 1996. WIPO was established under the World Intellectual Property Organization Convention (1967–1979) to promote the protection of intellectual property and administrative co-operation between the Unions established by the Paris Convention for Protection of Industrial Property, the Berne Convention and other international treaties and agreements. The 1996 treaties which it promoted were the WIPO Copyright Treaty (WCT) and the WIPO Performances and Phonograms Treaty (WPPT).

1.26   Like TRIPs, the WCT is also a special agreement within the meaning of Article 20 of the Berne Convention, and adds a new right of making available of a work to the public in such a way that members of the public may access the work from a place and at a time individually chosen by them (WCT, Art 8). The WCT also includes provisions relating to computer programs (Art 4) and to compilations of data (databases) (Art 5): these provisions require computer programs to be protected as literary works within the meaning of Article 2 of the Berne Convention, and protection of compilations of data or other material, in any form, which by reason of the selection or arrangement of their contents constitute intellectual creations (Art 5).

Article 11 of the WCT requires contracting parties to provide adequate legal protection and effective legal remedies against the circumvention of effective technological measures used by authors for the protection of their works against unauthorised acts, and Article 12 requires contracting parties to provide adequate and effective legal remedies against the removal of rights management information or the distribution of works or copies of works from which rights management information has been removed. These requirements motivated the inclusion of protection for technological measures and rights management information in the Directive.

1.27   The WPPT, adopted at the same 1996 diplomatic conference as the WCT, protects performers and producers of phonograms. The principle of national treatment applies. Protection is against reproduction, distribution, rental and making available on demand, and against circumvention of technological measures of protection. Rights management information is also protected. The WPPT does not derogate from or substitute for the Rome Convention.

EVOLUTION OF THE EU COPYRIGHT DIRECTIVES

1.28   The Commission of the European Communities issued its Green Paper on Copyright and the Challenge of Technology[10] in 1988 as a Consultative Document. Sub-titled 'Copyright issues requiring immediate attention' the Green Paper included chapters on distribution right, exhaustion and rental right, computer programs, databases and the role of the Community in multilateral and bilateral relations. It foreshadowed development of the *acquis communautaire* for which the Computer Programs Directive[11] provided the first building block. The Green Paper identified[12] the Community's fundamental concerns as:

–   ensuring the proper functioning of the Common Market so that creators and providers of copyright goods and services should be able to treat the Community as a single internal market;
–   developing policies to improve the capacity of the Community's economy in relation to its trading partners, particularly in such areas as the media and information; and
–   preventing misappropriation by others outside the Community of intellectual property resulting from creative effort and substantial investment within the Community.

1.29   The Green Paper recognised[13] that new dissemination and reproduction techniques had entailed the de facto abolition of national frontiers, increasingly making the territorial application of national copyright laws obsolete. These concerns and technological developments together required the harmonisation of national copyright laws.

1.30   Although expressed to be a Consultative Document limited to certain aspects of copyright, the Green Paper was the springboard from which the Community's

---

10   COM (88) 172 final.

11   Directive 91/250/EEC of 14 May 1991 on the legal protection of computer programs.

12   Paragraph 1.3.

13   Paragraph 1.4.1.

harmonisation policy and the *acquis communautaire* have been developed. It may be a matter for criticism that, without a single comprehensive policy put into effect through a pre-defined series of directives, development of the *acquis communautaire* by an iterative process has resulted in successive provisions lacking a single comprehensive scheme and coherent expression. Conversely, the development of successive directives dealing with particular aspects of copyright and meeting changing circumstances as they arise has enabled the *acquis* to be developed in a flexible way by responding to changing technology and commercial realities.

1.31   The first major component of the *acquis communautaire*, foreshadowed in the Green Paper,[14] was the Computer Programs Directive which, although titled generally as being on the legal protection of computer programs, is in fact limited to copyright issues. It includes definition of lawful user rights particularly with reference to a lawful acquirer's right to use a computer program for its intended purposes, a lawful user's right to make back-up copies necessary for lawful use, a lawful user's right to observe, study and test the functioning of a program in order to determine the ideas and principles which underlie it, and a lawful user's right of decompilation for the permitted purpose of ensuring interoperability (the ability of a computer program to run in conjunction with other independently created programs). The Directive is also concerned to ensure that copyright in computer programs (and the Directive's provisions extend to preparatory design material for computer programs) does not apply to ideas and principles which underlie any element of a computer program, including those which underlie its interfaces, and is available only for computer programs which are original in the sense that they are their authors' own intellectual creations.

1.32   The Computer Programs Directive is expressed[15] to be without prejudice to other legal provisions such as those concerning patent rights, trade marks, unfair competition, trade secrets, protection of semi-conductor products or the law of contract, except only that contractual provisions contrary to certain of the Directive's lawful user provisions are to be null and void. Competition law is left to limit the extent to which copyright may be applied and exercised in relation to computer programs, even when computer programs clearly fit within the Directive's framework of copyright protection. Notwithstanding that the Directive provides a right for a lawful user of a computer program to observe, study and test the functioning of the program in order to determine the ideas and principles which underlie any element of it, provided the user does so while performing any of the acts he is entitled to do, that right may not be denied by contract: nevertheless, any information obtained by exercise of the right may apparently be made subject to a separate obligation of confidence restricting the use of information so obtained. This illustrates the limits to which copyright may be applied to protect information relating to computer programs, but does not attempt to limit other non-copyright legal restraints on the use of such information, which restraints are not addressed by either this or subsequent Copyright Directives.

---

14   Chapter 5.

15   Article 9(1).

1.33   The Database Directive[16] followed the Computer Programs Directive but is more ambitious. It requires Member States to harmonise their copyright laws in relation to databases and defines the term 'database' as 'a collection of independent works, data or other materials arranged in a systematic or methodical way and individually accessible by electronic or other means'.[17] The Database Directive bases its copyright protection of databases on the Berne Convention, Article 2(5) of which requires collections of literary or artistic works which, by reason of the selection and arrangement of their contents, constitute intellectual creations, to be protected as such. The Database Directive provides, as a mandatory copyright exception in favour of the lawful user of a database, that the performance of any of the copyright-restricted acts set out in the Directive which are necessary for the purposes of access to the contents of the database and normal use of the contents by the lawful user shall not require the authorisation of the author of the database.[18] However, where the lawful user is authorised to use only part of the database this provision is to apply only for that part.[19] This mandatory exception may not be excluded by contract.[20] There are further permissive copyright exceptions which may, but need not, be transposed by Member States into their respective national laws,[21] so giving opportunities for disharmonisation: notably these permitted exceptions do not allow use of databases for commercial purposes, an element of the *acquis communautaire* which reappears, with added force, in the present Directive.

1.34   The Database Directive's most notable achievement is its creation of the new sui generis right in a database in favour of the database's maker where the maker can show that there has been a substantial investment in either the obtaining, verification or presentation of the contents of the database. The new sui generis right entitles the database's maker to prevent extraction and/or reutilisation of the whole or a substantial part of the contents of the database except with the maker's consent,[22] but the maker may not prevent a lawful user of a database which has been made available to the public in whatever manner from extracting or reutilising insubstantial parts of the database for any purpose whatsoever.[23] There are other permissive sui generis lawful user rights which Member States may adopt and which echo the permissive copyright lawful user rights in databases but, as for copyright, these permissive lawful user rights do not allow commercial use.

1.35   These complex provisions raise many issues in connection with access to and use of information contained in or derived from databases which have been made available to the public, as has been illustrated in the United Kingdom's first instance and Court of Appeal judgments in *British Horseracing Board and Others v William*

---

16   Directive 96/9/EC of the European Parliament and of the Council of 11 March 1996 on the legal protection of databases.

17   Article 1(2).

18   Article 6(1).

19   Article 6(1).

20   Article 15.

21   Article 6(2).

22   Article 7.

23   Article 8(1).

Hill Organization Limited.[24] The Court of Appeal's full judgment awaits the result of a reference by that Court to the European Court of Justice (ECJ), which reference is still pending as at February 2004.

1.36 In part, the failure of the *acquis communautaire* to answer these questions may be a consequence of the Commission's piecemeal development of a harmonised European copyright law, with successive Directives being expressed to be without prejudice to the provisions of earlier Directives.[25] In the result, lacunae in earlier Directives may be excluded from rectification by provisions of later Directives even when those later provisions might have provided answers to questions raised but unresolved by earlier Directives.

1.37 The Database Directive follows broadly the pattern established by the Computer Programs Directive but, because of the distinctive nature of databases, necessarily to some extent departs from that pattern. For example, 'Object of protection', 'Restricted acts' and 'Exceptions to restricted acts' appear as Article titles in both Directives, but the title 'Decompilation' in the Computer Programs Directive has no parallel in the Database Directive. This is an obvious consequence of the nature of the protection, and exceptions to protection, required for computer programs and databases respectively, but at a higher level the decompilation provision in the Computer Program Directive[26] springs from the same competition law motivation as the Database Directive's bar against a database maker's restriction of a lawful user's extraction and/or reutilisation of insubstantial parts of a database once that database has been made available to the public in any manner.[27] At the root of both computer program and database provisions is an awareness of, and some uncertainty about, the extent to which the protection provided by copyright, both in relation to computer programs and databases, and the protection provided by the sui generis right in relation to databases, should restrict access to, and subsequent use of, information as such. Perhaps it was felt that it was not sufficient to leave these issues to be separately dealt with by Community competition law. Resolution of these uncertainties may come from the ECJ's consideration and response to the pending reference to it by the Court of Appeal in *British Horseracing Board and Others v William Hill Organization Limited* referred to above, at least to the extent to which the sui generis right under the Database Directive should be allowed to control access to, and use of, information contained in or derived from a sui generis right protected database.

1.38 Other directives in the Commission's first series which have followed the Green Paper and which have formed part of the *acquis communautaire* are the Rental and Lending Right Directive,[28] the Broadcasting and Cable Retransmission Directive[29] and the Copyright and Related Rights Term Directive.[30]

---

24 [2001] RPC 612; [2001] EBLR 71; (2001) *The Times*, 23 February.

25 See, for example, Recital (20) to the Copyright Directive.

26 Computer Program Directive, Art 6.

27 Database Directive, Art 8(1).

28 92/100/EEC.

29 93/83/EEC.

30 93/98/EEC.

1.39   The E-Commerce Directive[31] has an indirect bearing on the Copyright Directive, and so on the *acquis communautaire* in relation to copyright, in that it includes limitations to the liability of internet intermediaries.[32] It is said that the E-Commerce Directive's provisions potentially provide sufficient protection against allegations of copyright infringement so as to have made unnecessary the mandatory exception contained in Article 5(1) of the Copyright Directive, which excludes from the harmonised reproduction right under Article 2 of the Copyright Directive temporary acts of reproduction which are transient or incidental and an integral and essential part of a technological process. A copy of Article 13 of the E-Commerce Directive appears at Appendix 8.

THE INTERNET AND THE DIGITAL AGENDA

1.40   The emergence of the internet as a universally available and widely used means of accessing, displaying and transferring content held on websites, with the ability to distribute copyright works, productions, performances and information at large from such websites, post-dated the publication of the Copyright Green Paper in 1988 and has become a dominant justification for the Directive.

1.41   The internet has moved the main focus of concern about piracy away from issues of one-to-one copying, home copying and distribution and rental rights of the kind which were canvassed in the Green Paper. New risks have emerged associated with digitisation, and subsequently untraceable reproduction, adaptation and distribution, of copyright material and of productions protected by related rights. The ability to access, download, transfer to third (non-EU) countries and subsequently to abuse, works and productions protected under harmonised EU copyright and related laws makes a harmonised body of EU copyright and related rights laws even more important. Although harmonisation within the European Union will not resolve wider global concerns, it can set a pattern which third countries may follow if they choose: it takes an initiative and may contribute to the creation of a more coherent global market and body of jurisdictions with common rules for dealing with the new range of problems raised by the internet and by digitisation of content. It also enables the European Union to conform to the WCT and the TRIPs Agreement and meshes with the US Digital Copyright Millennium Act (DCMA).

1.42   Within the European Union, the Directive requires harmonisation to WCT and TRIPs standards on the reproduction right, the right of communication to the public in relation to copyright works and the right of making available to the public other defined content protected by related rights.

1.43   The optional exceptions and limitations set out in Article 5(2) and (3) of the Directive have a counter-harmonisation effect. The extent to which they fragment the EU pattern of copyright and related rights will depend on the forms, and the extent to which, EU Member States choose to adopt these permitted derogations from the Community norm. Where optional exceptions and limitations are adopted by EU

---

31   2000/31/EC.

32   E-Commerce Directive, Art 13.

Member States, national laws will apply, although Community competition rules may override the application of national laws.

THE INFORMATION SOCIETY COPYRIGHT DIRECTIVE

1.44   The Directive has been described by Dr Jorg Reinbothe, Head of Unit at the Directorate General for the Internal Market at the European Commission, as the first of the second generation of the European Commission's Copyright Directives. He has described the first series of directives as the *acquis communautaire* and as a solid legislative framework, enacted between 1991 and 2001, concerning the 'pre-Information Society age'. He has said that the Information Society Copyright Directive is the most important initiative ever adopted at EU level in the area of copyright, filling gaps in the *acquis communautaire* of the first generation. It has harmonised the rights of reproduction and of making available content for all kinds of authors, performing artists, phonogram producers, film producers and broadcasting organisations. It has also introduced EU-wide protection of technological measures. The Directive came into force on 22 June 2001 and was required to be transposed into the laws of the Member States by 22 December 2002. Transposition of the Directive was a necessary precondition to ratification by the European Community and its Member States of the so-called 'internet treaties', the WCT and WPPT.

1.45   Although the Directive is important, it has been criticised on the following grounds:

–   it fails to achieve harmonisation, in particular in relation to its extended list of exceptions and limitations;[33]

–   the mandatory (Art 5(1)) exception for temporary acts of reproduction which are transient or incidental and an integral part of a technological process[34] is complex, unclear and arguably unnecessary having regard to Article 13 of the E-Commerce Directive.[35] Since the Article 5(1) exception does not apply either to computer programs or to databases it is also potentially defective; and

–   the Directive provides overly broad protection for technological measures to control access to and use of materials protected by copyright or by related rights.[36] This may provide legal protection for technological protection, where technological protection goes beyond the protection which copyright tradition-ally provides, by preventing access to materials, so preventing access to information as such where information is either contained in, or capable of being derived from, those materials.

These criticisms are fully considered in later chapters of this book.

---

33   Article 5(2) and (3).

34   Article 5(1).

35   See Appendix 8 below.

36   Article 6.

Chapter 2

DEVELOPMENT, SCOPE AND PROVISIONS OF THE COPYRIGHT DIRECTIVE

BACKGROUND TO DEVELOPMENT OF THE DIRECTIVE

2.1 Protecting copyright and related rights should stimulate creativity by allowing authors, performers, broadcasters and record and film producers the exclusive right to reproduce and disseminate their own creations. Much of the material that is protected by copyright tends to be recorded in physical goods such as cassettes, CDs, books, etc. However, in today's communication-driven environment and with the development of the information society, there has been a sharp increase in the distribution of such material in digitised form over electronic networks. Sophisticated technology has provided new forms of reproduction, such as the scanning of printed works and the storing of digitised material in computer memories. With its ability to distribute works worldwide at the push of a button, it is hardly surprising that the internet is such a popular means for circulating works.

2.2 Digitised copies can be 'perfect' reproductions of the original work. As a transmission medium, the internet is particularly suitable for communicating audio-visual material, software and databases, and so it is not surprising that internet piracy has so far had the greatest impact on the music and entertainment industries.

2.3 Delivering such products online has historically been governed by national legislation. However, the resulting imbalance between national laws of Member States was thought to be fragmenting the Single Market, distorting trade within the European Community. Consequently, the Commission Green Paper[1] contained proposals both to adapt and harmonise the principles of applying copyright protection to the new technology and to deal with the poor level of security associated with this medium. The Commission was concerned that the lack of regulation would make rightholders reluctant to provide their own content for insecure online services.

2.4 Following publication of the Green Paper, the Directive went through a turbulent 5 years of debate and aggressive lobbying, finally being adopted on 9 April 2001. The legislation itself has been heavily criticised as seriously flawed and has been accused of failing to provide sufficient harmonisation of copyright protection in the European Union – one of its primary objectives. 'Hard-fought compromises' and delicate balances struck during the tense negotiations are also said to be responsible for the lack of clarity in the Directive.

---

1   See **1.28** et seq.

2.5   Advocates for the adopted Directive, while accepting that some of the provisions are unclear, optimistically view the fierce negotiation as 'a positive contribution to the community legal order',[2] having forced a fundamental rethink of copyright's application to the information society. Conversely, critics of the Directive are in abundance. Due mainly to the ability of Member States to pick and choose from certain 'permitted exceptions' contained in the legislation, they argue that there is a complete lack of harmonisation. Similarly, the scope of the Directive is legally uncertain because it introduces new undefined terms such as 'voluntary agreements' and 'appropriate measures'.[3]

2.6   One thing is certain – the fierce debate that slowed the Directive's progress through the legislative process, and continued through its implementation at national level in Member States, is indicative of disagreements to come in future years during the review phase of its application.

AIMS OF THE DIRECTIVE

2.7   A proposal for a Copyright Directive was first put forward in January 1997. The draft Directive aimed to extend the nature of copyright protection to cover internet use and to implement international obligations contained in the 1996 WCT and WPPT.[4]

2.8   The Directive attempts to harmonise across Europe both the fundamental exclusive rights afforded to the owner of copyright and the exceptions to those rights. It also provides new rights favouring copyright owners who have tried to protect their works against unauthorised copying by using special technology such as copy control mechanisms and electronic rights management systems (ERMS).

2.9   During the legislative process, the Directive was the subject of prolonged lobbying by representatives from the music, film and publishing industries, the information technology and telecommunications sector and a large cross-section of artists and consumer groups. Groups such as authors and recording companies from the music industry lobbied to protect their rights from internet piracy, while consumer groups and IT/telecoms companies attempted to prevent heavy-handed measures affecting existing rights to copy and use an author's work (eg restricting temporary copying and private use).

2.10   It is important to note that the provisions of the Directive are expressly stated as being without prejudice to the Community provisions relating to computer programs, rental and lending rights, the broadcasting of programs by satellite and cable retransmission and the terms of copyright and database protections.[5]

2.11   In summary, the Directive provides for:

---

2   See Jeff Campbell and Walo Von Greyerz and Mark Hansen 'Why the Copyright Directive matters' (2001) VI(5) *Global Counsel* 15.

3   See, eg, Bernt Hugenholz 'Why the Copyright Directive is Unimportant and Possibly Invalid' [2000] EIPR 499.

4   See **1.25–1.27**.

5   See **1.31–1.38**.

- authors, performers, producers and broadcasting organisations to have exclusive rights over the reproduction by any means, communication to the public and distribution of their work;
- a narrow 'mandatory' exception to the exclusive right of reproduction for certain *temporary* acts of copying that form part of a technological process;
- protection against the circumvention of 'technological measures', in the form of new rights to act against persons circumventing or enabling others to circumvent them;
- a list of 'optional' exceptions to the exclusive rights of the copyright owner from which Member States can choose which they wish to implement; and
- the possibility of copyright owners receiving 'fair compensation' for certain excepted acts being carried out.

A full text of Directive 2001/29/EC is contained at Appendix 1.

RIGHTS

The reproduction right (Art 2)

2.12 The reproduction right set out in Art 2 provides protection for:

'authors in respect of their works, performers for fixations of their performances, phonogram producers for their phonograms, producers of the first fixations of films in respect of the original and copies of their films and broadcasting organisations for fixations of their broadcasts, whether they are transmitted by wire or air, including by cable or satellite'.

In each case, the author, performer or producer is given the exclusive right to authorise or prohibit copying – the most basic of all of the protections provided by copyright. It extends to reproduction whether 'direct or indirect, temporary or permanent ... by any means and in any form in whole or in part'.

2.13 Article 2 is drafted broadly so as to include temporary copies that may be made on computer networks. From the earliest Communications[6] released by the European Commission, the emphasis has always been on how material converted into electronic form and transmitted digitally has become more vulnerable to exploitation through copying. The Commission's aim was to reassess the level of protection provided across the European Union and to attempt to restore an equilibrium.

The communication to the public right (Art 3)

2.14 The Commission considered that 'on-demand' services were likely to be a major area of growth. Such interactive services were expected to allow members of the public to access digital material such as films, software or music, whatever their location and whatever their chosen time.

---

6 Communication on Copyright and Related Rights in the Information Society (20 November 1996).

2.15   Even from the original proposal,[7] it was clear that the exclusive rights granted under this Article were aimed at authors who chose to make their works available to the public on demand. The author's exclusive right therefore applies irrespective of the number of times the work or other subject matter is transmitted online. It is the act of offering *the service* which will need the authorisation of the rightholder.

2.16   Specifically, the rights in Article 3 are split into two sections: one dealing with the rights granted to authors and the other dealing with rights granted to 'related rights owners'. Article 3(1) gives *authors* an exclusive right to allow communication of their works by wire or wireless means *including* the making available to the public of their works in such a way that they may access them from a place and at a time chosen by them. As communications can be by wire or wireless means, the Article will cover both internet communications and conventional broadcasts on radio and television. Hence, Article 3.1 will provide authors with protection in the context of various media including websites.

2.17   Article 3(2) gives owners of so-called 'related rights' (ie performers, phonogram producers, film producers and broadcasting organisations) only the limited right of *making available to the public* by wire or wireless means their performances, phonograms, films and broadcasts so that members of the public may access them from a place and at a time individually chosen by them. In other words, these related rights owners only have control over the transmission of their works through interactive on-demand transmission.

Exhaustion

2.18   According to the principle of exhaustion of intellectual property rights, the holder of intellectual property rights in a work cannot control the distribution of a given physical copy of the work after that copy has been sold for the first time. Hence, for example, the buyer of a book or a CD is free to sell it on immediately should he or she so wish.

2.19   Recitals (28) and (29) draw a distinction between subject-matter exploited online and works that are distributed by being incorporated in a tangible article. An online delivery, as contemplated by Article 3, is considered by the Commission to be an online service and, as such, should not be subject to the principle of exhaustion. This is examined in more detail below.

2.20   Article 3(3) of the Directive therefore exempts the rights conferred by Article 3(1) and (2) from exhaustion. As a result an author, for example, will need to provide consent under Article 3 each and every time the work is communicated to the public.

The distribution right (Art 4)

2.21   Article 4 of the Directive provides an exclusive right to authorise or prohibit any form of distribution of original or copies of copyright works to the public. This right is available only to authors.

---

7   'Copyright and Related Rights in the Information Society – Proposal for Directive/Background' (Press release, 10 December 1997).

2.22   In this Article, distribution is defined to mean any form of distribution to the public, by sale or otherwise, of either the original works or tangible copies. The means of distribution can be by paper, CD, tape or other physical medium but the right does not extend to online distribution or to services in general.

2.23   Article 4(2) expressly applies the principle of exhaustion to this right to distribute 'tangible' articles, in line with Recital (28). Once a copy of a copyright work is sold for the first time in the European Union the rights owner cannot prevent further distribution of that copy of the work within the European Union. This provision has been specifically included to avoid confusion with the concept of 'international exhaustion' which applies in some Member States and can provoke significant obstacles to free trade. Where the principle of international exhaustion is accepted, the first sale of a work by the copyright holder or with his or her consent anywhere in the world is taken to have exhausted the copyright, so that the copy is thereafter in free circulation in any market.

Problems with exhaustion

2.24   Is the Commission right to classify online delivery as online services and make a distinction between this and a more tangible object? While it seems reasonable that online broadcasts and websites, which are intended to be accessed and viewed solely online, should not be subject to exhaustion, should the same rule apply to a purchase of an article, simply because it may be transmitted through the internet? After all, a purchaser of online products could transfer the downloaded item on to a carrier such as a diskette or CD-ROM, the sale of which *would* be subject to exhaustion.

2.25   Specifically, the Directive states:[8]

'The question of exhaustion does not arise in the case of services and on-line services in particular. This also applies with regard to a material copy of a work or other subject-matter made by a user of such a service with the consent of the rightholder. Therefore, the same applies to rental and lending of the original and copies of works or other subject-matter which are services by nature. Unlike CD-ROM or CD-I, where the intellectual property is incorporated in a material medium, namely an item of goods, every on-line service is in fact an act which should be subject to authorisation where the copyright or related right so provides.'

2.26   The Directive does not, however, differentiate between making a copyright work available to the public and a specific transmission of a work directed to an individual. An individual such as a purchaser has the direct consent of the copyright owner to make a permanent copy of the downloaded material. Conversely, there is no consent to copy by virtue of the works being broadcast.

2.27   It is arguable that a purchaser of a downloaded product who deletes his copy after selling it to a single third party should be allowed to make use of the doctrine of exhaustion. However, it is right that if the purchaser intends to keep a copy, further distribution of the product should be restricted. The current principle is that the owner should be compensated only for each single use of his copyright works, irrespective of whether the single use is subsequently transferred from one purchaser to another.

---

8   Recital (29).

2.28   Applying exhaustion to tangible objects does not, however, ensure that only a single use is made of the works. For example, software sold on CD-ROM may be copied to another tangible form or uploaded onto the internet for further distribution and is therefore just as susceptible to piracy as downloaded versions.

2.29   It is therefore somewhat illogical for the Directive to disapply the principle of exhaustion to individually sold products that are delivered online.

2.30   Notably, companies, such as Microsoft, that do provide products online are increasingly doing so on a licensing basis. This allows the copyright owner to impose conditions on the use of the software and avoid problems related to the exhaustion of rights altogether.

EXCEPTIONS UNDER ARTICLE 5

2.31   The Directive contains two types of exception to the exclusive rights in copyright work: mandatory and optional. All Member States are obliged to incorporate the mandatory exception when transposing the Directive into their respective national legislation. Member States do, however, have complete freedom to choose from a list of the 20 optional exceptions listed in the Directive. This list is exhaustive in that no Member State can provide any exception which does not appear on the list. Existing exceptions in force in Member States must be modified or deleted to the extent that they do not fall within the scope of the Directive's exhaustive list.

Mandatory exception

2.32   Only one exception is mandatory under the Directive. Article 5(1) obliges every Member State to provide an exception to the reproduction right in Article 2 for temporary acts of reproduction which:

(a)   are transient or incidental;
(b)   are an integral and essential part of a technological process;
(c)   have as their sole purpose to enable:
    (i)   a transmission in a network between third parties by an intermediary; or
    (ii)   a lawful use,
    of a work or other subject matter to be made; and
(d)   have no *independent economic significance*.

2.33   It is important to note that this mandatory exception relates only to the right of reproduction.

Historical development

2.34   The mandatory exception was intended to satisfy consumer groups concerned that, without an appropriate exception, acts of temporary copying such as internet browsing online servers making 'cache' copies of information would come within the scope of copyright infringement.[9]

---

9   See 'Copyright and Related Rights in the Information Society – Proposal for Directive/ Background' (10 December 1997).

2.35 The mandatory exception has been through some dramatic changes. The European Parliament first amended the Article to introduce the concept of allowing temporary copies that are an integral 'and essential' part of a technological process[10] but without any reference to or indication of purpose. Further, the authorisation of the rightholders was also required.

2.36 To better understand the motivations behind some of the amendments made to the legislation, it is necessary to look at the technology concepts in more detail.

Technical scope

2.37 An internet cache sits between the web server computer and the computers of clients who are making requests for HTML pages, images and files (known as objects) over the internet. In this sense, caching means saving a copy of this original information so that if there is another request for the same object it can be satisfied by using the existing copied version rather than requesting the same information again from the web server. Such 'server caching' reduces both the time taken for the information to return to the user and the amount of information that must be downloaded from the web server.[11]

2.38 Caching may also occur on the end user's system, rather than on the web server. During this 'client caching' the end user's browser may copy recently downloaded information to the end user's cache memory so that a request to access that information again does not necessitate having to fetch it from the internet. Again, this reduces the time taken and processing capacity needed to retrieve the information. Neither form of caching described here is permanent, although cached copies may be stored for up to a matter of days or weeks.

2.39 The caching mechanisms described help the systems and the internet environment to function efficiently, and so one would think they should naturally fall within the scope of the mandatory exception.

2.40 However, taken literally, this is not necessarily the case. The wording of the provision gives little guidance as to what may be considered to be an 'integral and essential part' of a technological process. Literally, caching by its nature is non-permanent or transient. Its incorporation into computer systems may also allow it to be described as integral. However, whether caching is essential for the operation of the internet is arguable. Without it, the speed of communication would be greatly reduced but information would nonetheless pass.

2.41 An obvious worry expressed by various information technology groups was that operations such as caching, while permissible, would, under the proposed amended legislation, require the individual authorisation of each rightholder. Specifically, the European Parliament amendments stated that 'Transient ... acts of reproduction ... shall be exempted from the rights set out in article 2. Such uses must be authorised by the right holders or permitted by law and must have *no economic significance* for the right holders' (emphasis added). This was rightly criticised as

---

10 EP Opinion 1st Reading, PE T4–0094/1999.

11 See Mark Nottingham 'Caching Tutorial for Web Authors and Web Masters' (21 June 1999) (www.wdvl.com/internet/cache/index.html).

impractical, if not impossible, since obtaining an owner's explicit permission for each act of temporary caching of copyright materials would cause unwarranted delay in the operation of the internet. The proposal was also misconceived since, if express permission were to be obtained, this would amount to a licence in each case, vitiating the need for an exemption from copyright. Similarly, the requirement of having *no* independent economic significance seemed very restrictive. Potentially, all works that are protected by copyright can be said to have at least some economic significance.[12]

2.42   The Common Position[13] reached in 2000 relieved many of these concerns by clarifying that the sole purpose of the reproduction should be '*a transmission in a network between third parties by an intermediary, or a lawful use*' in Article 5 and by removing the requirement for the copyright owners' authorisations. There was acceptance that the Directive should not unduly hinder the effective operation of the worldwide web for those who place copyright material on the internet or those who transmit or carry such material.

2.43   Recital (33) of the Directive now expressly refers to the mandatory exception including acts that enable browsing and 'caching to take place including those that enable transmission systems to function efficiently provided that the intermediary does not modify the information'.

2.44   The current wording of the provision has nevertheless continued to be criticised as swinging too far in favour of copyright owners. There is still some concern that such protection will stifle the internet's openness. The requirement that the copy have 'no independent economic significance' also remains. Although the Commission has acknowledged the controversial nature of the exception, it maintains that the extensive lobbying has now led to wording that provides a 'satisfactory balance'.[14]

Optional exceptions

Historical development

2.45   The Green Paper originally put forward by the European Commission recognised that the scope of the reproduction right needed careful consideration because so many national exceptions had been introduced by Member States, by virtue of Article 9(2) of the Berne Convention. The Commission warned that a 'degree of harmonization will be needed to resolve these problems', but has been criticised at the same time for not looking at the national problems or solutions in sufficient detail.

2.46   In reality, the national exceptions recognised by Member States represent the way business has developed in those jurisdictions and so are understandably largely different from one another in their scope and operation. To harmonise such different provisions across Member States, it has been argued, is worthy of its own separate

---

12   See, eg, Paul Festa 'Caching caught in copyright debate', CNET News.com, 3 March 1999.

13   Council Common Position, CSL 9512/1/2000.

14   'Commission welcomes Council agreement on directive on copyright in the information society' (Press release, 9 June 2000).

legislative exercise.[15] Although the Commission aimed to keep the exemptions to the reproduction right to a minimum, the complex negotiations of the Council Working Group resulted in many of the national exemptions being retained in the Directive.

The exceptions

2.47   There are 20 optional exceptions set out in the Directive.[16] These make up an exhaustive list. Each exception may be transposed into national law, in each case entirely at the discretion of the relevant Member State. As already mentioned, the use of such a varied range of exceptions has been heavily criticised as giving Member States too much leeway for creating their own rules and therefore defeating the point of harmonisation.

2.48   In addition, the idea of having a set of limitations set in stone has come under fire as being conceptually too inflexible to deal with those unforeseen situations that frequently arise in a context as fast moving as the internet environment. Of comparatively little consolation is the incorporation of a so-called 'grandfather clause', included to allow Member States to continue to apply existing exceptions but only in minor cases and only for analogue use.[17]

2.49   The optional exceptions are divided into:

(a)   those applicable only to the reproduction right;[18]
(b)   those applicable to both the reproduction right and the right of communication to the public.[19]

2.50   As exceptions to the reproduction right, the Directive permits:

(a)   reproductions on paper or any similar medium effected by photographic techniques (with the exception of sheet music), on condition that the rightholder receives fair compensation;[20]
(b)   reproductions on any medium by natural persons for private use for ends that are neither directly nor indirectly commercial, on condition that the rightholder receives fair compensation accounting for any technological measures used;[21]
(c)   reproductions by publicly accessible libraries, educational establishments, museums or archives which are not for direct or indirect economic or commercial advantage;[22]
(d)   ephemeral recordings of works made by broadcasting organisations using their own facilities and for their own broadcasts;[23] and

---

15   Bernt Hugenholtz 'Why the Copyright Directive is Unimportant and Possibly Invalid' [2000] EIPR 499.

16   Article 5(2) and (3).

17   See 'Commission welcomes Council agreement on a directive on copyright in the information society' (Press release, 9 June 2000).

18   Ie Article 2.

19   Ie Articles 2 and 3.

20   Article 5(2)(a).

21   Article 5(2)(b)

22   Article 5(2)(c).

23   Article 5(2)(d).

(e) a right for social institutions pursuing non-commercial purposes (such as hospitals or prisons) to make reproductions of broadcasts, on condition that the rightholder receives fair compensation.[24]

2.51 Seemingly the Directive contains different tests of commercial benefit for different exceptions. Should a Member State choose to implement an exception for publicly accessible libraries (see **2.50**(c) above) those libraries can only carry out specific acts of reproduction which are not for 'direct or indirect economic commercial *advantage*'. By comparison, the private use exception in Article 5(2)(b) (see **2.50**(b) above) provides that the reproduction must be for 'ends that are neither directly nor indirectly commercial'. There is likely to be much debate as to whether prohibiting the reproduction of copyright works for an indirect commercial advantage confers wider protection than prohibiting 'ends' that are indirectly commercial.

Private use and fair compensation

2.52 Article 5(2)(b) – the exception of copying for 'private use' – was also the subject of fierce lobbying. The resulting provision includes a concept of 'fair compensation' and of 'technological measures'.[25] Both the exception to reproduction by photographic or similar technique on a physical medium (**2.50**(a) above) and the exception to the reproduction by social institutions of broadcasts (**2.50**(e) above) are accompanied by the requirement that the rightholders should receive 'fair compensation'.

2.53 Levies have been used in continental Europe to compensate rightholders for the private copying of copyright works since the early 1980s. Levy systems allow the private reproduction of specific works in return for a payment distributed between affected rightholders. A levy is usually imposed on the importer or manufacturer of equipment or storage media (eg tape recorders, video tapes, etc).

2.54 Historically, levies of this type were introduced when it was difficult to control private reproduction of copyright works in analogue form. In today's environment of digital works it is much easier to track and control reproduction of copyright works using digital technology. One particular problem with the concept of compensatory levies is the idea of 'free riders'. Although not all technical equipment will be used for reproduction of copyright works, as the levy is imposed on every purchaser of the technical equipment at point of sale, those buyers who are not using the equipment for the reproduction of copyright works are subsidising or giving a 'free ride' to those who are.

2.55 To avoid free-riding, the UK legislature introduced the idea that compensation should only be paid if the copying caused economic harm to the rightholders. For example, the domestic use of a recording of a broadcast or cable programme to enable the works to be reviewed or listened to at a more convenient time ('time-shifting') causes no such harm, and was expressly permitted under UK legislation.[26]

---

24 Article 5(2)(e).

25 Technological measures are dealt with in detail in Art 6 of the Directive and are examined later in this chapter.

26 Copyright, Designs and Patents Act 1988 (CDPA 1988), s 70.

2.56   In drafting the proposal for the Directive, the Commission was of the view that it was too early to predict the future development of the digital copying market.[27] Accordingly, without having the experience of digital piracy occurring on the widespread level that it does today, the Commission was unable to predict whether technical systems would be sufficient to allow rightholders to control the private copying exception when exercising their exclusive rights. The Commission thought it premature to attempt to harmonise a solution in relation to digital private copying and so left the decision of whether and how to implement this exception to the Member States.

2.57   Any such exception implemented by a Member State would still have to satisfy the Berne Convention 'three-step test' incorporated into the Directive at Article 5(5). The three-step test is discussed later in this chapter at **2.65**.

2.58   Indeed, with the arrival of new technologies, such as MP3 compressed digital audio files, and equipment with greater copying capability, it will not be long before equipment and systems that can download entire music albums directly to customers' personal devices become widely available.[28] It therefore seems that there is a real prospect that Member States will be forced to start imposing national levies on items such as PCs and mobile phones.[29]

2.59   Recital (35) of the Directive provides guidelines for ascertaining the level of fair compensation. These include:

–   the harm to the rightholders resulting from the act in question;
–   whether rightholders have already received payment in another form (eg licence fee); and
–   the degree of use of technological protection measures (as referred to in Article 6).

2.60   Account must be taken of the particular circumstances of each case. Where the prejudice to the rightholder is minimal, no obligation for payment may arise. For the moment, there seems to be little guidance as to what would be considered as minimal harm and what level of prejudice would be necessary to give rise to an obligation to pay fair compensation.

2.61   The term 'technological protection measures' refers to copy control techniques, such as encryption, used by rightholders to prevent piracy of their works. If such technological measures are applied these must be taken into account in any assessment of what fair compensation should be. Although no rightholder should be obliged to use copy control technology, the rightholder should not be rewarded for failing to do so. Similarly, it would be unfair to impose a levy in return for allowing reproduction which was not then possible due to the implementation of a technological measure, preventing work from being copied. How these factors should be weighted is left to each Member State to determine. The legal protection provided

---

27   'Copyright and Related Rights in the Information Society – Proposal for Directive/Background' (10 December 1997).

28   Mark Ward 'Music downloads on your mobile', BBC News Online, 13 March 2003.

29   Michael Hart 'The Copyright in the Information Society Directive: An Overview' [2002] EIPR 63.

for technological measures by the Directive is considered in more detail below, from **2.67**.

Exceptions to rights of reproduction and communication to the public – Article 5(3)

2.62   Article 5(3) sets out the optional exceptions from both the exclusive rights of reproduction and communication to the public. The precise text is set out at Appendix 1 but, in brief, the exceptions are:

(a)   use for the sole purpose of illustration for teaching, scientific research so long as it is justified by the non-commercial purpose to be achieved;

(b)   use for the benefit of people with a disability, such use being directly related to the disability and of a non-commercial nature;

(c)   reproduction by the press, communications to the public or making available published articles on economic, political or religious topics in cases where use is not expressly reserved;

(d)   quotations for criticism or review relating to a work that has already been lawfully made available to the public;

(e)   uses for public security, performance or reporting of administrative, parliamentary or judicial proceedings;

(f)   use of political speeches, public lectures;

(g)   use during religious or official celebrations organised by a public authority;

(h)   use of works to be located permanently in public places;

(i)   incidental inclusion of a work in other material;

(j)   use for advertising the public exhibition or sale of artistic works, as necessary to promote the event but excluding other commercial use;

(k)   use for caricature, parody or pastiche;

(l)   use for the demonstration or repair of equipment;

(m)   use of an artistic work in the form of a building, drawing or plan of a building for reconstructing the building;

(n)   use by communication or making available for research or private study to members of the public by dedicated terminals on the premises of public libraries, educational establishments, etc[30] of works contained in their collections and which are not subject to purchase or licensing terms; and

(o)   use in 'certain other cases of minor importance' that have already been implemented under national law provided they only relate to analogue uses, do not affect the free circulation of goods within the Community and are without prejudice to the other exceptions.

2.63   Importantly, under Article 5(3)(a), use for the sole purpose of scientific research is accepted 'to the extent justified by the non-commercial purpose to be achieved'. This is a major departure from the historical position in the United Kingdom which imposed no requirement that the research be non-commercial.[31] This will be good news for bodies such as the Copyright Licensing Agency, which will be seeking to extend their licensing schemes to cover companies carrying on research for commercial purposes.

---

30   As referred to in Article 5(2)(c).

31   CDPA 1988, s 29(1).

2.64 Examining the precise wording of Article 5(3), it is interesting to note that many of the optional exceptions are dependent on the need to include with the copyright works information identifying the source (such as the author's name) unless this turns out to be otherwise impossible. More specifically, this applies to reproduction for teaching or scientific research (Article 5(3)(a)), by the press (Article 5(3)(c)), for criticism or review (Article 5(3)(d)) and use of political speeches and extracts of public lectures (Article 5(3)(f)).

The three-step test

2.65 The Berne Convention for the Protection of Literary and Artistic Works provides the international framework for copyright protection. Article 9(1) of the Convention confers on a copyright-holder the exclusive right to authorise the reproduction of copyright works, in any manner or form. Article 9(2) then sets out a so-called 'three-step test' which must be satisfied by any exception to the exclusive rights of reproduction introduced by a Berne Convention country.[32]

2.66 Article 5(5) of the Directive follows the wording of the Berne Convention and states that the exceptions:

–   shall only be implied in certain special cases,
–   which do not conflict with a normal exploitation of the work or other subject matter, and
–   which do not unreasonably prejudice the legitimate interests of the rightholder.

Accordingly, whenever a Member State introduces an Article 5 exception, it must also satisfy this three-step test.

TECHNOLOGICAL MEASURES AND CIRCUMVENTION

2.67 Article 6 of the Directive deals with protection against the circumvention of measures designed to prevent or restrict copyright infringement under the Directive, the so-called technological measures.

Background to technological measures

2.68 The technological measures provision caused more controversy than any other Article of the Directive. From an early stage the Commission was advocating not only that protection should be afforded against acts of circumvention themselves, but also that there should be controls on the products and services that facilitate the circumvention.[33]

2.69 It was a requirement in both 1996 WIPO Copyright Treaties that the signatory States provide legal protection to forms of technology implemented to control the copying or use of and access to works subject to copyright protection. For example, a

---

32 See also Article 10 of WIPO Copyright Treaty 1996 and Article 13 of the Agreement on Trade-related Aspects of Intellectual Property Rights.

33 See 'Copyright and Related Rights and the Information Society – Proposal for Directive/ Background' (10 December 1997).

copy-control mechanism might allow a record company to stop a potential infringer from making a reproduction of a CD.

2.70   The need for protection technology such as encryption software or other copy-control mechanisms has increased due to the flawless nature of digital copies and the ease with which they can be distributed, for example, using the internet. It simply is not feasible for a copyright-holder to identify and pursue in the courts every potential infringer, since enormous numbers of individuals can each be making small numbers of copies. Without technological (as opposed to legal) protection right-holders have a greatly reduced ability to enforce the exclusivity of their rights and so there is less incentive to make their works available through such an insecure environment. As copy-control mechanisms have progressed in sophistication, so have the means used to defeat them. However, there are problems with providing legal protection for such technological solutions. Although it is true that the Commission has tried to balance the increased vulnerability of copyright material in digital form with the appropriate level of protection, questions remain over issues such as how the new provisions operate alongside the increased use of technological means installed specifically to prevent the reproduction of copyright works in digital form.[34]

The provisions

2.71   Article 6(1) obliges Member States to provide adequate legal protection against the circumvention of 'effective technological measures' that are carried out in the knowledge of pursuing that objective (or where the perpetrator has reasonable grounds to know they are pursuing that objective). Article 6(3) defines technological measures as any technology, device or component that, in the normal course of its operation, is designed to prevent or restrict acts not authorised by the rightholder. Article 6(3) goes on to say that technical measures are 'effective' where:

> 'the use of a protected work is controlled by the rightholders through application of an access control or protection process (such as encryption or a copy control mechanism) which achieves the protection objectives'.

2.72   For example, a hacker who successfully cracks encryption technology being used on software, with the intention of obtaining unauthorised access to the source or object code, would fall within the ambit of the protection envisaged by Article 6(1).

2.73   Article 6(2) obliges Member States to give legal protection against the manufacture, import, distribution, sale, rental, advertisement for sale or rental, or possession for commercial purposes of devices, products or components, or the provision of services which:

- are promoted, advertised or marketed for the purposes of circumvention of; or
- have only limited commercially significant purpose or use other than to circumvent; or
- are primarily designed, produced, adapted or performed for the purpose of enabling or facilitating the circumvention of,

any effective technological measures.

---

34   Michael Hart 'The Copyright in the Information Society Directive: An Overview' [2002] EIPR 63.

2.74   Therefore, the legislation will even catch circumvention devices which have uses other than the circumvention of technological measures, if those other uses have either a limited commercially significant purpose or if the device is 'primarily designed' to circumvent such technology. It is also worth noting that the protection against circumvention also covers the provision of services. Therefore, any instructions or details on how to circumvent copy-protection mechanisms, posted on the internet or otherwise, will also be covered by the Directive's provisions.

2.75   Although it seems that Article 6 has a broad scope covering both the act of circumvention and the trafficking of any tools used to circumvent (tools which are in themselves a broad category), Recital (48) states that it should not prohibit devices that have a commercially *significant* purpose other than to circumvent the technical protection and that all legal protection should respect 'proportionality'. However, there is no guidance in the Directive as to what is considered proportional.

2.76   The protection provided by Article 6 should not prevent the normal operation of electronic equipment and there is no obligation to design devices, products, components or services to correspond to technological measures. Consequently, technology companies do not have to respond to new copy-control mechanisms that are unilaterally introduced by rightholders by introducing new equipment to avoid anti-circumvention liability. Nonetheless the provision has in turn given rise to a need for 'industry to industry' agreements on standards for copy-control mechanisms such as encryption types. This approach has been applauded by some as 'technologically-neutral' legislation which avoids imposing any requirement for manufacturers to comply with technical standards laid down in law.[35] Instead of focusing on the technology, the legislation can focus on protection against pirates and whatever processes they use to gain unauthorised access.

2.77   However, despite the benefits of 'technologically-neutral' legislation, many problems still remain with the drafting of Article 6 of the Directive. For example, the Directive is without prejudice to the Computer Programs Directive, Article 7 of which provides legal protection against any means, the 'sole intended purpose' of which is to facilitate the circumvention of any technical device which may have been applied to protect a computer program. Hence, if there is another intended purpose which is lawful and exists alongside an intended purpose to circumvent, such means are not outlawed under the Computer Programs Directive. Under the Copyright Directive a broader test is applied in that the means are outlawed if any other intended purpose they have is of limited commercial significance or the products are 'primarily' designed to facilitate circumvention. Different standards would appear to apply to acts of identical intent.

Technological measures versus copyright exceptions

2.78   The major debate in relation to Article 6 was the interaction between the protection of technological measures and the lawful exceptions included in Article 5. If rightholders are able to have and enforce complete control over access and use of copyright works through technological measures such as encryption, users wishing to

---

35   See Jeff Campbell, Walo Von Greyerz and Mark Hansen 'Legal Recognition for Copy Protection Systems' (1999) IV *Global Counsel* 14.

exercise their lawful rights under an Article 5 exception may be prevented from doing so, contrary to the spirit of the legislation which confers the right in the first place. Furthermore, should the user wishing to use the technologically protected works attempt to do anything about the lack of access, he or she would then be liable for circumventing technical measures under Article 6(1). Negotiations surrounding the relationship between technological measures and limitations to copyright were so intense they nearly halted the entire Directive. The resulting solution is the less than legally certain compromise found in Article 6(4).

2.79   Article 6(4) states that:

'Notwithstanding the legal protection provided for in paragraph 1, in the absence of voluntary measures taken by rightholders, including agreements between rightholders and other parties concerned, Member States shall take appropriate measures to ensure that rightholders make available to the beneficiary of an exception or limitation provided for in national law in accordance with Art. 5(2)(a), (2)(c), (2)(d), (2)(e), (3)(a), (3)(b) or (3)(e) the means of benefiting from that exception or limitation, to the extent necessary to benefit from that exception or limitation and where that beneficiary has legal access to the protected work or subject-matter concerned.

A Member State may also take such measures in respect of a beneficiary of an exception or limitation provided for in accordance with Art. 5(2)(b), unless reproduction for private use has already been made possible by rightholders to the extent necessary to benefit from the exception or limitation concerned and in accordance with the provisions of Art. 5(2)(b) and (5), without preventing rightholders from adopting adequate measures regarding the number of reproductions in accordance with these provisions . . .'

2.80   There is little to assist in interpreting 'voluntary measures by rightholders including agreements between rightholders and other parties concerned'. It has been suggested that such measures could by their nature allow only eligible users to access the works,[36] although it is not clear how this would operate. Similarly, what will be the nature of agreements between rightholders and other parties and when, in relation to accessing the works, will such agreements be entered into?

2.81   Recital (51) of the Directive attempts to resolve the situation by obliging Member States to take 'appropriate measures' to ensure that the beneficiaries of any of the exceptions in Article 5 are provided with the necessary means to benefit from those exceptions. However, Recital (51) only imposes this obligation on Member States if voluntary measures are absent after a 'reasonable period' of time.

2.82   It is unclear both what a 'reasonable period' should be for rightholders to give beneficiaries the use of lawful exceptions under the Directive and what is meant by Member States taking 'appropriate measures'.

2.83   Article 6(4) specifically deals with the interaction between technological measures and the private use exception in Article 5(2)(b). Member States may take appropriate measures to ensure that lawful users can benefit from the private use exception but they are under no obligation to do so. Further, Member States are specifically excluded from taking such appropriate measures if a reproduction for private use has already been made possible by the rightholder to the extent necessary

---

36   See Bernt Hugenholtz 'Why the Copyright Directive is Unimportant and Possibly Invalid' [2000] EIPR 499.

for those who wish to benefit from the private use exception. Consider, for example, a technological protection measure such as encryption that is introduced to prevent ordinary television viewers from recording a transmitted programme. Although such recording is explicitly allowed under UK law as time-shifting,[37] the UK Government would not be *obliged* under the Directive to do anything to bring the broadcaster into line to make the programme available.[38]

2.84 These provisions, dealing with the overlap between technological processes and the exceptions to the exclusive rights, apply solely to the prohibition of circumvention in Article 6(1) and not to the preparation of circumventing devices prohibited under Article 6(2). This produces a bizarre result: where a rightholder has protected copyright works by means of a technological measure, although circumvention may be exempted under Article 6(4), the means by which the exempted use is facilitated remains outlawed by virtue of Article 6(2).

2.85 Although Article 6(4) has been subject to considerable criticism, it has also been praised for having the clear intention to allow Member States to require copyright works to be made available and to give them the flexibility to do it in a way that does not contradict national laws.[39] It remains to be seen how the balance will ultimately work out.

Technological measures and fair compensation

2.86 The exceptions permitted by the Directive may also provide for fair compensation to be received by the rightholder. The provisions suggest that a rightholder should not be rewarded for failure to adequately protect its copyright work with copy-control mechanisms by way of remuneration through compensation. (A good comparison with home insurance policies has been made.[40] Any insurance company will require the home owner holding the policy to comply with certain safeguards, such as locking the front and back doors when leaving. If these tasks are not carried out it would invalidate the protection provided by the policy and compensation would not be payable by the insurance company if the house is burgled.)

2.87 However, it is unclear how the proposed fair compensation system will operate in practice or how it will affect existing levying schemes. It will no longer be possible for levies to be set at arbitrary levels. Existing mechanisms for the collection of copyright levies – for example, through collection societies – will need to be adapted to reflect that the compensation must account for the income lost by the rightholder. The actual losses incurred through exceptions such as private copying will be difficult to quantify and such losses should be clearly distinguished from the damage incurred through piracy.

---

37 CDPA 1988, s 70.

38 See Michael Hart 'The Copyright in the Information Society Directive: An Overview' [2002] EIPR 63.

39 Jeff Campbell, Walo Von Greyerz and Mark Hansen 'Why the Copyright Directive Matters' (2001) VI(5) *Global Counsel* 15.

40 Ibid.

Types of technological measures

2.88   In practice, it will take some time for sectors such as the music and video industries to decide how to integrate technological protections allowing for limited private copies to be made, how this system should operate between the rightholder and the vendor of the commercial recording and how fair compensation to the rightholders is quantified and levied. Undoubtedly, this will depend upon the extent to which copy control mechanisms are used in practice and how easily they are installed. Currently, rightholders have various technological measures available to them to ensure some protection against circumvention. These are:

(a) **Encryption techniques**

Works may be sold in encrypted format, and then decrypted by the user by means of a key. This key may come in the form of a password or by decryption software installed on a user's machine. However, once the encryption has been broken, decryption keys can become widely available through media such as the internet. As a result, the main disadvantage of encryption protections will be a vulnerability to hacking.

(b) **Tracing techniques**

'Digital watermarks' may be used to track copies of works. For example, such techniques can register copying and further distribution of the works and provide a direct link, tying the copyright owner to the works. The watermark operates much like those found on bank notes and consists of only minor changes that are practically undetectable. However, problems do exist with digital watermarks such as incompatibility with older playing systems and their susceptibility to removal. Unlike encryption techniques, tracing helps only to identify the infringing users; it does not prevent copying from taking place. It is still necessary for the copyright to be enforced by the rightholder.

(c) **Hardware**

It has been proposed that the physical hardware used to play, for example, film or music works, could contain anti-circumvention mechanisms. Again, this solution is far from perfect and would call for unified industry standards. Although not as susceptible as encryption to widespread circumvention, permanently modified equipment could potentially prevent reproduction which is permitted under a copyright exception. Further, periodic upgrading of the technology, once redundant, would be costly for consumers.

Although there are some obvious problems with all of the technological measures listed above, they should go some way to prevent copyright infringement by the less determined users.

Electronic rights management information (ERMI)

2.89   During the early stages of the Directive it was thought that to impose a rights management information scheme would have the effect of imposing formalities which are not permitted under the Berne Convention.[41]

2.90   The initial proposal from the Commission[42] emphasised the importance for rightholders better to identify their work and to provide information about the terms and conditions of use of the work. It was thought particularly important in the light of the increasingly wide scope of distribution available through means such as computer networks.[43] Copyright owners who incorporate ERMI into their works would 'render easier the management of rights attached to them'.

2.91   Indeed, the concept of properly attaching identifying information to copyright works pervades some of the exceptions in Article 5(3), where the permitted copyright use is available only if the source and author's name are acknowledged.

2.92   Typically, rights management information systems include providing for digital watermarking and digital object identifiers. The inclusion of rights management information on copyright works is at the discretion of the rightholder under the Directive.

2.93   Article 7 of the Directive states that Member States must provide protection against the removal or alteration of ERMIs or against the distribution, broadcasting, importation for distribution, communication or making available to the public of works where the ERMI has been removed or altered without authority. However, the protection applies only if the person in question knows or has reasonable grounds to know that by doing so he is 'inducing, enabling, facilitating or concealing' an infringement of any copyright or similar rights such as database rights.

2.94   This is a potentially broad Article and would cover many acts: from the detailed removing of a digital watermark from a protected work to the distribution of a piece of software where the electronic on-screen copyright notice has been altered or removed.

2.95   In addition, ERMI is likely to include some form of processing of personal data, not only of the copyright owner but also potentially of the user if the user's online behaviour is being monitored or recorded. Accordingly, any rights management information systems must incorporate appropriate safeguards to comply with data protection legislation.

---

41   See Opinion of the Economic and Social Committee on the 'proposal for a European Parliament and Council Directive on the harmonization of certain aspects of copyright and related rights in the Information Society'.

42   COM (97) 628, submitted by the Commission on 21 January 1998.

43   Recital (33) of COM (97) 628.

COMMON AND FINAL PROVISIONS

Sanctions and remedies

2.96 Article 8 derives largely from the enforcement provisions in the TRIPs Agreement. Member States are obliged to provide 'appropriate' sanctions and remedies which are required to be 'effective, proportionate and dissuasive'.[44] The Recitals state that the sanctions should include the possibility of seeking damages and/or injunctive relief and, where appropriate, the possibility of applying for seizure of infringing material. It is clear from the wording of the Recitals[45] that the conditions relating to the grant of injunctions are for Member States to determine.

2.97 Article 8(3) of the Directive specifically ensures that rightholders will have the ability to apply for injunctions against intermediaries whose services are used by a third party to infringe copyright. This accords with Article 13 of the E-Commerce Directive, which relieves internet service providers of liability for damages where their systems are used to infringe copyright, but does not prevent them from being injuncted.

Final provisions (Art 12)

2.98 The Commission has provided for a report to be submitted by the Council and the Economic and Social Committee on 22 December 2004 and every 3 years thereafter. The report will review the application of the Directive and will examine in particular the application of the optional exceptions as implemented throughout the Member States (Article 5), assessing the development of appropriate levies relating to fair compensation, the extent of the use of technological measures (Article 6) and the development of ERMI (Article 7). Article 12 also makes express mention of the need to examine whether the technological measures under Article 6 are adversely affecting the operation of the permitted exceptions under Article 5. From the date of writing, there is less than a year to go before this report is due to be submitted, a number of Member States have yet even to implement the Directive. The report may therefore fail in its objectives; if the original difficulties involved in implementing the Directive are any indication, appropriate levies to provide fair compensation and mechanisms to permit lawful beneficiaries to make use of the exceptions to copyright may still be some way off.

---

44 Recital (58).

45 Recitals (58) and (59).

Chapter 3

THE COPYRIGHT AND RELATED RIGHTS REGULATIONS 2003

INTRODUCTION

3.1 The Copyright and Related Rights Regulations 2003 ('the Regulations'),[1] implementing the Directive in the United Kingdom, were eventually laid before Parliament on 3 October 2003. They were adopted and came into effect on 31 October 2003, more than 10 months after the deadline for implementation. Draft Regulations and commentary ('the Consultation Paper') had been published on 7 August 2002 as part of an extensive consultation process on the implementation of the Directive, but a combination of the difficult issues raised and other matters requiring the Government's attention led to successive postponements in publication of the final text.

3.2 The Regulations run to 61 pages, but although their sheer length might lead one to expect numerous major changes to copyright law in the United Kingdom, this is not the case, although one or two of the changes may be seen as profound. Rather, a large part of the complexity of the Regulations reflects the complexity of the existing legislation, already revised and extended multiple times, which has now had to be further revised to conform to the requirements of the Directive.

3.3 The changes involve the introduction of two new rights: a copyright of electronic communication to the public; and a related right for performers to make available their performances to the public through on-demand services. Neither of these was controversial in principle, although the former, in particular, occupies a considerable proportion of the text of the Regulations. More hotly debated were the rights given to copyright owners and the manufacturers of technological protection mechanisms to prevent circumvention of such mechanisms or the removal of electronic rights management information. The status of technological protection measures has been elevated from a matter of contract between the suppliers of copy-protected products and their customers, to a matter of generally applicable rights or, from the converse point of view, denial of rights, to all parties regardless of any pre-existing contractual relationship.

3.4 The other area of major controversy surrounding the draft Regulations was the amendment of the existing exceptions to copyright protection for copying for the purposes of research and education. Since the invention of the photocopier, students and researchers of all kinds have come to expect to be able to photocopy materials rather than relying upon taking laborious notes from them for future reference. Libraries around the world have been grappling with the copyright implications of

---

1 SI 2003/2498.

photocopying for almost the same period. Prior to the introduction of the Regulations, the United Kingdom had a relatively liberal regime as regards such photocopying – although even so those library staff who took seriously their role of policing authorised copying found the requirements burdensome. Nevertheless, the system functioned, and collective licensing schemes have gradually come into existence to streamline the process of obtaining permission for institutions which need to carry out regular copying, although these are as yet neither comprehensive in their coverage nor extant in every Berne Convention jurisdiction. In the negotiation of the Directive, the UK Government's position was to maintain existing UK exceptions to infringement as far as possible, and this is what the Regulations aim to achieve. However, one of the changes imposed – removing the exception insofar as it applied to copying for the purpose of commercial research or study – will have a major impact by removing the exception from a very large number of organisations.

3.5   This chapter reviews the details of the changes made to copyright law in the United Kingdom by the Regulations, including, where appropriate, explanation of the intention underlying those changes. The extent to which the Regulations have complied with either the Directive or the United Kingdom's other international obligations is considered in Chapter 4. Potential future controversies in the application of the amended law are the subject of Chapter 5.

NEW RIGHTS

3.6   The rights described below came into existence on 31 October 2003. Although their provisions in general apply to all forms of work, whether made or done before or after commencement, no act done before that date will be actionable as an infringement of any of the new or extended rights,[2] although if an act was actionable under the law as it applied at the date of the act it will remain possible to bring proceedings under that law.[3] Further, even acts done after the commencement date will not infringe the new or extended rights if done in pursuance of an agreement made before the date on which the Directive was due to have been implemented: 22 December 2002.[4]

Communication of a work to the public

3.7   The new right of communication to the public, mandated by Art 3 of the Directive, is a right to control the electronic transmission of particular categories of copyright works, including broadcasting or making the work available for on-demand access by the members of the public at times and places individually chosen by them.[5] This is perhaps the most fundamental change to UK copyright law effected by the Regulations. Not only has it involved broadening the scope of the acts previously restricted under s 20 of the Act (broadcasting or inclusion in a cable programme service), to cover 'communication to the public by electronic transmission' but it has

---

2   Regulation 31(2).

3   Eg reg 40.

4   Regulation 32(2).

5   CDPA 1988, s 20(2).

also involved redefining what constitutes a 'broadcast' and abandoning the separate right subsisting in a 'cable programme service'. The Consultation Paper had proposed seeking exhaustively to define the expression 'communication to the public'. The Regulations no longer seek so to do.

3.8 The main problem with implementing Art 3 has been the treatment of different types of material on the internet and the borderline between broadcasting and other activities. As the law which previously applied in the United Kingdom was less than transparent, the amendments required to adapt it to implement the new regime are complex – although it is to be hoped that the result is a simpler law. In order to understand the difficulties which the Government faced in introducing this new right, it may be helpful first to review the law as it previously stood on broadcasts and cable programmes.

3.9 Copyright in radio and television broadcasts was first introduced in the Copyright Act 1956 at s 14, for all broadcasts made on or after 1 June 1957. Broadcasts made before this date are not protected by copyright at all, although, of course, where the material broadcast consisted of a copyright work such as a film or a sound recording, copyright subsisted in the work itself and could be infringed by copying. The copyright in a broadcast is only significant in respect of transmissions of live footage of news or sports events, where there is no separate recording attracting an independent copyright.

3.10 Copyright[6] protection was first conferred on cable programmes (other than mere relays of existing broadcasts) as a species of 'work or other matter' in their own right by the Cable and Broadcasting Act 1984, inserting new s 14A into the Copyright Act 1956. Since the cable and satellite transmissions of the time were protected by encryption to prevent non-subscribers from tapping into them, a related right was also provided by s 54 of this Act: a right infringed by the provision of devices or the publication of information enabling people to receive programmes without payment.

3.11 The Cable and Broadcasting Act 1984 further complicated the area by bringing in a new definition of a broadcast which defined what forms of broadcast would have copyright protection on or after 1 January 1985. The Copyright, Designs and Patents Act 1988 (CDPA 1988) further amended that definition, and also amended the definition of cable programme service.

3.12 The CDPA 1988 defined as a broadcast a transmission by wireless telegraphy – electromagnetic energy travelling over paths not provided by a material substance, other than microwave energy passing between terrestrial fixed points – of visual images, sounds or other information. This definition was expressly tailored[7] to separate entirely the treatment of cable programme services. By s 7 of the CDPA 1988 a cable programme service was a service of sending visual images, sounds or other information by a telecommunications service *other than* by wireless telegraphy. In

---

6   This is using the term 'copyright' in the broad sense in which the term is used in the Act, so as to include all related rights except the rights of performers. From the perspective of most others in Europe the right that subsisted in cable programme services in the United Kingdom, now repealed, would be a related right.

7   An amendment to exclude microwave energy was introduced for the purpose by the Copyright and Related Rights Regulations 1996 (SI 1996/2967).

other words, the information is transmitted as electromagnetic energy but travels along a path provided by a material substance, save where short microwave links are included.

3.13   However, these definitions were not applied throughout the CDPA 1988 in a manner consistent with their apparent meanings. For example, under former ss 6(6) and 20 copyright in a broadcast could be infringed by the inclusion of the broadcast in a cable programme service and vice versa. Such inclusion is impossible as a matter of physics since a transmission made by wireless telegraphy cannot be included in a transmission sent by a telecommunications service other than wireless telegraphy. The reality which ss 6(6) and 20 reflected was that the material protected by copyright in each case was not the transmission either by wireless telegraphy or through a material path, but the information content of that transmission – that is, the images, sounds and other information.

3.14   Something of the nature of the problem the legislative draftsmen faced in attempting to reform UK copyright treatment of these media in order to implement the new right of communication to the public can be seen from the definitions proposed in the Consultation Paper for 'broadcasting' and 'communication to the public' respectively in amended ss 6 and 20 of the 1988 Act:

'6(1) In this Part a "broadcast" means a transmission by electronic means of visual images, sounds or other information which –
(a)   is transmitted for simultaneous reception by members of the public and is capable of being lawfully received by them, or
(b)   is transmitted for presentation to members of the public
and which is not excepted by subsection (1A), and references to broadcasting shall be construed accordingly.

(1A) Any transmission included in an interactive service which operates in such a way that members of the public may at their individual request access a transmission from its commencement at a time they select or determine, is excepted from the definition of "broadcast".'

'20(1) . . .

(2) References in this Part to communication to the public are to communication to the public by electronic transmission, and in relation to a work include –
(a)   the broadcasting of the work;
(b)   inclusion of the work in an on-demand service or other interactive service.

(3) In this Part, "on-demand service" means an interactive service for making a work available to the public by electronic transmission in such a way that members of the public may access the work from a place and at a time individually chosen by them.'

Subtly, different types of 'interactive service' were described in the proposed ss 6(1A) and 20(3), and their interrelation would inevitably have caused uncertainty.

3.15   In the event, the Regulations as finally adopted use a different approach, defining broadcast in a positive sense by excluding internet transmissions altogether save in specified cases. Under the new s 6(1) of the CDPA 1988 a broadcast means:

' . . . an electronic transmission of visual images, sounds or other information which –
(a)   is transmitted for simultaneous reception by members of the public and is capable of being lawfully received by them, or

(b)   is transmitted at a time determined solely by the person making the transmission for presentation to members of the public,

and which is not excepted . . . .'.

The exception[8] is for:

'. . . any internet transmission unless it is –

(a)   a transmission taking place simultaneously on the internet and by other means,

(b)   a concurrent transmission of a live event, or

(c)   a transmission of recorded moving images or sounds forming part of a programme service offered by the person responsible for making the transmission, being a service in which programmes are transmitted at scheduled times determined by that person'.

3.16   The intended effect is to provide that, as regards internet transmissions, only those which are of a conventional broadcast character will qualify as broadcasts. Concerns had been raised in the consultation process that the new communication right would be so broad as to encompass any copyright work transmitted electronically, including individual images or pieces of text. The revised definition of broadcast avoids that problem. It also excludes interactive services as they are currently produced, since to the best of the author's knowledge no interactive services are yet being produced which involve simultaneous transmission on the internet and by conventional broadcasting or which are transmitted live.

3.17   Although the new definition of broadcast is broadened to include transmissions which were formerly cable programme services, like the former definition, it includes only broadcasts capable of being lawfully received by members of the public or transmitted for presentation to them – to avoid the accidental inclusion of police or taxi radio messages and the like.

3.18   Since the revised definition has subsumed cable programme services within broadcasts for the purpose of copyright protection, the concept of a cable programme as a separate protected work is abolished entirely by the deletion of s 7 of the CDPA 1988. The change brings UK copyright law closer to the international mainstream, which does not recognise separate protection for cable programmes, and draws a line under an interesting, but flawed, experiment in the creation of a new type of right. The most notable feature of the United Kingdom's former approach was the finding that the cable programme right could be applied to activities on the internet in the well-known case of *Shetland Times v Wills*,[9] and, much more recently, in *Sony Music Entertainment (UK) Ltd v Easyinternetcafé Ltd*.[10] Despite such cases, given the extraordinarily complex definition of what constituted a 'cable programme service', and the absence of any corresponding right in most other copyright and related rights systems, few will mourn its passing.

3.19   Other references to cable programme services have also been deleted from the CDPA 1988, such as the definition of the author of such a service (former s 9(2)(c)),

8   CDPA 1988, s 6(1A).

9   [1997] FSR 604; [1997] EMLR 277.

10   [2003] ECDR 297. The case is discussed in Chapter 5.

and references which continue to apply under the new definition of broadcast or communication to the public are amended to refer to broadcasts only.[11]

3.20   The new copyright of communication to the public is set out in a new s 20 CDPA 1988 which provides that communication to the public of a work is an act restricted by copyright. This section is substituted for the former s 20 of the CDPA 1988, which restricted broadcasting of a work or its inclusion in a cable programme service. The right governs only electronic transmission, including (but not limited to):

'(a)   the broadcasting of the work;
(b)   the making available to the public of the work by electronic transmission in such a way that members of the public may access it from a place and at a time individually chosen by them.'

Thus, on-demand internet services, although excluded from the definition of broadcasting, are included in the definition of communication to the public.[12] The works to which the new right applies are literary, dramatic, musical or artistic works, sound recordings, films and broadcasts.[13] These are unchanged from the previous protected categories, save for the omission of cable programmes as a separate category.

3.21   This new arrangement appears more logical than the regime of the past 14 years, since, as discussed above, transmissions by wireless or cable means are in fact directed to the same end – providing real-time sound and images of events of interest to viewers remote from the scene – and there is no apparent reason why the technology by which the transmission takes place should affect the copyright position.

3.22   Unfortunately, the definitions still do not appear to be totally clear. For example, Part I of the CDPA 1988 still refers either to a person making a broadcast or to a person making a transmission which is a broadcast – when the definition of a broadcast is an electronic transmission of images, sounds and so on. Thus, no person can make a broadcast who does not make a transmission which is a broadcast; and there is no apparent reason why a person making a transmission which is not a broadcast need be referred to. The two forms of reference therefore appear to overlap entirely, and the Act would be marginally easier to follow if only a single term were used consistently. The point is a minor one, but in an Act of the size and complexity of this one every contribution to clarity and simplicity is greatly to be welcomed, and any change which perpetuates the plethora of overlapping terminology must be seen to some extent as a missed opportunity.

3.23   The only other amendment made by the Regulations in respect of broadcasting, and hence the right of communication to the public of copyright works by electronic transmission, is the inclusion of a new subsection, in s 6(5A) of the Act. This makes it express that the act of receiving in the United Kingdom a broadcast and immediately re-transmitting it is to be regarded as a separate act of broadcasting from the making of

---

11   See list of consequential amendments to both the CDPA 1988 and other statutes and statutory instruments which formerly referred to cable programme services, in Schs 1 and 2 to the Regulations.

12   This aspect of the communication to the public right is sometimes referred to as the 'on-demand availability right'.

13   Section 20(1) as amended.

the broadcast which is being relayed. The owner of the relaying transmitter in the United Kingdom will therefore be liable for infringement of any copyrights included in such a broadcast, along with the entity responsible for the original broadcast. This confirms the former UK treatment.[14]

3.24 Section 73 of the CDPA 1988, which deals with the situation where a wireless broadcast is relayed by cable,[15] is reworded in the light of the new definition of broadcast and the deletion of the separate concept of cable programme service, but the effect remains the same. It is not an infringement of copyright in a broadcast to transmit it onward by cable if the broadcast falls under s 78A of the Broadcasting Act 1990 (inclusion of certain services in local delivery services provided by digital means), or Sch 12, Part III, para 4 to that Act (inclusion of certain services in diffusion services originally licensed under the Cable and Broadcasting Act 1984), and the carrier is responsible for transmitting the service outside the broadcast reception area. If the area in which the service is received by cable overlaps with the area in which it is received by wireless broadcast, and the transmission by cable is not otherwise licensed, then a reasonable royalty may be payable for the inclusion in the cable service (to be fixed by the Copyright Tribunal if not agreed).

3.25 A criminal offence of unauthorised communication to the public is introduced at s 107 of the CDPA 1988. This is discussed further at **3.108**.

Making a performance available to the public

3.26 The second new right introduced under the Regulations is a 'making available right' also mandated by Article 3 of the Directive, which in turn expands on Article 10 of the WPPT.[16] This right is intended to enable performers to control on-demand transmission of recordings of their performances. Prior to the adoption of the Regulations, a performer could not prevent transmission of authorised recordings. Section 182 of the CDPA 1988 gave the performer the right to prevent anyone recording the whole or any substantial part of a qualifying performance directly from the live performance, broadcasting the same live, or including it live in a cable programme service, or making a recording of the same for public or commercial purposes directly from a live broadcast or cable programme. Once a recording had been made with consent, the performer could prevent copies being made, issued to the public, or rented or loaned,[17] but no longer had control over its use in the broadcasting context; his or her only entitlement was to receive equitable remuneration for any such use.

3.27 The relevant new provision is s 182CA, which specifies that:

'(1) A performer's rights are infringed by a person who, without his consent, makes available to the public a recording of the whole or any substantial part of a qualifying performance by electronic transmission in such a way that members of the public may access the recording from a place and at a time individually chosen by them.'

---

14 However, the same may not apply in other European countries: see discussion at **4.50–4.51**.

15 And corresponding para 19 of Sch 2.

16 Article 10 of the WPPT, unlike Art 3 of the Directive, only confers the right in relation to performances fixed in phonograms.

17 Sections 182A–182C.

This echoes the formulation of on-demand services used in defining the right of communication to the public, intentionally, since the performer's right is intended to be an equivalent right which required separate treatment only because it is not a copyright but a related right. The right to equitable remuneration for such use is simultaneously withdrawn.[18]

3.28   This right of making available is a property right in the same way as the reproduction, distribution and rental and lending rights (amended s 191A), so that the right may be assigned or licensed in whole or in part or transmitted by operation of law (for example, upon death) in the same way as any other personal property. An assignment must be in writing and signed by the assignor in order to be legally effective (s 191B(3)). As with copyright and other related rights, an assignment of future making available rights can be made in advance of a performance (s 191C(2)). The provisions of Sch 2A to the Act, relating to collective licensing schemes for performers' rights, are amended to bring the making available right within the ambit of such schemes.[19]

3.29   The pre-existing provision providing the right of equitable remuneration for performers for the broadcast of commercially published sound recordings (s 182D) is amended so that performers continue to have only a right to equitable remuneration for communication to the public by ordinary (ie other than on-demand) broadcasting. The amount of remuneration is fixed by agreement between the parties (which need not be in advance of transmission) or, failing agreement, by the Copyright Tribunal. This leaves a curious anomaly in that a broadcaster must obtain consent before including an authorised recording of a performance in an on-demand service, or else be found to have infringed the performer's rights, but can include it in a normally scheduled programme without consent and simply negotiate an appropriate level of equitable remuneration after the event. At present, on-demand transmissions are likely to be greatly in the minority of instances so that it may be questioned whether the scale of exploitation of performances in this limited sector of electronic transmissions justifies an additional layer of administrative burden upon operators. However, it may be that in respect of performances such as music videos or films in their post-video- or DVD-release phase, on-demand services will, once widely available in real-time and at low cost, begin to match scheduled programmes in popularity. At that point broadcasters dealing in those particular entertainment sectors will need to negotiate a set of agreements in addition to those required by broadcasters transmitting mainly less repeat-worthy performances.

3.30   The existing rights enabling a performer to control the dissemination of authorised copies of recordings are subject to exhaustion once a copy has first been released with the performer's consent. This means that such copies, once in authorised circulation, are beyond the performer's control and subject to no further remuneration right. The new 'making available' right is not subject to exhaustion of rights, as this was considered unnecessary since the controlled transmission is an act not capable of further 'circulation' unless a recording or other copy is made of it. Such a copy would be an infringement of the performer's right to control copying of

---

18   Regulation 34.

19   Regulation 7(4).

recordings of a performance, under s 182A. No amendments have been made to specify the absence of exhaustion of the making available right.

3.31 A corresponding new criminal offence is introduced into s 198 of the CDPA 1988, discussed below.

Protection for technical protection measures

Background

3.32 Even prior to the amendments brought about by the 2003 Regulations, the CDPA 1988 incorporated one provision relating to technological methods of protection of copyright works in electronic form. Section 296(2) gave, to any person (being either the copyright owner or his or her licensee) who issued copy-protected electronic copies of a work to the public, rights against any person who, knowing or having reason to believe that it would be used to make infringing copies, made, imported, sold or let for hire, offered or exposed for sale or hire, or advertised for sale or hire, any device or means specifically designed or adapted to circumvent the form of copy protection employed, or published information intended to enable or assist persons to circumvent that form of copy protection ('the copy protection right'). This regime was later slightly modified in respect of computer programs, in order to bring UK law into compliance with Article 7(3) of the Computer Program Directive.[20] Under the special computer program regime[21] advertising for sale or hire is actionable only if the advertising takes place in the course of a business.[22]

3.33 The definition of copy protection measures was broad: copy protection included any device or means intended to prevent or restrict copying of a work or to impair the quality of copies made. It was not necessary that the copy protection mechanism actually *did* prevent or restrict copying, merely that it be intended to do so.

3.34 The rights conferred under the former s 296 were the same as those which the copyright holder has against a copyright infringer: the right to obtain an injunction and/or damages, including aggravated damages for flagrant infringement conferring a benefit upon the infringer;[23] and the statutory rights to seize[24] or have delivered up[25] copies which are indubitably infringing copies. Once in possession of the goods, the

---

20 Article 7(3): 'Without prejudice to the provisions of Articles 4, 5 and 6, Member States shall provide, in accordance with their national legislation, appropriate remedies against a person committing any of the acts listed in subparagraphs (a) (b) and (c) below:

   . . .

   (c)   any act of putting into circulation, or the possession for commercial purposes of, any means the sole intended purpose of which is to facilitate the unauthorised removal or circumvention of any technical device which may have been applied to protect a computer program.'

21 CDPA 1988, s 296(2A).

22 The former s 296 did not appear to permit action to be taken against a person who simply possessed the means for circumvention for commercial purposes, as the Computer Program Directive would appear to require; but no action was ever taken by the European Commission requiring the United Kingdom to amend its implementation.

23 CDPA 1988, s 96.

24 Ibid, s 100.

25 Ibid, s 99.

rightholder could apply to court for an order that they be forfeited to him or destroyed,[26] although there was no actual requirement to do so. If, nevertheless, such an application was made, then any other rightholders with an interest in the infringing goods would also need to be notified in order to have the opportunity to be heard as to what order should be made. Conversely, the person from whom they have been seized could, if convinced that the goods were not infringing the copy protection right, apply to court for an order for their return.

3.35   The right applied, however, subject to the rightholder being able to show that the person in possession of the copy circumvention means had that device or means with the intention that it should be used to make infringing copies of copyright works. Unless the holder of the device was caught in the act of running off additional copies by using the device to circumvent copy protection measures, or advertises their possession of the device for that purpose, it could well be a little more difficult to demonstrate this intention than it is to show the purely objective fact that copies found on a market stall or on sale outside a pop concert are copyright-infringing copies. The stall holder could for a start argue simple ignorance of the use of the device, although any form of advertising of its usefulness, by crying or otherwise, would negate this. This constraint was equivalent to the requirements for seizure of articles adapted for making infringing copies. It did not apply to the same measures of statutory seizure or delivery up when invoked against actual copyright infringements.

3.36   This relatively straightforward provision is substantially revised and expanded by reg 24 of the 2003 Regulations, so much so that it is enlarged into seven separate sections: ss 296 and 296ZA–296ZF. A new Schedule, Sch 5A, is also added to the CDPA 1988.

3.37   The substantive provisions are the new s 296, which relates to circumvention of technical devices applied to computer programs, continuing the separate regime established under the Computer Program Directive,[27] and ss 296ZA and 296ZD, which relate to the remedies available against, respectively, persons who circumvent technological measures applied to copyright works other than computer programs and devices which are designed or promoted for circumventing such measures. Of the remaining sections, ss 296ZB–296ZC relate to the criminal sanctions and associated procedural issues such as search warrants and forfeiture. These are discussed in the section on sanctions later in this chapter.

Protection measures for computer programs

3.38   The new s 296 gives several categories of person the right to bring proceedings against anyone who supplies devices or information which enable or assist the circumvention of a technical device applied to a computer program. A technical device is any device intended to prevent or restrict copyright-restricted acts which are not authorised by the owner of copyright in the program.[28] The reference to a device could be read to suggest, in contrast to the definition of technological measures in s 296ZF (discussed below), that some mechanical or electronic object may be

---

26 CDPA 1988, s 114.

27 Since by Art 1(2) the provisions of the Copyright Directive are expressed not to affect existing Community provisions relating to the legal protection of computer programs.

28 CDPA 1988, s 296(6).

required to bring the section into effect, rather than a purely software copy protection mechanism. However, in the context of computer programs Parliament must be taken to have realised that software protection mechanisms are the form of technical protection most likely to be applied, and therefore must be taken to have intended them to be covered.[29]

3.39 The right to bring proceedings is given to any of:

- the copyright holder,
- an exclusive licensee of the copyright,
- a person who issues or communicates to the public copies of the protected program, and
- the owner or exclusive licensee of any intellectual property rights in the technical device itself.[30]

3.40 The same persons have the right to apply for delivery up[31] or to execute a seizure of any means for facilitating the unauthorised removal or circumvention of a technical copy protection device under prescribed conditions.[32] The conditions are that:

- the articles must be on display in a place to which the public have right of access,
- the person proposing to make the seizure must notify the local police station beforehand of the intention to carry out a seizure at a particular time and place, and
- a notice in the prescribed form containing the prescribed particulars as to the person by whom or on whose authority the seizure is made and the grounds on which it is made must be left at the place from which the seizure has been made.

Once infringing devices have been delivered up or seized the claimant can (but need not) apply to the court for an order under s 114 of the CDPA 1988 that these be forfeited to him or her or destroyed.

3.41 As in the case of copyright infringement, defendants' rights not to provide information which would incriminate themselves are withdrawn, by amendment of s 72 of the Supreme Court Act 1981. However, the safeguards provided by s 72(3), namely that any information obtained in the course of such an action cannot be used to bring criminal proceedings against the defendants, also apply.

3.42 This right of action is entirely new as regards all prospective wielders other than the copyright holder or exclusive licensee. It is a relatively natural extension of the United Kingdom's traditional approach of treating copyright as a right in favour of the commercial interests in publishing works rather than the more continental approach of foregrounding the interests of the author. Clearly, all of these parties have a commercial interest in keeping copyright works within the scope of royalty-bearing

---

29 At the very least Parliament cannot have intended a debate over the meaning of 'technical', such as that which bedevils the status of patent protection for software, to be introduced also in this context.

30 CDPA 1988, s 296(2).

31 Ibid, s 99.

32 Ibid, s 100.

sales. For example, it may be a valuable negotiating tool for the manufacturer of copy protection devices to offer to take on the enforcement of technical protection in a computer program if its products are chosen to provide that protection, since enforcement costs in the digital environment can be substantial and ongoing. To make such an offer would also amount to a very strong and potentially persuasive statement of confidence in the effectiveness of the protection means concerned.

3.43   The various potential claimants' rights are concurrent, such that as soon as any of them brings any proceedings going beyond the stage of an application for an interim injunction, the others must either agree to join the action as co-claimants or be added as defendants, unless the court grants permission for them not to be parties. However, if a potential claimant is added as a defendant it will not be liable for any share of the costs of the action whichever side prevails, unless it opts to take an active part in the proceedings.[33] Any damages awarded at the conclusion of proceedings under s 296 will be apportioned between the potential co-claimants as the court sees fit, regardless of whether or not they were in fact parties to the action. Where any potential claimant intends to apply for an order for delivery up or exercise the right of seizure of infringing products, it must notify its potential co-claimants beforehand.[34] There is no requirement for the potential co-claimants to approve of the action or participate, but an obligation to notify does at least minimise the risk that due to simple lack of communication one party sets out to obtain delivery up or a seizure of articles which another party has authorised, by providing a mechanism under which the latter has the opportunity to intervene before any third party's rights are infringed.

3.44   A party bringing an action under the new s 296 is given the benefit of the presumptions set out in ss 104–106 inclusive of the CDPA 1988. These relate to establishing subsistence of copyright in a work, by reference in the case of literary, dramatic, musical or artistic works to a person named, on copies as published or on the work when made, as the author or publisher, or in the case of sound recordings and films to the named copyright owner or director. In respect of computer programs, the presumptions most relevant to the new s 296 are the presumptions under s 105(3) as to the fact that a person named as owner of copyright in the program in electronic copies was the copyright owner at the date of issue of the copies, or that the program was first published in a specified country or that copies of it were first issued to the public in electronic form in a specified year.[35]

Protection of copyright works other than computer programs, and works in which performers' rights, publication right or database right subsist

(i) What are effective technological measures?
3.45   The interpretation of new ss 296ZA and 296ZD depends upon the definitions set out in s 296ZF as to what constitute technological measures and what it means for these to be effective. This section is therefore considered next before turning to the substantive provisions.

---

33   CDPA 1988, s 102(2).

34   Ibid, s 102(5).

35   Section 105(3) also includes a direction that such statements are admissible as evidence of the facts stated, a requirement which seems somewhat outdated in these days of extensive disclosure of e-mails and other forms of electronic evidence, but which was considerably more valuable as reassurance in 1988.

3.46 Section 296ZF follows Article 6(3) of the Directive closely. The definition of technological measures is straightforward: it encompasses any technology, device or component which is designed, in the normal course of its operation, to protect a copyright work other than a computer program. Protection means the prevention or restriction of copyright-restricted acts where these have not been authorised by the copyright owner. The most pertinent such act is, of course, copying.

3.47 Although software is not expressly mentioned, it is not realistically arguable that software in this context is not a form of technology and therefore included. This is confirmed by the definition of 'effective', which requires that the technological measure enable the copyright owner to control the use of the work through either an access control or protection process such as encryption, scrambling or other transformation of the work, or by a copy protection mechanism. Encryption, scrambling and other transformations are ordinarily performed by software.

3.48 The definition of technological measures does not include, expressly at any rate, a constraint present in the Directive upon the forms of technology which are intended to be protected. Recital (48) explicitly excludes from the Directive's objectives any technological measures which prevent the normal operation of electronic equipment and its technological development. It appears from the Consultation Paper that the Government considers this recital to be implicit in the definitions themselves.

3.49 Any technological approach will be treated as 'effective' if it achieves the intended protection. Like the old s 296, this does not require the copy protection mechanism actually to prevent all-comers being able to make any copies at all; it depends upon the subjective intent of the person who has applied copy protection. If his or her only concern was to make it difficult for the ordinary user to make copies by simply putting the protected work on a CD into a CD recorder, then a signal at the beginning of each track which instructs the recorder not to copy may suffice. Such a mechanism would not stop even a moderately competent hacker from copying, simply by ripping the CD into a computer file and editing it to remove the 'no copying' signal. Nevertheless, if this low level of protection was all that the copyright owner intended to achieve, then this technological protection will be effective within the meaning of the CDPA 1988 as amended. This is entirely consistent with the approach taken under the former s 296.

3.50 It would therefore be advisable for any person issuing copy-protected copies to the public to ensure that the objectives for the effectiveness of the copy protection are not set too high, since in litigation over the circumvention of such a measure documents may have to be disclosed to establish exactly what the intended level of protection was. A memo or minute demonstrating that the protection was intended to be absolute could arguably be used to show that, as the mechanism had been circumvented, it had not achieved the intended level of protection and therefore was not 'effective' within the definition. In these circumstances, it is arguable that the technological protection measures do not gain the benefit of the remaining provisions introduced by the Regulations. Of course, such an argument raised by the hacker would not be very attractive.

3.51 Note that under s 296ZF(3)(b) mechanisms which are applied to control a use of the work which is not an act restricted by copyright will not benefit from the provisions of the Act protecting technological measures. So, for example, if a company were to release a CD-ROM encyclopaedia which for some reason was technologically protected against simply being read in private on a particular manufacturer's computers, this technological measure would not benefit from protection under the Act, since the act of releasing and selling the disk implies a licence to the purchaser to make any temporary copies necessary to play it. Selective protection of such a kind could also constitute anti-competitive conduct.

(ii) Protection against circumvention

3.52 The first substantive new section, s 296ZA, applies where any person deliberately (or with reasonable grounds to know that it will have that effect) does anything which circumvents effective technological measures applied to any copyright work other than a computer program,[36] or to any works in which rights in performances, publication rights or database rights subsist.[37]

3.53 There is an express exception for anyone carrying out research into cryptography. This exception was required by Recital (48) of the Directive, which said that nothing in the Directive should hinder research into cryptography. However, the benefit of that exception is removed if, in circumventing the protection measure or disclosing information derived from that research, the researcher then affects prejudicially the rights of the copyright owner. In all likelihood, copyright owners will argue that any disclosure of research results may assist another person to circumvent copy protection based upon the form of encryption in question, and therefore does prejudicially affect their rights.[38] Dissemination and peer review of research are therefore likely to be considerably constrained. The exception as phrased in the final version of the Regulations is considered to be a compromise between the public interest in research to further the level of technological knowledge, and the interests of those involved in using the current level of knowledge to protect their commercial interests in copyright works. The ability to research de-coupled from the right to discuss and disseminate that research is only half worth having, since the rate at which cryptographic knowledge advances will be substantially slowed, although not completely stalled, by the need for every researcher in effect to discover a way around any given technological protection measure for himself.

3.54 Cryptography researchers aside, any other person who does anything which circumvents a technological measure, knowing or having reasonable grounds to know that circumvention is the objective, will potentially face legal action by either the person who issues copies of the work to the public or communicates the work to the public in protected form, or the copyright owner or exclusive licensee, if that is someone different. Notably, the owners of intellectual property rights in the

---

36 CDPA 1988, s 296ZA(1).

37 Ibid, s 296ZA(6).

38 See, for instance, the threats made against Professor Felten by the Recording Industry Association of America in the US in April 2001 to prevent him disclosing the results of his research into the Secure Digital Music Initiative. The letter stated: 'Unfortunately, the disclosure that you are contemplating could result in significantly broader consequences and could directly lead to the illegal distribution of copyrighted material. Such disclosure is not authorized ... and would subject your research team to enforcement actions under the Digital Millenium Copyright Act and possibly other federal laws.' (Cited in the Complaint subsequently filed in *Felten et al v RIAA et al.*)

technological measures themselves are not given any right of action under this section. The rights of action are concurrent, as under s 296, and most of the same presumptions apply. In addition, where proceedings are brought under this section in respect of a protected database, the presumptions raised by reg 22 of the Copyright and Rights in Databases Regulations 1997[39] (as to a named person being the maker of the database and the database having been made in circumstances where that person[40] owns the database right) apply.

3.55 The remedies are also almost the same as those provided under s 296. This will simplify proceedings where these are bought in respect of the circumvention of technological measures applied to a computer program which is used in the operation of a non-copyright database, so that the program is not itself a database, in circumstances where the object of the circumvention is the contents of the database and the circumvention enables access to those contents. It may well be necessary to invoke both ss 296 and 296ZA in order to be sure of establishing liability, since reliance on s 296 alone could be met by an argument that the program is not in fact a protected program but merely a technological measure protecting the database. However, once the court has established that some form of protection has been circumvented, the combination of these sections will give rise to essentially the same remedies as either of them taken separately.

3.56 Section 296ZA does not, however, give the claimant the right to apply for destruction of the products in respect of which technological measures have been circumvented. Where copies have been made by virtue of the technological measures having been circumvented, they will be infringing copies and therefore subject to forfeiture or destruction under s 114 on that basis; but the formerly protected copy does not infringe copyright despite having been de-protected. The essence of s 296ZA is to prohibit an act or activity, namely the circumvention of the technological protection measures, not to give the rightholders rights over any device or mechanism used to perform or enable the activity or over the resulting 'clean' copy. Devices or mechanisms used to perform or enable circumvention are addressed by new s 296ZD, discussed below. If there is any evidence of its use or intended use for making unauthorised copies, then the de-protected copy itself infringes the copyright in the work by virtue of s 24 of the CDPA 1988, which provides:

'(1) Copyright in a work is infringed by a person who, without the licence of the copyright owner –

(a)　makes,
(b)　imports into the United Kingdom,
(c)　possesses in the course of a business, or
(d)　sells or lets for hire or offers or exposes for sale or hire,

an article specifically designed or adapted for making copies of that work, knowing or having reason to believe that it is to be used to make infringing copies.'

3.57 An unprotected copy is an article specifically designed or adapted for making copies unless it has been de-protected with the consent of the copyright owner, and it is hardly credible that someone who has intentionally removed the copy protection

---

39　SI 1997/3032.

40　Rather than his employer or another third party.

without that consent does not have reason to believe that it is to be used to make infringing copies. One issue which may arise in invoking this section is whether an electronic copy of a copyright work is an 'article'. However, even if it is not, it is arguable that the CD, floppy or hard disk upon which it is recorded is such an article. Note that as regards the person who makes the article, ie removes the copy protection, or imports a de-protected copy, the copyright is infringed whether or not the activity takes place in the course of a business.

3.58   A transmission over the internet using a de-protected copy will also infringe copyright by virtue of s 24(2) of the CDPA 1988:

> '(2) Copyright in a work is infringed by a person who without the licence of the copyright owner transmits the work by means of a telecommunications system (otherwise than by broadcasting), knowing or having reason to believe that infringing copies of the work will be made by means of the reception of the transmission in the United Kingdom or elsewhere.'

New s 296ZG, discussed below, may also assist in circumstances where the copy-protected copy included electronic rights management information and this has been removed along with the copy protection.

(iii) Devices for the circumvention of technological protection measures
3.59   New s 296ZD relates to the production, import, supply or advertisement or possession for commercial purposes of any device or component either promoted, advertised or marketed for the circumvention of technological protection measures or which has only a limited commercially significant other purpose, or which is primarily designed, produced, adapted for that purpose. It also covers the provision of services for that purpose.

3.60   Where a person does any of the prohibited acts, the right to bring proceedings is given to any of:

–   the copyright holder,
–   an exclusive licensee of the copyright,
–   a person who issues or communicates to the public copies of the protected program, and
–   the owner or exclusive licensee of any intellectual property rights in the effective technological protection measures.[41]

As can be seen, s 296ZD substantially mirrors new s 296, granting to the same potential co-claimants the same rights of enforcement and remedies. The same presumptions are also applicable.

3.61   Section 296ZD includes only one additional provision. Subsection 7 varies the construction of s 97(1) of the CDPA 1988, which prevents a copyright holder from obtaining damages from a defendant who infringed 'innocently', that is to say without knowing and having no reason to believe that copyright subsisted in the copied work. Where this provision is being invoked in connection with the production, distribution or advertisement of means for circumventing effective technological protection measures, the defendant will benefit from s 97 if able to show that he neither knew nor had reason to believe that his acts enabled or facilitated an infringement of copyright.

---

41   CDPA 1988, s 296ZD(2).

(iv) Access for the purpose of permitted uses

3.62   One of the most hotly debated issues with the use of technological measures to prevent copying of copyright works is that in some circumstances copying is permitted under copyright law both in the United Kingdom and elsewhere. Obvious examples are the fair dealing exceptions to copyright infringement, where part of a work may be copied for purposes of criticism and review, or the reporting of current events. Another example is the copying of copyright works for the production of versions accessible by visually impaired people. Once technological protection measures have been applied, such exceptions may be eviscerated since copying may simply not be possible. Considerable anxiety has been expressed that enactments such as this are:

> 'replacing copyright law with technology ... the balance between society and authors is being replaced with arbitrary rules governed by the software or hardware you use to access a copyright work. Software is unable to determine whether the circumvention is for copyright infringement, or extraction of a quote which would otherwise be fair use. All copies, however innocent, become illegal.'[42]

3.63   Accordingly, the Directive required Member States to provide some mechanism whereby the beneficiaries of such exceptions could continue to enjoy them. Section 296ZE is the United Kingdom's response.

3.64   Section 296ZE must be read in parallel with the new Sch 5A. Part 1 of the new Schedule lists all of the permitted acts in respect of copyright; Parts 2 and 3 list the permitted acts in respect of performance rights and database right.

3.65   The Government's intention, echoing the hopes of the European Commission, is that the tricky balancing of rights may be sorted out between copyright holders and consumers by means of voluntary measures or agreements which will enable consumers to carry out the permitted acts notwithstanding the technological protection. If this does not transpire within a reasonable time and as a result a person is unable to carry out a permitted act in the United Kingdom, his or her remedy is to issue a notice of complaint to the Secretary of State. However, the Secretary of State is under no obligation to do anything at all in response to such a notice. The Secretary of State *may*, in his or her sole discretion, direct the copyright holder or his exclusive licensee in writing to do various things (discussed below). If directions are given, the recipients must respond. But not giving directions at all is also an option. Nor is there any time-limit for the Secretary of State to decide whether to give any directions, and no provision for any appeal from a failure to do so. It would be left to the disgruntled complainant to apply for judicial review of the Secretary of State's failure to act, or giving of inadequate or inappropriate directions – a substantial burden for the complainant to undertake, with a high threshold of unreasonableness to be established before the Secretary of State can be required to reconsider his or her decision.[43]

3.66   Commentators on the draft form of the Regulations considered this arrangement a serious flaw in the level of protection provided to ordinary users of copyright.

---

42   Per Julian Midgley, Campaign for Digital Rights. See various discussions of this issue at www.ukcdr.org.

43   *Associated Provincial Picture Houses Ltd v Wednesbury Corporation* [1948] 1 KB 223, and subsequent cases. The decision must be one which no reasonable body acting with due appreciation of its responsibilities would have decided to adopt.

Although, by providing the possibility of complainants bringing class actions[44] to share the cost and risk, the Regulations as passed are somewhat more user-friendly than the draft, the magnitude of the Secretary of State's discretion leaves considerable room for disagreement. There is still no express provision whereby a mechanism imposed to permit an individual to benefit from a particular exception may be applied for the benefit of all members of the same class, for example – although of course this too is within the Secretary of State's discretion. Challenges may be raised in the future as to whether so potentially toothless a scheme complies with the United Kingdom's obligations under Article 6(4) of the Directive.

3.67 The directions which the Secretary of State may give are: first, to establish whether there is any voluntary measure or agreement in place which assists, and secondly, if not, to ensure that the complainant is given the means to carry out the permitted act to the extent necessary to benefit from the act. This could be absolutely anything, including requiring the copyright holder to give the complainant a non-copy-protected version of the work, but it is highly unlikely that such a direction will be given since to do so would effectively undermine the copyright holder's ability to control the dissemination of the work in electronic form thereafter. Clearly, it would be possible to permit the copyright holder to require the complainant to enter into an agreement not to copy beyond the permitted extent, and not to permit any other person access to the unprotected copy, but the remedy for any breach – of suing the complainant once the damage has been done – is hardly likely to compensate for the fact that the unprotected copy is now at large. It remains to be seen how industry will respond to requests for access to unprotected copies, and what form of compromise arrangements successive Ministers may attempt to broker. If directions are given but the respondent fails to comply with them, the onus is left upon the complainant to enforce the directions by bringing legal proceedings for breach of statutory duty – a substantial burden, reversing the normal position whereby the copyright holder must take the initiative to prevent infringement.

3.68 The Secretary of State is empowered to give directions as to the form in which complaints must be made and how the complaint procedure shall operate; no such directions had yet been given at the time of writing.

3.69 There is no express limitation of the copy protection right such that once a work ceases to be copyright the circumvention of technological measures becomes permissible. Archivists in particular expressed concerns in connection with the draft Regulations that they should have a right to retain a copy in unprotected form for use once the work passes out of copyright. Permission to de-protect may still be required in these circumstances. Section 296ZA is not expressed to apply 'where a copyright work *is* protected by effective technological measures' which, in view of the definition of technological measures in s 296ZF would result in the remainder of the section ceasing to apply once the work was no longer a copyright work. Instead, it applies 'where effective technological measures *have been* applied to a copyright work', which may require only that the work was protected by copyright at the time when the technological measures were applied. To arrive at the contrary construction it would be necessary to argue that a technological measure ceases to fall within the definition once the protected work ceases to be a copyright work, and therefore once

---

44 CDPA 1988, s 296ZE(6).

the work is no longer copyright, technological measures have no longer been applied, which is somewhat strained. Thus, the result is potentially to extend the monopoly right of the copyright holder indefinitely – for so long, at least, as the copyright continues to have a value sufficient to warrant enforcement of the copy protection right. This is potentially a major encroachment on what is seen as the historic freedom of the public to share copyright works after expiry of the rights.

3.70 But in fact it must be questioned on what basis there is assumed to be a right to have all copyright material in the public domain? The fine arts first arose and flourished in the secular context under the Renaissance system of patronage of the arts, under which the public had no rights of access whatsoever. The owner of a commissioned painting could display it or not as he or she saw fit and, if so desired, destroy it altogether without it ever being observed by any other person.[45] Even if the work survived, it would have every chance of spending its entire existence in a private house unseen by the public at large, and many works by major artists remain virtually unknown in private hands. Similarly, manuscripts of unpublished literary and musical works have survived centuries in private ownership without any opportunity to view, let alone copy, ever being made available. The right to retain a unique work in private ownership has not yet been subjected to the barrage of protest which has accompanied the passage of the Directive and its various national implementations, which appears to assume almost a universal human right to access and copy works once their copyright has expired.

3.71 Nevertheless, the freedom to use works which their producers have brought into public access by publication is long-standing. It is likely that any use by one-time copyright holders of the copy protection right to extend the exclusivity of their control of a published work will incur the disapproval of both European Commission and the European Court of Justice, neither of which is wholly in favour of monopolistic intellectual property rights in general.

Protection for electronic rights management information

3.72 The right to enforce copying restrictions is of limited value in the digital context unless there is some way to track back to the source of any given copy. The solution which the rightholders have come up with is the inclusion in any digital copy of a work of information as to the authorship, creation date, copyright ownership and so on. The scope of any licence may also be included. Such 'rights management information' can then be used to identify infringing copies and their origins, giving the rightholder a point at which to strike to attempt to limit unauthorised copying. This sort of information has been in use in connection with source code for computer software, for example, for many years, leading to the inclusion in the CDPA 1988 of the references to labels and marking in s 105.

3.73 The pirates' obvious response to such measures is to alter or delete the rights management information itself which, since it is also bound to be electronic in form, is technologically simple in principle. Sophisticated mechanisms such as digital

---

45 Consider, eg the fate of Graham Sutherland's fêted portrait of Sir Winston Churchill, which met with much approval save from its subject and was destroyed by him.

watermarking of documents have made it more difficult, but there is no totally secure way to prevent such interference.

3.74   The Regulations introduce a new s 296ZG into the CDPA 1988. This section gives the copyright owner, an exclusive licensee of the copyright or a person issuing copies to the public or communicating the work to the public, rights against anyone who either removes or alters electronic rights management information or imports for distribution or communicates to the public copies of a copyright work from which the electronic rights management information has been removed or altered without authority. The same rights apply to the owner of rights in performances, publication right and database right.[46] Since the entire concept of protecting rights management information is new to UK law, the Regulations closely follow the wording of Article 7 of the Directive.

3.75   Rights management information is defined as any information provided by the copyright owner or the holder of any right under copyright which identifies the work, the author, the copyright owner or the holder of any intellectual property rights, or information about the terms and conditions of use of the work, and any numbers or codes that represent such information.[47] Since there was no special regime established for the protection of rights management information under the Computer Program Directive, this provision applies to all forms of copyright work.

3.76   The new provisions do not in any way alleviate the claimant's task of proving that the allegedly infringing copy has originated from a copy which formerly included rights management information. They merely serve to discourage potential infringers from removing such information by adding a further cause of action to the copyright owner's armoury.

3.77   The rightholders have, concurrently, the same rights as a copyright owner has in respect of an infringement of copyright. As in the other new sections, s 296Zx, the statutory presumptions of ss 104–106 of the CDPA 1988 and reg 22 of the Copyright and Rights in Databases Regulations 1997 as regards labelling and ownership of copyright are applied. The information is therefore not only legally protected against removal or alteration, but it is presumed to be correct and is admissible in evidence. Notably, it is only the software presumption (s 105(3)) which refers to the work being issued to the public in electronic form, so that it might be arguable that none of the other presumptions apply where the work and the rights management information are electronic. However, such a construction would clearly defeat the object of the Directive and the Regulations.

3.78   There is no defence under s 296ZE that the person altering rights management information did so in order to correct an error in the information. This was another concern of archivists and librarians expressed in the consultation process. It could of course be argued that the copyright owner may be taken to have given implied consent to such corrections being made, since it must be in his or her interests for the rights management information to be accurate. However, it would equally be arguable that the correct approach would be to notify the copyright owner and request permission – which in the circumstances ought reasonably to be forthcoming.

---

46   CDPA 1988, s 296ZG(8).

47   Ibid, s 296ZG(7)(b).

3.79   There are no criminal sanctions proposed or introduced for the removal of or interference with electronic rights management information.

CHANGES TO THE EXCEPTIONS TO COPYRIGHT

Copying for research

3.80   By far the most far-reaching change introduced by the Regulations is the restriction of the exception, formerly permitted under copyright in literary, dramatic, musical or artistic works in the United Kingdom, for copying for purposes of research, whether private or commercial. In future the exception in respect of these categories of works only applies for purely private research, that is research which is for a non-commercial purpose. The exception for private study remains in effect, although to emphasise the restriction being placed upon the exception as a whole the definition of private study has been tightened to exclude any study which is directly or indirectly for a commercial purpose.

3.81   The exception to the neighbouring right in respect of typographical arrangements has alone been preserved for all forms of research and private study.[48]

3.82   On the day the Regulations came into effect, the Copyright Licensing Agency Limited (CLA), a non-profit-making organisation representing UK authors, artists and publishers, warned: 'the effect of the change in the law is that, with very few exceptions, any commercial organisation wishing to copy or scan extracts from published books, journals or magazines will require a CLA licence or will need to seek the permission of the copyright owner on each occasion'. However, the CLA is not empowered to grant licences in respect of all works published in the United Kingdom and abroad. A list of excluded publications is available on its website;[49] in many cases, individual licences must be sought from the copyright owner. Nor does it grant licences for copying from newspapers, which are separately represented by the Newspaper Licensing Agency Ltd.

3.83   This change affects the majority of commercial organisations in the country, most of which will to some extent have been relying upon this exception in the ordinary course of their business, in many cases without even being aware that an exemption was required for the copying of news items, articles from technical journals, or extracts from textbooks and other readily available sources. There is no definition of what constitutes commercial research, but it would be prudent to assume that any research with even an indirectly commercial purpose will require a licence for any copying involved. For instance, as well as commercial research and product development, market research and competitive intelligence are clearly commercial purposes, as is regulatory work undertaken to acquire the necessary licences or approvals for an organisation to carry on its trade. The preparation of a book which will earn royalties may be considered a commercial activity, as would preparation of an article for which the author expects to be paid. A tricky question may arise in connection with journal papers and conference presentations for which the author does not expect to be and is not paid. Although the preparation work is not itself

---

48   CDPA 1988, s 29(2), as amended.

49   www.cla.co.uk.

commercial here, where the author is employed in a commercial organisation the work may still be considered commercial since the author would be unlikely either to undertake it or to be permitted to take time to carry it out, if it was not perceived as forwarding the interests of the organisation to some extent, however minimal.

3.84 Even apparently academic research may not be immune. Many universities seek to attract commercial sponsorship for scientific research, and this may well be considered to have a commercial purpose, if the sponsorship contract gives the sponsor the right to direct the subjects of research and privileged access to the results. There must, however, come a point at which a remotely commercial connection will not 'taint' research to the point where it is considered commercial. Many scholarships are funded by commercial sponsors, but involve no commitment on the part of the student to act in his or her sponsor's interests, which can hardly render the research the student undertakes commercial any more than a project carried out by an unfunded student which turns out ultimately to have commercial potential, but was not carried out for that purpose, should be considered commercial research. To decide otherwise would be to render practically all research in the sciences, engineering and professional disciplines such as management, law and accountancy, research for a commercial purpose, since a commercial application may eventually be found. The test as to whether or not research is commercial can only meaningfully be applied at the time when the research is taking place, rather than hindsight being applied once the fruits of the research are known.

3.85 Note that it is the research which must be private for copying to be exempted, not the organisation carrying it out. It is therefore of no assistance, for example, for a large charity to claim that its copying is exempt because it is not a commercial organisation. Many not-for-profit organisations operate trading businesses as part of their fundraising activities, which will certainly fall within the definition of 'commercial'. Research as part of those activities would be categorised as commercial. Likewise, although perhaps less significant, in some contexts it could be conceivable that a commercial organisation might carry out private research, although this would have to be exceptional. For example, a small privately owned biotech company might include among its activities research into a rare genetic disorder which happens to affect the founder's only child, but for which a cure, even if discovered, is unlikely to be a commercial proposition due to the rarity of the condition. It could be argued that this research is not for a commercial purpose, although it would take considerable evidence to convince a court that the results of the research would not be commercially valuable either in demonstrating the company's expertise to potential backers, or through the potential for applying the knowledge gained to other, commercially viable projects.

3.86 Librarians and archivists are permitted under the CDPA 1988 as it stands to provide copies to library users of various categories of materials[50] provided that the appropriate conditions are met. The majority of these conditions are unchanged, but a librarian or archivist asked to provide copies may not do so in future unless satisfied

---

50 An article in a periodical, a copy of part of a literary, dramatic or musical work from a published edition, or the whole or part of an unpublished literary, dramatic or musical work, a recording of an unpublished folksong of unknown authorship: set out in ss 38–43 and 61.

that the copies are for the purpose of research for a non-commercial purpose or for private study.[51]

3.87 As a result of this change, libraries around the country will need to amend the copyright declaration forms which are completed before a copy can be provided, to specify that the copy requested is exempted because it is for a non-commercial research purpose or for private study. Of course, it is unlikely that libraries within commercial organisations will be providing any exempt copies; they will instead have to attempt to get all necessary licences for the copies which they make. This is not a trivial task. In response to the Government consultation over the draft Regulations, various organisations representing librarians commented that many publishers, particularly overseas publishers in countries where there is no copyright licensing scheme in place, are simply not set up to provide copyright clearances. Numerous requests may be submitted without obtaining a response, and significant administration is involved in keeping track of outstanding unanswered requests. It is possible that in some cases the charges incurred in staff time and telephone calls may be substantially higher than the additional fees, if any, paid to publishers for permission to copy the occasional article – which may in turn have to be paid for by reductions in subscriptions.

3.88 The amendment to s 29 also introduces the need for the copier to include a sufficient acknowledgement of the source of the material, in line with the Berne Convention, unless this is impossible for reasons of practicality or otherwise.[52] Some user organisations[53] hoped that the amendments would include the express incorporation of the Berne three-step test since this might provide a threshold below which copying would not infringe and remove doubts as to the applicability of the test under UK law. However, this does not appear to have transpired expressly save in specified instances, none of which are relevant to the permissions given to librarians and archivists. The Explanatory Note to the Regulations does acknowledge that the three-step test is applicable under Article 5(4) of the Directive to all the permitted areas for exceptions set out in Article 5 (that is all permitted exceptions) so that there can be little doubt that the test must be considered by the courts in determining liability for copying in any future copyright infringement action.

Copying for education

3.89 Section 32 of the CDPA 1988 includes various exceptions for copying for the purposes of education: copying of literary, dramatic, musical or artistic works, sound recordings, films and broadcasts. These were formerly permitted provided they were made in the course of instruction (including setting or communicating questions to exam candidates) or of preparation for instruction, provided the copying was done by a person giving or receiving instruction, and was (in the case of literary, dramatic, musical and artistic works) not by means of a reprographic process. Reprographic

---

51 Regulation 14, amending ss 38, 39 and 43 of the CDPA 1988.

52 CDPA 1988, s 29(1B).

53 For example, the Society of College, National and University Libraries in its response to the Consultation Papers.

copying was permitted only if not more than 1 per cent of any published work is copied by or on behalf of an establishment in any quarter.[54]

3.90   Educational establishments had the additional right to record broadcasts[55] for educational purposes without infringing copyright in them, unless there was a licensing scheme in place under which they could have obtained a licence. Exempted copies remained exempted, however, only so long as they were not subject to further dealings. If later sold or let for hire, or offered for either, they became infringing copies.

3.91   These exceptions are narrowed by the Regulations for all non-commercial education to include a requirement that the copier give a sufficient acknowledgement of the source. However, where copying for education is for a commercial purpose further constraints are imposed:[56] that the copying is permitted only in respect of works which have been made available to the public, and that the copying must be fair dealing. It is not easy to assess what forms of education will be affected by this narrower exclusion. It is presumably intended to restrict private providers of courses leading to professional qualifications and other vocational training which are privately or commercially funded. This may lead to some disagreements between copyright owners and users, since in many cases vocational or professional qualifications are indeed run for profit and paid for by the student in the hope of obtaining commercial employment as a result, but it is difficult to see why such providers and their students should be penalised if universities or other publicly funded colleges providing courses leading to equivalent qualifications are not.[57] It can credibly be argued that virtually all education today is ultimately for a commercial purpose: to provide a skilled and hence employable workforce. It is merely that some elements are compulsory for and available to all, and some further elements are funded in whole or in part from the public purse. The distinction to be drawn here between private and publicly funded education would therefore appear unsatisfactory, and it may be that the courts will interpret these provisions as being directed only at courses provided for commercial organisations or their employees.

3.92   Educational establishments recording broadcasts are given the additional right, where a broadcast has been recorded, to rebroadcast it (communicate it to the public) within their own premises, provided that the broadcast cannot be received by any person situated outside the premises.[58]

New exception for transient or incidental copies

3.93   The mandatory exception required by Article 5(1) of the Directive is implemented by the introduction of new s 28A in the CDPA 1988. The exception is for transient or incidental copies which are an integral and essential part of a

---

54   CDPA 1988, s 36.

55   Ibid, s 35.

56   Ibid, s 32(2A) (new).

57   Particularly in view of the emphasis the Government is currently placing on the claimed increase in potential earnings a graduate enjoys, as a justification for making top-up fees a material element of the funding of higher education.

58   CDPA 1988, s 35(1A) (new).

technological process and which have the sole purpose of enabling either a transmission of the work in a network between third parties by an intermediary or a lawful use of the work, but having no independent economic significance. This transposes the wording of the Directive almost exactly, and as a result leaves the interpretation of these multiple preconditions to the courts without further guidance. The Government took the view that the laws of the United Kingdom already complied, but concluded that it should anyway amend the CDPA 1988 to make it explicit that Part II covers temporary copies.

3.94   The criteria may be satisfied by a copy which is either transient, which seems clear enough – having a duration short enough that it would not appear to qualify as a permanent or semi-permanent copy – or incidental, which does not. A copy which is not transient must endure for some material length of time, but nevertheless may not infringe if it was created only incidentally and has no independent economic significance. In view of the rapid and unpredictable evolution of the internet and the services operating over it, it must be difficult to say in advance what copies have independent economic significance and which do not. Imagine, for example, that a brilliant computer science student develops an application which tracks music files being transmitted across the internet and identifies their contents. The application might vitiate the peer-to-peer arrangements now in vogue by substituting a mechanism for downloading copies not from static directories on identifiable and unvarying servers, but from incidental copies appearing from time to time on the servers of legitimate organisations which have no intention of participating in music piracy. The person who had put the arrangements in place for a pirate copy to be taken would, as under the peer-to-peer system, have taken no copy at all himself, but in this case the users would also be protected to some extent since there would be no reason to advertise one's participation in the scheme at all by allowing it to catalogue the files available on one's own system. Unless the copyright owners were able to identify a copy being taken and trace the destination, or access 'request lists' enforcement would become a further order of magnitude harder. Of course, the downloads might be slower – the system would have to wait until such a copy happened to be identified rather than giving the users instant gratification – but it would almost certainly still appeal to a large number of users more than the alternative, of paying a fee for their copies. If so, the incidental copies being used as source material could certainly be said to have independent economic significance.

3.95   It is likely to be easier to ascertain whether the making of a copy is an integral and essential part of a technological process, simply by attempting to identify whether there is any way in which the process might operate which would not result in the copy being made. If expert investigators cannot identify any such way, then it must be fair to say that the making of the copy is integral and essential to the particular process.

3.96   The remaining elements of the test, whether the purpose of making the copy is to enable either a transmission of the work across a network between third parties by an intermediary or a lawful use of the work, are questions of the intent of the maker of the copy. These can be investigated by evidence in the usual way. In any case, the history of lobbying over the Directive suggests that there is no real dispute as to the intentions of the internet service providers in making temporary copies. The real issue was whether the copyright holders should be entitled to make good the economic damage they are suffering through internet piracy by bringing their claims against the established and relatively financially sound service providers, leaving them to pursue claims for indemnification or damages against the users who are fundamentally responsible for the making of permanent, economically illegitimate copies. As in the case of the E-Commerce Directive[59] before it, this debate appears to have been won by the internet service providers.

Changes to the provisions regarding computer programs

3.97 The regime for the protection of computer programs is generally unaffected save in specified, limited respects. For example, the right to control on-demand communication to the public will apply to computer programs as to other copyright works.

3.98 Further, s 29 of the CDPA 1988, providing the exception to infringement for any copying which is fair dealing with a copyright work, is amended by the addition of a new subs (4A), which expressly provides that observing, studying or testing the functioning of a computer program in order to determine the ideas and principles which underlie any element of it is *not* fair dealing. However, this is purely by way of clarification as to what the fair dealing exception covers, since a new s 50BA is introduced[60] which exempts the lawful user of a computer program from copyright infringement for observing, studying or testing a program for this purpose if he or she does so while performing any of the acts of loading, displaying, running, transmitting or storing the program which he or she is entitled to do. This right, which cannot be excluded by contract, actually derives from the 1991 Computer Program Directive[61] but was not previously incorporated into UK law as a positive right under the implementing regulations for that Directive, although contract terms excluding the right to do so were rendered void by s 296A(1)(c) at that time.

3.99 It remains unclear, and is perhaps a matter of construction of the licence agreement in each case, whether running a program solely for the purpose of observing its functioning is within the acts which a lawful user is entitled to do. It is, however, clear that the right to observe by running a program does not go so far as to permit decompilation of the software, since that right is expressly given only in very limited circumstances, to which no change has been made.

Other amendments to existing exceptions

Unpublished works

3.100 The exception for copying provided in s 30 of the CDPA 1988 for criticism and review of the copied work now explicitly covers only those works which have been made available to the public. A separate definition of making a work available to the public is inserted for the purpose of this provision only, which includes issuing,

---

59 Directive 2000/31/EC of the European Parliament and of the Council of 8 June 2000 on certain legal aspects of information society services, in particular electronic commerce, in the Internal Market: OJ L 178, 17.7.2000, p 1. The E-Commerce Directive came into force on 17 July 2000, with national implementation due by 17 January 2002.

60 Regulation 15.

61 Article 5(3).

renting or lending copies to the public, or making them available for electronic retrieval, communication to the public or the performance, exhibition, playing or showing of the work in public. However, none of these acts will make a work available to the public if the act is unauthorised. Thus, a researcher who came across an unpublished manuscript of a famous author and uploaded it in electronic form onto the internet accompanied by a detailed commentary would infringe the copyright since the uploading, not being authorised, would not make the work available to the public so that the associated criticism and review would not bring the copying within the exception.

Clubs and societies

3.101 The exception permitting the playing of sound recordings in charitable, religious, education or social welfare clubs or societies is also narrowed. Where formerly this was permitted as long as the proceeds of any charge for admission to the place where the recording was to be heard were applied solely for the purposes of the organisation, the permission is now limited by the addition of extra requirements. First, the sound recording must be played by a person who is acting primarily and directly for the benefit of the organisation and not with a view to profit (ie no commercial DJs at club social events). Secondly, as well as the admission charge the proceeds of any goods or services sold by or on behalf of the organisation at the time must be applied solely for the purposes of the organisation.[62] Provided that these conditions are met, there will be no infringement of copyright.

Public broadcast to a non-paying audience

3.102 The provisions dealing with the situation where a broadcast is played in public but to a non-paying audience[63] have also been narrowed. The existing exception applied to any public playing of a broadcast, including sound recordings and films included in it, unless the audience had paid an admission fee or were paying prices for goods and services on the premises which were attributable at least in part to the facilities for seeing the broadcast. This was intended to enable copyright holders to claim royalties from bars and cafés which provide a television as part of the entertainment facilities, and may have been able to charge higher prices for their food and drink accordingly. This exception was drafted so as to permit the showing of a broadcast in public generally save in the specified circumstances, in other words in an inclusive rather than an exclusive fashion. It is now drafted[64] exclusively, to permit only not-for-profit organisations and TV or hi-fi sales and repair shops to play broadcasts without paying a royalty. All other organisations can now expect to be visited by the relevant collecting societies, which are in effect invited, by the insertion into the CDPA 1988 of new ss 128A and 128B dealing with licensing schemes for such purposes, to set up a licensing scheme for all other organisations which wish to play broadcasts in public. However, the existing anomaly, that the exception exonerates the broadcast from infringing copyright in sound recordings and films but not from infringing copyright in any literary, artistic or dramatic work which happens to be included, has not been corrected.

---

62 Regulation 18, amending CDPA 1988, s 67.

63 CDPA 1988, s 72.

64 Regulation 21.

Time-shifting

3.103   The existing permissions set out in ss 70 and 71 of the CDPA 1988 for private recording of broadcasts for the purpose of time-shifting, that is watching at a time other than that at which it is broadcast, or photographing images from broadcasts, are also tightened up. Under the amended section, such a recording or photograph is exempt only if it is made not only for private and domestic purposes but also in domestic premises. If the recording is subsequently sold or let for hire, offered for the same or communicated to the public it becomes an infringing copy.[65] These changes, which did not appear in the Consultation Paper, follow from concerns as to the possible scope of the exception, in the wake of an attempt, since the publication of the Consultation Paper, to use it in relation to an internet café in *Sony v Easyinternetcafé*.[66]

3.104   The right of time-shifting has even been extended by new para 17A of Sch 2 to the CDPA 1988, to cover rights in performances insofar as a performance is incorporated in a broadcast. In contrast to most other European countries, which provide a generalised exception for private copying, coupled with a levy on recording media and equipment, there is no generalised exception for private copying in the United Kingdom. Neither is there a levy in the United Kingdom, but the Government maintains that s 70 is consistent with Article 5(2)(b) of the Directive, which requires that for private copying the rightholders 'receive fair compensation', in view of the last sentence of Recital (35) of the Directive, providing that 'in certain situations where the prejudice to the right-holder would be minimal, no obligation for payment would arise'.

3.105   There appears to be a typographical error in the new para 17B of Sch 2, such that the definition of what dealings (sale, hire etc) will convert an exempted photograph into an infringing photograph instead refers to recordings, having presumably been cut and pasted from the equivalent new para 17A relating to recording for time-shifting; but Parliament's intention is clear.

3.106   A corresponding exception is introduced which applies to rights in performances.

NEW SANCTIONS

Criminal offences

3.107   Article 8 of the Directive requires Member States to implement criminal sanctions, which are considered to reflect the TRIPs Agreement requirement for effective, proportionate and dissuasive sanctions and remedies.

---

65   Regulations 19 and 20.

66   This required giving the term 'cable programme' a broad interpretation so as to cover transmission of material via the internet, as indeed it had been in *The Shetland Times Ltd v Wills and Another*. The defence was, however, held not to be available to the defendant in *Sony v Easyinternetcafé* as 'the interposition of the Defendant in the copying exercise for commercial gain [was] fatal to this defence'.

3.108   The CDPA 1988 already included criminal sanctions for infringement of the existing copyrights, but the relevant sections have been amended[67] to bring in new offences of breach of the rights of communication to the public[68] and the making available right.[69] In both cases the breach must take place in the course of a business or, if not in the course of a business, to such an extent as to affect prejudicially the owner of the right. Further, in both cases a criminal offence is committed only if the defendant had the necessary state of mind (mens rea) of knowing that the act infringed the relevant right, or had reason to believe that it did so. It is not intended to criminalise inadvertent or innocent acts.

3.109   The maximum penalties for both offences are identical to those for other criminal infringements of copyright: for summary conviction, imprisonment for up to 3 months and/or a fine, and for conviction on indictment imprisonment for up to 2 years and/or a fine. The maximum penalty has been applied subject to the limitations arising from the legislative route chosen.

3.110   Sections 296ZB and 296ZC concern the criminal options for enforcement of the revised copy protection right. There was no equivalent under the CDPA 1988 prior to amendment; copy protection right was a purely civil affair. It is therefore open to question whether these new provisions respect the requirement laid down in Recital (48) of the Directive, that the legal protection Member States confer should respect proportionality. This is particularly relevant given that these provisions do not address the underlying mischief of copyright infringement directly, but merely mechanisms applied by copyright holders to prevent such infringement. The Government's position is that these new provisions were intended to be transparent, targeted and consistent with existing copyright offences given the parallel work in the United Kingdom on making and dealing in infringing copies.

3.111   The first objective is to enable the police to remove from circulation devices and components for devices which are primarily designed or adapted for the purpose of enabling or facilitating the circumvention of effective technological measures. Section 296ZB(1) therefore renders it a criminal offence to manufacture for sale or hire, import other than for private and domestic use or, in the course of a business sell, let for hire, offer or expose or advertise for sale or hire, possess or distribute such a device. It is also an offence to distribute such devices even on a non-commercial basis if it is done to such an extent as to affect the copyright owner prejudicially. It is also an offence, under s 296ZB(2), to provide, promote, advertise or market a service, the purpose of which is to enable or facilitate the circumvention of effective technological measures in the course of a business or, if on a non-commercial basis, to do such acts to such an extent as to affect the copyright holder prejudicially.

3.112   In both cases, it is a defence to show that the accused did not know and had no reasonable grounds for believing that the device, component or service enabled or facilitated the circumvention of effective technological measures.[70]

---

67   Regulation 26.

68   CDPA 1988, s 107(2A).

69   Ibid, s 198(1A).

70   Ibid, s 296ZB(5).

3.113 There is no guidance as to how much distribution of devices or service provision will be such as to affect copyright holders prejudicially, and this is clearly a very subjective test. It derives from the 'three-step test' laid down in the Berne Convention, which may mean that it is legitimate for the English courts to look at the decisions of other jurisdictions' courts over the years to gauge the appropriate level. However, copyright holders have become increasingly determined – or desperate – in the face of the level of piracy which the advent of digital copying has engendered, to begin taking proceedings against individuals.[71] This contrasts with the traditional UK approach of treating individual copying as sufficiently innocuous not to merit even the introduction of the sorts of levies on copying technology which continental European countries have used in the past to compensate copyright holders for inevitable copyright infringement at a minor level. It remains to be seen, then, what level of activity the UK courts will consider meets this requirement, particularly bearing in mind that the sanctions are criminal rather than civil. A single CD copied across to permit a copy to be kept in the car may, if a significant proportion of the population do likewise, be portrayed as prejudicial to the interests of copyright holders who will argue that they would otherwise have sold twice as many copies. This is, of course, highly uncertain: it is axiomatic in economics that there is an unlimited demand for any free good or service, but that demand falls off as the price increases. Predicting how many people, deprived of the ability to make a second copy for use in the car, would instead have gone out and bought a second copy is a subject for endless argument. The courts' approach will no doubt be considerably more rough and ready.

3.114 The offences are triable either way, and will on summary conviction carry a penalty of up to 3 months' imprisonment or a fine, while on indictment a sentence of up to 2 years' imprisonment can be imposed as well as a fine.

3.115 An exception to the new offences is provided for the national law enforcement and intelligence agencies for circumventing copy protection where necessary. These agencies may, for example, need to decrypt messages in the pursuit of criminals or terrorists. Since any electronic message is likely to comprise a copyright text, encrypting it amounts to applying effective technological measures. Decrypting messages could therefore conceivably be a criminal offence, although it is unlikely that the police or GCHQ would be seen as businesses and therefore their activities would not be criminal unless carried out to such an extent as to affect prejudicially the copyright owner. Of course, having criminal plans thwarted would no doubt be seen as prejudicial by the copyright owners concerned, but there is an interesting question as to whether the interests which the Berne Convention intends to protect go wider than the purely economic interests which copyright confers. If not, and it is difficult to see how the Convention could be taken otherwise, then intelligence activities would appear unlikely to fall within the definition of the s 296ZB offences anyway, since the copyright in messages of the sort contemplated is unlikely ever to be of any economic or moral value to the owners. However, it may be best not to have the intelligence and law enforcement agencies at risk of having to try to convince a court of this.

---

71 Eg the cases brought by the Recording Industry Association of America in the United States in 2003, discussed in Chapter 4.

3.116   There is, despite lobbying, no such exception for professional music studios which sample or otherwise copy tracks, or for companies selling professional DAT systems which circumvent the music industry's Source Copy Management System to enable this kind of use. These users therefore face criminal liability in future unless able to negotiate specific permission from the copyright holders.

3.117   Sections 297B, 297C and 297D of the CDPA 1988, governing the criteria for the issue of search warrants and the forfeiture of unauthorised decoders, apply by virtue of s 296ZC.

Actions against internet service providers

3.118   The Regulations insert a new s 97A into the CDPA 1988 giving the High Court or, in Scotland, the Court of Session, the express power to grant injunctions against an internet service provider[72] which has actual knowledge of another person using its services to infringe either copyright or a performer's property right. Actual knowledge can be ensured by the copyright owner notifying the service provider of the presence on its systems of infringing material since, in determining whether a service provider has actual knowledge:

' ... a court shall take into account all matters which appear to it in the particular circumstances to be relevant and, amongst other things, shall have regard to:

(a)   whether a service provider has received a notice through a means of contact made available in accordance with regulation 6(1)(c) of the Electronic Commerce (EC Directive) Regulations 2002 ... and

(b)   the extent to which any notice includes:
   (i)   the full name and address of the sender of the notice;
   (ii)   details of the infringement in question.'

3.119   The Electronic Commerce (EC Directive) Regulations 2002 require internet service providers to make available a contact[73] through which copyright holders can give such notice. To be effective, the notice should include the full name and address of its sender and proper details of the infringement in question.

3.120   In practice the courts of the United Kingdom arguably already had this power since a transient electronic copy of a copyright work was an infringing copy by virtue of s 17(2) and (6), respectively affirming that an electronic copy is a copy and that the making of copies which are transient or incidental to some other use of the work is copying within the meaning of the CDPA 1988. Accordingly, an internet service provider (ISP) which hosted a bulletin board or website on which unauthorised electronic copies were posted, or which provided a connection over which a third party transmitted unauthorised electronic copies, was itself liable as an infringer. The

---

72   Service provider is defined by reference to reg 2 of the Electronic Commerce (EC Directive) Regulations 2002 (implementing in the United Kingdom the E-Commerce Directive) as:
   'any person providing an "information society service"',
   which is in turn:
      'any service normally provided for remuneration, at a distance, by means of electronic equipment for the processing (including digital compression) and storage of data, and at the individual request of a recipient of a service)'.

73   The contact information must include an e-mail address.

E-Commerce Directive gave an exception from liability for damages if the service provider took down the infringing material upon being given notice of the infringement, but the remedy of being able to obtain an injunction to prevent further copying was left. The additional section now added to the CDPA 1988 would therefore arguably have been superfluous were it not for the need to implement Article 5(1) (discussed above) which in future will make an ISP's transient copies non-infringing. The result could have been uncertainty as to whether the participation of an ISP in production of infringing copies at the instigation of a third party was capable of being the object of an injunction.

Actions by non-exclusive licensees

3.121   The intellectual property laws of the United Kingdom generally give rights to bring infringement proceedings to the right owner and any exclusive licensee. A non-exclusive licensee has in the past had no immediate right of recourse to the courts.[74] However, such a delay can reduce the value of legal proceedings, for example where small traders and counterfeiters are concerned whose stock may have turned over within that period, or who may simply have ceased trading and re-emerged in another location or with a different trading identity. This can cause great frustration for a licensee where the copyright owner is not located in the United Kingdom and does not consider the returns from bringing proceedings to be warranted by the costs and risks.

3.122   A new s 101A is therefore introduced into the CDPA 1988, giving a non-exclusive licensee the right, concurrent with that of the copyright owner, to bring proceedings in some circumstances, provided that a written licence signed by the copyright owner expressly grants that right. The circumstances in which the right is effective are where the infringing act is directly connected to some prior licensed act of the licensee. The definition of a non-exclusive licensee is a licensee with authority to exercise a right which remains exercisable by the copyright owner. This is broad enough to include both non-exclusive licensees as the term is generally understood, and also sole licensees where the copyright owner retains the right to use the copyright but gives up the right to grant any further licences.

AMENDMENTS TO DURATION OF RIGHTS IN SOUND RECORDINGS

3.123   The Regulations extend the period of protection for sound recordings in accordance with Article 11(2) of the Directive. Previously, the copyright in a sound recording expired at the end of the period of 50 years from the end of the calendar year in which it was made, or, if it was released during that 50-year period, 50 years from the end of the calendar year in which it was released. 'Released' was defined to include publication, playing in public or including in a broadcast or cable programme. This meant that sound recordings which were not released but were nevertheless made

---

74   Although in the special case of trade marks a non-exclusive licensee could bring proceedings if the proprietor failed to do so within 3 months of having been requested: Trade Marks Act 1994, s 31(3).

available, for example through on-demand services, received only the shorter period of protection specified for unpublished recordings.

3.124   The Regulations extend the duration of copyright for the latter category of sound recordings so that, like recordings which are released, they will remain in copyright until 50 calendar years have expired from the end of the year in which the recording is first made available by being played in public or communicated to the public, unless the making available is unauthorised. If a recording is first made available through, for example, an on-demand service but later published, the copyright will nevertheless expire 50 years from the end of the calendar year in which it is first published.

3.125   As a result of this change, copyright in some sound recordings may be extended.[75] It is therefore necessary to introduce transitional provisions regarding ownership during the extended period and the effect of the extension on existing agreements which are still in effect at the date when the extension takes place. Where the duration of copyright in a sound recording is extended by the Regulations, the owner of the extended copyright will be the person who owned the copyright immediately before 31 October 2003. Existing licences, whether commercial or imposed by the Copyright Tribunal, which were for the full term of the unextended copyright will continue in effect for the extended duration unless agreed otherwise.[76] Further, any agreement made before 31 October 2003 relating to the ownership of the future extended copyright will be effective to vest the extended copyright in the beneficiary of the agreement, provided that the agreement is effective to entitle the assignee as against all other persons to require the title to be vested in him or her.[77] A licence of the future extended copyright will bind the licensor and any successors in title, save for a purchaser in good faith for value without notice.

---

75   No copyrights will be truncated: reg 39.

76   Regulation 38.

77   Regulation 37.

Chapter 4

INTERNATIONAL ISSUES

COMPLIANCE WITH EXISTING INTERNATIONAL INSTRUMENTS

Introduction

4.1 The Copyright and Related Rights Regulations 2003 ('the Regulations') are expressed to implement the Directive, which is expressed in turn[1] to 'implement a number of the new international obligations' imposed by the WCT and WPPT (together, 'the WIPO Treaties'). Article 13 of the Directive required national implementation to have taken place by 22 December 2002, a relatively short period after the Directive came into force on 21 June 2001, but some 6 years after the passage of the WIPO Treaties, the delay being largely occasioned by the European Commission's ambitious determination to use the Directive not only to address those matters that were essential for ratification of the WIPO Treaties but also to harmonise exceptions and reservations in copyright and related rights laws throughout the European Union. In part, the importance of the Directive lies in the scope that it will give the European Union to accede to the WIPO Treaties.[2] Member States cannot do so individually, copyright and related rights being a shared competence between the European Union and the Member States.[3]

4.2 The Directive, and the WIPO Treaties which it in part implements, should be seen against the background of the rapid development, at an international level, in the law of copyright and related rights which took place in the 1990s, after the stagnation which the international development of copyright (under the Berne Convention), and certain related rights (under the Rome Convention) had for many years experienced. The impetus provided by the TRIPs Agreement of 1994, in both building on the Berne

---

1   Recital (15) of the Directive.

2   Under Art 17(3) of the WCT and Art 26(3) of the WPPT, the European Union (as the European Community) may become party to these Treaties, and by Council Decision 2000/278/EC ([2000] OJ L89/6 of 11 April 2000), the Council agreed to ratify both the WIPO Treaties simultaneously with the Member States. See Council Document 13212/02 of 29 October 2002 on the concerns of the Commission in this regard as to the consequences of the likely failure by some Member States to meet the implementation deadline specified by the Directive.

3   Opinion 1/94 – *Re the Uruguay Round Treaties – Competence of the Community to Conclude International Agreements Concerning Services and the Protection of Intellectual Property* [1995] 1 CMLR 205, [1994] ECR I-5267, ECJ. However, several of the countries which will join the European Union on 1 May 2004 have already ratified both the WIPO Treaties, namely the Czech Republic, Hungary, Latvia, Lithuania, Slovakia and Slovenia; and Poland has ratified the WCT.

Convention,[4] and incorporating much of the Rome Convention,[5] was then adopted in negotiating and agreeing the WIPO Treaties. The European Union, as well as the EFTA countries which together with it constitute the EEA, had for some time already, under the EEA Agreement, had to adhere to the 1971 (Paris Act) Revision of the Berne Convention and the Rome Convention.[6]

4.3 It has never seriously been questioned that the substantive law of copyright and related rights as already harmonised at EU level, before the passage of the Directive,[7] conformed to, and indeed in many respects exceed, the requirements of TRIPs,[8] but in certain respects, such as the obligations regarding technological measures and the obligations concerning rights management information, it is apparent that the law at EU level did not, until the passage of the Directive, conform to the requirements of, and so enable ratification of, the WIPO Treaties. It should be noted, however, that since adherence to the WIPO Treaties is not mandated by TRIPs, then insofar as they extend beyond the standards set by TRIPs, failure to adhere to such 'TRIPs plus' standards does not expose WTO Member States, whether or not they are parties to the WIPO Treaties, to the TRIPs Dispute Resolution Procedure and the sanctions available for failure to comply with its determinations.

4.4 This section explores to what extent the Regulations, in implementing the Directive, render the CDPA 1988 consistent with the WIPO Treaties. Such an enquiry is most readily conducted in two parts: first, as to the extent to which the Directive itself is consistent with the WIPO Treaties; and secondly, as to the extent to which the Regulations are consistent with the Directive. The second enquiry is dealt with in three parts: first, as to the restricted acts; secondly, as to the exceptions and

---

4   By virtue of Art 9 of TRIPs, 'Relation to the Berne Convention'. Articles 1, 2, 3 and 4 of TRIPs also deal with the relationship between TRIPs and the Berne Convention.

5   As Art 14 of TRIPs, 'Protection of Performers, Producers of Phonograms (Sound Recordings) and Broadcasting Organizations'.

6   See Case 13/00, *Commission v Republic of Ireland* [2002] 2 CMLR 10, [2002] ECDR 17, ECJ, in which Ireland, already a member of the Community, was found to be in breach of the EEA Agreement by not having adhered in due time, as required under the EEA Agreement, to the 1971 (Paris) Revision of the Berne Convention. The EEA Agreement had in this respect been preceded by Council Regulation of 14 May 1992 on increased protection for copyright and neighbouring rights (OJ C 138, 28.5.1992, p 1) (replacing an abandoned proposal for a Council Decision in similar terms: OJ C 24, 31.1.1991, p 5), Art 1 of which provided that 'The Council notes that the Member States of the Community, in so far as they have not already done so, undertake, subject to their constitutional provisions, to become by 1 January 1995 parties to the Paris Act of the Berne Convention and the Rome Convention, and to introduce national legislation to ensure effective compliance therewith'.

7   By virtue of Directives 91/250/EEC, 92/100/EEC, 93/98/EEC and 96/9/EC discussed in Chapter 1. Other harmonising Directives in the field of copyright and related rights, namely Directive 93/83 on the coordination of certain rules concerning copyright in and rights related to copyright applicable to satellite broadcasting and cable retransmission ('Satellite Broadcasting Directive'), Directive 98/44/EC on the legal protection of services based on, or consisting of, conditional access ('Conditional Access Directive') and Directive 2001/84/EC on the resale right for the benefit of the author of an original work of art, were relevant to other issues.

8   Indeed, of all the countries in the world it is only the United States which has to date been found wanting in this respect, as its law of copyright and related rights has, in the matter of exceptions and reservations, been found not to comply with the standards set by TRIPs: see the Report of the WTO Panel in WT/DS160/R – Section 110(5) of the US Copyright Act (15 June 2000).

reservations to these; and thirdly, as to the protection of anti-circumvention measures and rights management information.

Relationship between the WIPO Treaties and the Directive

4.5   The relationship between the minimum standards set by each of the WIPO Treaties and the Directive can, in simplified terms, be seen from the following tabulation, which also sets out the degree to which these issues had already also been expressly addressed by TRIPs:[9]

	TRIPs	**WCT**	**WPPT**	**Directive**
Subsistence	Article 10 as to computer programs and compilations of data Article 14(1) as to rights of performers in their performances and fixations of these on a phonogram Article 14(2) as to rights of producers in phonograms	Articles 4 and 5 as to computer programs and compilations of data		Not addressed[10]
Term	Article 12 as to most copyright works – plus 50 years[11]	Article 9 – Art 7(4) of Berne to apply to photographic works	Article 17 – As to phonograms, for performers, fixation plus 50 years and, for	Article 11(2) as to producers of phonograms[12]

---

9   TRIPs also mandated adherence to the standards of the Berne Convention (1971) with the exception of Art 6 bis, concerning moral rights, so further provisions as to copyright works are in effect mandated by TRIPs, but the table in general omits provisions which are not expressly set out in TRIPs.

10 As to computer programs and databases the Computer Program Directive and the Database Directive had respectively addressed these issues, and the Rental Lending and Related Rights Directive had done so as to the rights of performers and producers in phonograms.

11 TRIPs, Art 12 'Term of Protection': 'Whenever the term of protection of a work, other than a photographic work or a work of applied art, is calculated on a basis other than the life of a natural person, such term shall be no less than 50 years from the end of the calendar year of authorized publication, or, failing such authorized publication within 50 years from the making of the work, 50 years from the end of the calendar year of making.'

12 The Harmonisation of Term Directive had already addressed the term of copyright in photographs by Art 6, and the term of the rights in phonograms for performers and for producers by Art 3(1) and (2) respectively. Article 3(2) of the Harmonisation of Term Directive, as to the rights in phonograms of producers, has been replaced by a new provision by virtue of Art 11(2) of the Directive. This new provision modifies slightly such term for phonograms, which have been lawfully published or lawfully communicated to the public within 50 years of the date of fixation, which the Regulations also follow.

	TRIPs	WCT	WPPT	Directive
	Article 14(5) as to rights in phonograms of performers and producers		producers, publication plus 50 years or, failing publication within 50 years of fixation, fixation plus 50 years	
Right of Reproduction	Article 14 (1) as to performances fixed in phonograms Article 14(2) as to phonograms	Not addressed as already addressed by Art 9 of Berne	Article 7 as to performances fixed in phonograms Article 11 as to phonograms	Article 2
For copyright works, communication to the public of such works, including 'on-demand availability right', and for other matter the subject of the WPPT, 'on-demand availability right'[13]	Article 14 (1) for performers, as to broadcasting by wireless means and communication to the public of their live performance	Article 8 as to communication, (including 'making available'), to the public but without prejudice to certain Articles of Berne	Article 10 as to 'making available' performances fixed in phonograms to the public Article 14 as to 'making available' phonograms to the public	Article 3
Right of distribution		Article 6	Article 8 as to performances fixed in phonograms Article 12 as to phonograms	Article 4, except as to related rights where already addressed by the Rental Lending and Related Rights Directive

---

13   As to copyright works the subject of the Berne Convention and the WCT, the right by Art 8 of the WCT of authorising ' … communication to the public of … works by wire or wireless means, including the making available to the public of … works in such a way that members of the public may access these works from a place and at a time individually chosen by them', but as to those related rights the subject of the WPPT, the right by Arts 10 and 14 of authorising ' … the making available to the public of [the subject-matter of such rights], by wire or wireless means, in such a way that members of the public may access them from a place and at a time individually chosen by them'. The 'making available … ' aspect of these rights can be termed the 'on-demand availability right' as discussed at **4.9** below.

	TRIPs	**WCT**	**WPPT**	**Directive**
Right of rental	Article 11 as to computer programs and cinematographic works Article 14(4) as to phonograms	Article 7 – computer programs, cinematographic works and works embodied in phonograms	Article 9 as to performances fixed in phonograms Article 13 as to phonograms	Not addressed as already addressed by Rental Lending and Related Rights Directive
Limitations and exceptions	Article 13 – Berne 'three-step test' applied to all restricted acts as to copyright works[14] Article 14(6) as to, inter alia, rights in phonograms	Article 10 – Berne 'three-step test' applied to all restricted acts	Article 16 – Same kinds as for copyright, and Berne 'three-step test' applied to all rights	Article 5[15] Also, as to certain restricted acts in relation to related rights, Art 11(1)(b), amending Art 10 of the Rental Lending and Related Rights Directive
Protection of anti-circumvention measures	None	Article 11	Article 18	Article 6, except as to computer programs, already addressed by Computer Program Directive
Protection of rights management information	None	Article 12	Article 19	Article 7
Enforcement[16]	Articles 41–61	Article 14	Article 23	Article 8

---

14 TRIPs, Art 13 'Limitations and Exceptions': Members shall confine limitations or exceptions to exclusive rights to certain special cases which do not conflict with a normal exploitation of the work and do not unreasonably prejudice the legitimate interests of the rightholder.

15 Except as to computer programs and databases in which copyright subsists, where specific provisions as to exceptions and reservations in the Computer Program Directive and the Database Directive respectively are retained.

16 Since the coming into force of the Directive, the Commission has published a Proposal for a Directive on measures and procedures to ensure the enforcement of intellectual property rights: COM (2003) 46 final; 2003/0024 (COD) 30 January 2003.

4.6   As is evident from the above table, the Directive does not deal with certain issues within the scope of the WIPO Treaties because they have already been covered by certain of the previous Directives harmonising the laws of copyright and related rights. Indeed, by Article 1(2) the Directive expressly provides that it does not affect existing Community provisions, except as to certain specific cases referred to in Article 11.[17] These 'specific cases' are described as 'Technical Adaptations' which, according to Recital (61) of the Directive, are amended 'in order to comply with the [WPPT]'. This leaves some cases, such as copyright in computer programs and databases in which copyright subsists, where certain provisions of, for example, the Computer Program Directive are somewhat differently expressed to the corresponding ones in the Directive, a distinction which is retained (and has indeed even been emphasised) in the UK implementation of the Regulations.[18] The Commission can, however, be expected to take the view that such provisions, despite their different formulation, equally meet the requirements of the WIPO Treaties.[19]

4.7   The Directive goes further than required by the WIPO Treaties in its treatment of related rights, so as to maintain consistency in the structure of EU law in this area as established under the Rental Lending and Related Rights Directive. This, inter alia, mandated protection of four types of related right:

–   for performers, of fixations of their performances;
–   for phonogram producers, of their phonograms;
–   for the producers of the first fixations of films, in respect of the originals and copies of their films; and
–   for broadcasting organisations, of fixations of their broadcasts.

4.8   The WPPT only addressed the rights in phonograms (ie sound recordings) of producers of phonograms and, for performers, their performances and the fixations of these in phonograms. Thus the WPPT did not address the rights of performers in audiovisual performances and their fixations,[20] or the fixation rights in films[21] or in

---

17   Namely, in relation to related rights, the restricted act of reproduction and the issue of exceptions and reservations, and the term of protection of the rights of producers of phonograms, discussed further in Chapter 5 at **5.31**.

18   See, eg, the wholly differing provisions found in the CDPA 1988 as a result of the Regulations as to the protection of technological measures for computer programs and for other copyright works, discussed in Chapter 3.

19   The issue of inconsistencies and lacunae in the law of copyright and related rights at an EU level (which are reflected in the CDPA 1988), resulting from this piecemeal approach to legislation, is further discussed in Chapter 5 at **5.28** et seq.

20   Work has been underway in WIPO on the question of the rights of performers in their audiovisual performances for a number of years (including a Diplomatic Conference in December 2000, which however failed to agree on a Treaty), and is continuing.

21   These related rights in film fixations, the first owner of which is the producer of a film, are conceptually different from the copyright in a film, the first owner of which is, under EU law in this area, inter alia, the director of the film, in recognition of the director's creative contribution. The distinction is not, however, reflected in the laws of copyright and related rights in the common law jurisdictions such as the United States and the United Kingdom, with the consequence in the latter case that the CDPA 1988 conflates the two rights in the 'copyright' in the film, which accounts for the somewhat unsatisfactory and specific treatment that such 'copyright' receives in the CDPA 1988.

broadcasts.[22] Thus the Directive has gone further than the WPPT by applying, except insofar as this had already happened by virtue of the Rental Lending and Related Rights Directive, the restricted acts which are the subject of the WPPT to all these types of related right. The Directive has been of greatest practical significance, since EU legislation already applied the other restricted acts established under the WPPT to all such related rights, in applying by Article 3 the 'on-demand availability' right mandated by Articles 10 and 14 of the WPPT to all of these related rights.

4.9   The introduction of this new right (and the corresponding one for copyright works, expressed as included within the broad right of communication to the public by Article 8 of the WCT) is one of the most important contributions of the WIPO Treaties, as it confers on the rightholder 'the exclusive right of authorising the making available to the public of their [performances fixed in] phonograms, by wire or wireless means, in such a way that members of the public may access them from a place and at a time individually chosen by them' and so confers exclusive rights over the most relevant acts for the provision of interactive services which make subject-matter available on demand, such as those encountered over the internet. Indeed, the term 'making available' right or 'internet making available' right sometimes used for this right is somewhat misleading in failing to convey the critical 'on-demand' aspect of the right and its distinction from the general right of authors to authorise the communication to the public of their works by wire or wireless means (within which, by Article 8 of the WCT it is expressed to be comprised), and a better expression is the term 'on-demand availability' right, as used by Sterling.[23]

4.10   The Directive has also, in its provisions as to the protection of technological (namely anti-circumvention) measures in Article 6 (which, however, do not apply to computer programs, as such provisions are already found in the Computer Programs Directive), considerably elaborated on the vague and generally expressed provisions of Article 11 of the WCT and Article 18 of the WPPT. For example, Article 11 states:

> 'Contracting Parties shall provide adequate legal protection against the circumvention of effective technological measures that are used by authors in connection with the exercise of their rights under this Treaty or the Berne Convention and that restrict acts, in respect of their works, which are not authorised by the authors concerned or permitted by law.'

4.11   Article 6(3) defines the 'technological measures' which are the subject of the Article. Article 6(1) mandates protection against acts of circumvention of such 'technological measures' and Article 6(2) mandates protection against various acts which are preparatory to or which facilitate such circumvention. Article 6(4), which was only introduced during the passage of the Directive, and which has no express basis in the WIPO Treaties, is a significant, although limited, provision which restricts the application of Article 6(1) where circumvention is necessary to allow users to

---

22   Work is currently underway in WIPO on the question of the rights of broadcasting organisations in their broadcasts, and a Diplomatic Conference may take place on this in 2004.

23   Sterling discusses its nature and scope in more detail in *World Copyright Law* (Sweet & Maxwell, 2nd edn, 2003). For further discussion of the nature and scope of this right, see also Ficsor *The Law of Copyright and the Internet* (Oxford University Press, 2002), and Reinbothe and von Lewinski *The WIPO Treaties 1996* (Butterworths, 2002).

enjoy the benefit of certain specified exceptions and reservations.[24] It thus provides a mechanism to limit the scope for 'locking up content' by the use of technological protection measures, where the use of such content would otherwise be permitted by certain of the exceptions and reservations set out in Article 5. In contrast to Article 6, the implementation in Article 7 of the Directive of the provisions as to the protection of rights management information set out in Article 12 of the WCT and Article 19 of the WPPT, very closely follows the structure and the wording of these Articles.

4.12   In one notable respect, however, the Directive falls short of the minimum standards set out under the WIPO Treaties – namely that of the moral rights of performers, as mandated, albeit only as regards 'live aural performances or performances fixed in phonograms', by Article 5 of the WPPT. This issue is not addressed by the Directive because the Commission has never as yet undertaken any initiative in relation to the area of moral rights, whether for authors of copyright works as mandated by the Berne Convention (but not by TRIPs) or performers.[25] As the Directive does not address this issue, the Regulations cannot serve to bring UK law into conformity with the requirements of the WPPT in this respect. Quite how the UK authorities will address this problem is not clear, although it has been suggested that primary legislation, with its demands on parliamentary time, may not in fact be necessary as once the European Union becomes a party to the WPPT, the European Communities Act 1972 would allow the necessary amendments to be made to UK law by delegated legislation under the 1972 Act.[26]

Restricted acts under the Directive and the Regulations

4.13   As is evident from the table at **4.5** above, the Directive harmonises within Europe, to the extent as yet unharmonised by previous measures,[27] for works and other subject matter, the restricted acts of:

–   reproduction (Art 2);
–   communication (including 'on-demand availability') to the public of copyright works and 'on demand availability' for other matter (Art 3);
–   distribution (Art 4).

Finally, by Article 5, the Directive harmonises, to a considerable degree, exceptions and reservations from each of these restricted acts.

---

24   The balance that Art 6(4) seeks to draw is further discussed in Recitals (38) and (39) of the Directive. A less flexible mechanism, albeit one which equally recognises that circumvention ought not to be treated as unlawful in all instances, can be found in the United States in the deferred implementation of s 1201(a)(1) of the WIPO Copyright and Performances and Phonograms Treaties Implementation Act of 1998 (part of the Digital Millennium Copyright Act), and is discussed below.

25   Authors' moral rights were identified as a potential area for action by the Commission in the *Follow Up to the Green Paper – Working programme of the Commission in the field of copyright and neighbouring rights* of 17 January 1991: COM (90) 584 final. However, no proposals on moral rights have ever emerged from the Commission.

26   See the Consultation Paper from the Copyright Directorate of the Patent Office *Moral Rights for Performers* of January 1999.

27   Namely the Computer Program Directive, the Database Directive, the Rental Lending and Related Rights Directive, the Harmonisation of Term Directive and the Satellite Broadcasting Directive.

4.14 As to restricted acts, the most difficult aspect of implementing the Directive in the United Kingdom has been Article 3 of the Directive. Here, the main problem faced has not been in conforming the CDPA 1988 to wording of the Directive, but in addressing the consequential redefinition in the Act of what constitutes 'broadcasting'. 'Broadcasting' is now expressed to fall, along with the new 'on-demand availability' right of 'making available to the public of the work by *electronic transmission* in such a way that members of the public may access it from a place and at a time individually chosen by them' (emphasis added) within the scope of the restricted act of 'communication to the public'.[28] Although the new definition of broadcasting in s 6 of the CDPA 1988 has been the subject of criticism, the Directive does not mandate any particular approach to its definition.[29]

4.15 The Regulations do, however, introduce language into the CDPA 1988 which speaks of communication to the public 'by electronic transmission' rather than the 'by wire or wireless means' wording of the Directive and the WIPO Treaties. Consistent with their general approach to construing UK legislation in the field of intellectual property which reflects EU directives, the English courts will no doubt look to the Directive wording in preference to that in the CDPA 1988, and will not attribute any significance to the different wording now found in the CDPA 1988.

4.16 A further disparity between the Directive and its implementation by the Regulations is a consequence of the structure of the CDPA 1988, the passage of which preceded the programme of harmonisation of copyright and related rights in the European Union. That structure does not reflect EU law in this area by distinguishing between copyright in works (in the strict sense of the types of works protected only under the Berne Convention and the WCT, namely 'literary and artistic works' which term is so defined as to include music and films), and the related rights in phonograms (ie sound recordings) and in broadcasts.[30] In contrast, the CDPA 1988 has always adopted, consistent with the historical development of UK law in this area, a different approach to related rights in performances and their fixations. A consequence of this structure is that the Regulations go rather further than the Directive (which already, as explained above, goes further than required by the WPPT), in protecting related rights other than those of performers. Thus by s 20 the restricted act of communication to the public, including 'the on-demand availability right', applies not only to copyright works in the strict sense (as mandated by Article 3(1) of the Directive) but also to phonograms and broadcasts, even though Article 3(2) of the Directive only mandates introducing for such related rights the restricted act of 'making available to the public, by wire or wireless means, in such a way that members of the public may access them from a place and at a time individually chosen by them'. In contrast to their treatment of other related rights the Regulations, as ever, perpetuate the different treatment meted out to performers by the CDPA 1988 by implementing as s 182CA the

---

28 The expression 'communication to the public' is not defined, in contrast to the proposals made in the Consultation Paper.

29 The issue of the territorial scope of the restricted acts of 'communication to the public', and that of 'broadcasting' included within it (and to some extent already addressed by the Satellite Broadcasting Directive), is not addressed by the Directive, and is discussed later in this chapter at **4.48–4.52**.

30 There is also the fixation right to consider under EU law in this area but, as noted above, the CDPA 1988 conflates the copyright (in the strict sense) in films with the fixation right in films.

restricted act of making a recording of a performance available to the public, as also mandated by Article 3(2) of the Directive, termed the 'making available right'.

Exceptions and reservations to the restricted acts, under the Directive and the Regulations

4.17 Neither of the WIPO Treaties contains specific provisions as to limitations and exceptions. Moreover, despite the title of the Directive, the problematic issue of exceptions and reservations, the subject of Article 5 of the Directive, has very little to do with any issues raised by the 'information society'.[31] Instead of the list of exceptions and reservations set out in the Directive, the WIPO Treaties, as with the Berne Convention[32] and TRIPs,[33] provide, by Article 10 of the WCT, and by Article 16 of the WPPT, a generalised test by which the acceptability of specific exceptions and reservations can be assessed – the 'three-step test'.

4.18 This three-step test is also set out at Article 5(5) of the Directive in such a way that its hierarchical superiority to the specific exceptions listed in the previous paragraphs of Article 5 is made clear (splitting it into the 'three steps'):

> '5(5) The exceptions and limitations provided for in paragraphs 1, 2, 3 and 4 shall only be applied in
> – certain special cases
> – which do not conflict with a normal exploitation of the work or other subject matter and
> – do not unreasonably prejudice the legitimate interests of the rights holder.'

4.19 Article 11(1)(b) makes a corresponding amendment in relation to certain related rights to the provisions as to exceptions and reservations for those restricted acts which are retained in the Rental Lending and Related Rights Directive and to which, by virtue of Article 1(2), Article 5 does not apply – namely fixation, broadcasting and communication to the public and distribution. The compatibility of the specific exceptions and reservations set out in the Directive with the three-step test has not been the subject of detailed study, although Ricketson has suggested that certain specific provisions might not be.[34] However, the Regulations omit any counterpart to Article 5(5) or 11(1)(b), the view having been taken by the UK authorities that such considerations were taken account of in striking the balance in

---

31 Moreover, the Commission's initial proposals as to exceptions and reservations (which were modified considerably during the progress of the measure) were, unlike other Commission legislative proposals in the field of copyright and related rights, made without any prior comparative law exercise.

32 Article 9(2) as to the restricted act of reproduction.

33 Article 13, but in relation to all restricted acts under copyright and related rights. This was reviewed and interpreted fully by a WTO Panel in WT/DS160/R 'Section 110(5) of the US Copyright Act' (15 June 2000), which found certain US legislation as to exceptions and reservations inconsistent with this aspect of TRIPs.

34 Ricketson: *WIPO Study on Limitations and Exceptions of Copyright and Related Rights in the Digital Environment*: Tabled at Ninth Session of the WIPO Standing Committee on Copyright and Related Rights (23–27 June 2003), referring in this connection to Art 5(2)(a) and (3)(b), (e), (g), (i) and (k) (the latter incorrectly referred to in the paper as (g)).

the exceptions and reservations contained in the Regulations.[35] The English courts cannot, however, be precluded from considering Article 5(5) in appropriate circumstances.

4.20   Article 5(1), (2), (3) and (4) of the Directive set out exhaustive lists of various specific exceptions and reservations, of which the only mandatory one, Article 5(1) (implemented by the Regulations as s 28A of the CDPA 1988), has no basis in the WIPO Treaties. Because of its specific nature in the context of transient copying, it is discussed in Chapter 5. Article 5(2) and (3) each set out lists of specifically drawn exceptions and reservations, optional in that they are not obligatory, but proscriptive in that no other exceptions and reservations than these are permitted. Those in Article 5(2) are from the restricted act of reproduction and those in Article 5(3) are from both the restricted acts of reproduction and of communication to the public (including 'the on-line availability' right) including at Article 5(3)(o) a 'wrap-up' permitting the retention of traditional national analogue exceptions of minor importance. Article 5(4) extends these principles to the restricted act of distribution.

4.21   The UK authorities took the decision to try to implement Article 5(2) and (3) in such a way as to change as little as possible the existing (and already highly detailed by most standards in Europe) provisions in the CDPA 1988, which has caused them some difficulty. The Consultation Paper observed:

> 'While there is no obligation on member states to provide for any of these exceptions in national law, it is not permitted to continue with existing exceptions, or introduce new exceptions, which fall outside the scope of any one or more of the categories defined in Article 5.2 and 5.3. (An important point that was borne in mind during preparation of the draft amendments to the Act is the lack of hierarchy between the various optional exceptions and limitations.)'

4.22   The passage in brackets would appear to have provided the rationale for the approach adopted by the UK authorities of, on occasion, amending the exceptions and reservations in the CDPA 1988 by 'mixing and matching' exceptions found in Article 5 of the Directive. While convenient from the point of view of trying to make as little change as possible to the literal wording of the CDPA 1988 (except to make it even more complicated), such an approach is somewhat convoluted and counterintuitive, in that it does not leave all the exceptions and reservations set out in the CDPA 1988 as amended by the Regulations in a convenient one-to-one correspondence with those set out in Article 5(2) and (3) of the Directive, as can be seen from the following (non-exhaustive) table of such 'combined exceptions'.

---

35   As noted in the Consultation Paper: 'It is not proposed to introduce the test as such into UK law as a general constraint on exceptions; rather, it is proposed to continue with existing practice in the [CDPA 1988] of using the test as a standard in framing exceptions to rights. It follows that the exceptions amended as proposed, as well as other unamended exceptions to copyright and related rights in the [CDPA 1988], are considered to comply with the three step test.' In this context the Consultation Paper then went on to canvass, in relation to exceptions and reservations to certain related rights as harmonised under the Rental Lending and Related Rights Directive and as to which by virtue of Art 11(1)(b) of the Directive the three-step test was to be applied, the approach to be adopted as to ss 67 and 72 of the CDPA 1988. As a result of this these exceptions have been narrowed in the Regulations.

Title of Exception in CDPA 1988	Provision of CDPA 1988	Corresponding Provisions in Directive
Research and private study	Section 29	Article 5(2)(b), (3)(a)
Things done for purposes of instruction or examination	Section 32	Article 5(3)(a), (d)
Copying by librarians: articles in periodicals	Section 38	Article 5(2)(b), (3)(a)
Copying by librarians: parts of published works	Section 39	Article 5(2)(b), (3)(a)
Copying by librarians or archivists: certain unpublished works	Section 43	Article 5(2)(b), (3)(a)
Recordings of folksongs	Section 61	Article 5(2)(b), (c), (3)(a)

4.23   Such an approach also increases the number of overlapping exceptions and reservations which may potentially be applicable to any particular restricted act. Allied to the undoubted relevance in any English court (and on a reference by it to the ECJ) of the three-step test mandated by Articles 5(5) and 11(1)(b) of the Directive, irrespective of the approach adopted by the Regulations, the intricate interrelation between the CDPA 1988 as amended (and as highlighted by the above table) and the Directive is hardly calculated to clarify or facilitate the task of such court if the basis for any such provision in the CDPA 1988 is challenged.

Protection of anti-circumvention measures, and of rights management information under the Directive and the Regulations

4.24   The provisions of Articles 6 and 7 of the Directive, mandating, consistent with the WIPO Treaties, legal protection of technological (namely anti-circumvention) measures and of rights management information, are not the first such measures to have been part of European or UK legislation. Thus the Computer Program Directive, by Article 7(1)(c), mandated the protection of anti-circumvention measures. Moreover, the Conditional Access Directive, by Article 4, also mandated the prohibition of various activities in relation to 'illicit devices', being 'any equipment or software designed or adapted to give access to a protected service in an intelligible form without the authorisation of the service provider', where the term 'protected services' included various conditional access services such as broadcasting or information society services. Although the CDPA 1988 did not, until amended by the Regulations, provide for criminal sanctions in connection with the circumvention of copyright protection, it did, by s 297, provide for a criminal offence of fraudulently receiving programmes and, by s 297A,[36] a criminal offence for dealing in unauthorised decoders.

---

36   Inserted by the Broadcasting Act 1990, and subsequently replaced by a differently worded provision by the Conditional Access (Unauthorised Decoders) Regulations 2000, SI 2000/1175, to implement the Conditional Access Directive. See also CDPA 1988, ss 297B, 297C and 297D for associated provisions.

4.25 By Article 6 the Directive mandates protection for technological (namely anti-circumvention) measures protecting copyright and related rights. However, Article 1(2) of the Directive has the effect of preserving Article 7(1)(c) of the Computer Program Directive, which provides as to this that:

'1   Without prejudice to the provisions of Articles 4, 5 and 6, Member States shall provide, in accordance with their national legislation, appropriate remedies against a person committing any of the acts listed in subparagraphs (a) (b) and (c) below:

. . .

(c)   any act of putting into circulation, or the possession for commercial purposes of, any means the sole intended purpose of which is to facilitate the unauthorised removal or circumvention of any technical device which may have been applied to protect a computer program.'

4.26 The corollary of Article 1(2) is that Article 6 of the Directive does not apply to 'computer programs' to the extent that they are the subject of the Computer Program Directive.[37] The position would presumably be taken by the Commission that despite the much more elaborate language of Article 6 of the Directive, Article 7(1)(c) of the Computer Program Directive remains adequate to meet the somewhat general standards set by Article 11 of the WCT.

4.27 In consequence, the Directive envisages a different approach to the protection of anti-circumvention measures as to computer programs from that for other works and matter the subject of related rights, which difference is also reflected in the Regulations, at least as regards civil rights of action. The Regulations also recognise the arguably inadequate prior UK implementation of Article 7(1)(c) of the Computer Program Directive in s 296 of the CDPA 1988 by totally recasting the provision.[38] The section had, before such replacement, been expressed to cover all copyright works where 'issued to the public, by or with the licence of the copyright owner, in electronic form which is copy-protected'.[39] The new version of s 296 is expressed to apply where 'a technical device has been applied to a computer program'. To add causes of action to protect, consistent with the Directive, anti-circumvention measures for copyright works other than computer programs, as well as matter the subject of related rights, the Regulations also add ss 296ZA and 296ZD, broadly corresponding to Article 6(1) and (2) respectively, which apply where 'effective technological measures have been

---

37   The term 'computer program' is not defined in the Computer Program Directive, but Art 1(1) of the Computer Program Directive does provide that 'For the purposes of this Directive, the term "computer program" shall include their preparatory design material.'

38   Section 296 had in fact preceded the Computer Program Directive, having been in the CDPA 1988 as originally enacted. It underwent a small modification as from 1 January 1993, by the insertion of subs (2A), under the Copyright (Computer Programs) Regulations 1992, SI 1992/3233, in purported implementation of the Computer Program Directive. As replaced by a new provision under the Regulations it is expressed significantly differently.

39   CDPA 1988, s 296, before its replacement by the Regulations, was considered in *Sony Computer Entertainment Inc v Owen* [2002] EWHC 45, [2002] EMLR 34.

applied to a copyright work other than a computer program'.[40] New s 296ZF corresponds to Article 6(3) of the Directive.

4.28 However, the new criminal offence introduced by the Regulations as s 296ZB, which also corresponds to Article 6(2) in addressing various acts which are preparatory to or which facilitate such circumvention (it is entitled 'Devices and services designed to circumvent technological protection measures'), also covers computer programs, as it does not distinguish between these and other works and matter the subject of related rights. The Directive does not mandate the introduction of criminal sanctions for any particular acts,[41] but the UK authorities took the view that it was appropriate to introduce such an offence 'drafted to be consistent with existing copyright offences given the parallel work relating to UK intellectual property criminal offences concerning making and dealing in illegal material'.[42] The new offence has many parallels with the existing criminal offence under s 297A of the CDPA 1988 for dealing in unauthorised decoders, but does not render criminal the act of circumvention itself, despite calls from rightholders' organisations to do so.

4.29 There is considerable latitude as to how Article 6(4) of the Directive can be implemented and it would appear that is proving to be one of the most variable in its manner of national implementation. In the United Kingdom this is achieved by new s 296ZE (with its associated Sch 5A of permitted acts to which the section applies), providing a mechanism which ultimately gives administrative power to the relevant Government Minister to give appropriate directions.

4.30 Unlike anti-circumvention measures, the Computer Program Directive did not provide legal protection for rights management information, and so Article 7 of the Directive applies to all types of copyright work, as well as those matters the subject of related rights, as is recognised by the Regulations, which closely follow its wording in the new s 296ZG which they introduce. No corresponding criminal sanctions have been introduced despite calls from rightholders' organisations to do so.

---

40 New ss 296ZA and 296ZD apply also to copyright in databases, as, in contrast to the Computer Program Directive, the Database Directive does not mandate legal protection for anti-circumvention measures, and so Art 6 of the Directive applies to copyright in databases, as is recognised by the Regulations. Indeed, Art 6 of the Directive is expressed also to apply to the sui generis right in databases established under the Database Directive, which is effectively a type of related right not within the scope either of TRIPs or the WIPO Treaties. By virtue of ss 296ZA(6) and 296ZD(8) these new provisions also apply to the sui generis right in databases ('database right').

41 Although it does require, by Art 8, that there be 'appropriate sanctions and remedies' and that such sanctions be 'effective, proportionate and dissuasive'.

42 As noted in the Consultation Paper from the Copyright Directorate of the Patent Office on Implementation of the Directive of 7 August 2002. The parallel work to which reference was made was the Copyright, etc and Trade Marks (Offences and Enforcement) Act 2002, which harmonised some of the copyright and trade mark criminal remedies.

EQUIVALENT UNITED STATES LAW AND PERSPECTIVES

Introduction

4.31 It has become traditional, especially given the high profile accorded to litigation in the United States, to characterise the Directive as a response to, and equivalent of, the Digital Millennium Copyright Act (DMCA) in the United States. Some comment about the Regulations has been to similar effect. In that both the Directive (and thus the Regulations) and the DMCA respond to the WIPO Treaties, there are bound to be similarities, but there are also significant differences.

4.32 The Digital Millennium Copyright Act of 1998 has several parts.[43] For the purposes of comparing its response to the WIPO Treaties with that of the Directive one need only concentrate on two of these: the Online Copyright Infringement Liability Limitation Act; and the WIPO Copyright and Performances and Phonograms Treaties Implementation Act of 1998. The issues that have arisen under them are briefly summarised below, although, as these have only limited relevance to most of the litigation which has taken place in relation to the issue of file-sharing and P2P networks, such litigation is discussed separately in the context of such matters in Chapter 5.

Online Copyright Infringement Liability Limitation Act

4.33 The Online Copyright Infringement Liability Limitation Act sets out what have come to be known as the 'safe harbours' for service providers and serves to limit the liability of such service providers, in a new s 512, for the following:

- transitory digital network communication (s 512(a));
- system caching (s 512(b));
- information residing on systems or networks at direction of users (s 512(c));
- information location tools (s 512(d)).

All of these safe harbours, apart from that for transitory digital network communications, are subject to intricately drafted 'notice & take down' procedures, by which the service provider can no longer avail itself of the safe harbour if it fails to remove, or to block, infringing material once notified of it.

4.34 These exceptions have no basis in the WIPO Treaties. In Europe, although Article 5(1) of the Directive provides an exception to the restricted act of reproduction, which addresses certain transient activities in which service providers are involved, it is the E-Commerce Directive, which, albeit in rather less detailed language, most closely tracks the provisions of the Online Copyright Infringement Liability Limitation Act. The application of these provisions to transient activities in which service providers are involved is discussed in Chapter 5 in relation to transient copying.

---

43   I – WIPO Copyright and Performances and Phonograms Treaties Implementation Act; II – Online Copyright Infringement Liability Limitation [etc] Act; III – Computer Maintenance Competition Assurance Act; IV – Miscellaneous Provisions; V – Vessel Hull Design Protection Act.

4.35   The relevance of the Online Copyright Infringement Liability Limitation Act to copyright infringement issues on the internet has until recently been limited. Thus in *A&M Records Inc v Napster Inc*[44] it was considered that the defendants in such litigation would be unlikely to be able to bring themselves within its safe harbours. This case (and subsequent ones involving other peer-to-peer (P2P) networks than Napster) instead turned on issues of fair use and of authorisation, which have interesting parallels in Europe, and are discussed in Chapter 5 in relation to P2P networks and file-sharing.

4.36   More recently, however, the Online Copyright Infringement Liability Limitation Act has been used not as a potential defence for service providers, but as a weapon in the war against P2P networks and file-sharing activities. Such use involved s 512(h), which permits a copyright owner to obtain and serve a subpoena on a service provider seeking the identity of a customer of that service provider alleged to be infringing the owner's copyright. *RIAA v Verizon*[45] concerned an action to enforce such a subpoena against a service provider to identify an internet user, tracked down by a 'bot', where the user had downloaded more than 600 songs from the internet in a single day. The Recording Industry Association of America, Inc (RIAA) argued that the subpoena mechanism in s 512(h) applied irrespective of under what safe harbour (s 512(a)–(d)) the ISP fell. The service provider, Verizon, argued that the subpoena should only be available where the safe harbour under s 512(c) applied and the material in issue was stored on the network, which it did not in this case, where Verizon availed itself of the safe harbour under s 512(a) for information transmitted over the network.[46]

4.37   At first instance, in January 2003, the District Court, looking to what it saw as the history and purpose of the measure, agreed with the RIAA, and made an order to enforce the subpoena. On appeal, the Court of Appeal (in December 2003), looking to the plain wording of the provisions in question, found little difficulty in overturning this, and noted that in any case P2P file-sharing had not been in the contemplation of the legislators. In so doing it set out something of the background to the matter and the attempts by the RIAA to identify certain internet users:

> 'The RIAA now has begun to direct its anti-infringement efforts against individual users of P2P file sharing programs. In order to pursue apparent infringers the RIAA needs to be able to identify the individuals who are sharing and trading files using P2P programs. The RIAA can readily obtain the screen name of an individual user, and using the Internet Protocol (IP) address associated with that screen name, can trace the user to his ISP. Only the ISP, however, can link the IP address used to access a P2P program with the name and address of a person – the ISP's customer – who can then be contacted or, if need be, sued by the RIAA. The RIAA has used the subpoena provisions of § 512(h) of the Digital Millennium Copyright Act (DMCA) to compel ISPs to disclose the names of subscribers whom the RIAA has reason to believe are infringing its members' copyrights. *See* 17 U.S.C. § 512(h)(1) (copyright owner may "request the clerk of any United States district court to

---

44   239 F 3d 1004, 57 USPQ 2d 1729 (US CA (9th Cir) 2001).

45   257 F Supp 2d 244, 65 USPQ 2d 1574 (DC, 2003) reversed 19 December 2003 (US CA (DC Cir), 2003). For copies of the various submissions filed in the case, see http://www.eff.org/Cases/RIAA_v_Verizon/.

46   The subpoena mechanism in s 512(h) was expressed to involve the provision of a notification given under s 512(c).

issue a subpoena to [an ISP] for identification of an alleged infringer"). Some ISPs have complied with the RIAA's § 512(h) subpoenas and identified the names of the subscribers sought by the RIAA. The RIAA has sent letters to and filed lawsuits against several hundred such individuals, each of whom allegedly made available for download by other users hundreds or in some cases even thousands of .mp3 files of copyrighted recordings. Verizon refused to comply with and instead has challenged the validity of the two § 512(h) subpoenas it has received.'

4.38 Since the decision at first instance in *Verizon* in January 2003 and before the appellate decision, numerous further subpoenas had been secured, enabling the RIAA to start to threaten and to commence action against individual users. This approach has become more important for the RIAA as it has become increasingly difficult for rightsowners to shut down file-sharing networks, as such networks become ever more widely disseminated and out of the control of any one particular entity. It remains to be seen how much of a setback to rightsowners this decision will be (it related only to those ISPs relying on the safe harbour under s 512(c)) and what their response will be. Subpoenas have also been granted against entities other than ISPs – such as universities in relation to the activities of their students – although some of these have been successfully challenged on jurisdictional grounds largely unconnected with the Online Copyright Infringement Liability Limitation Act.[47]

4.39 In Europe, Article 8(3) of the Directive mandates Member States to ensure that 'rightholders are in position to apply for an injunction against intermediaries whose services are used by a third party to infringe a copyright or related right', which the Regulations implement in the United Kingdom by new ss 97A and 191JA of the CDPA 1988. Although these do not provide in terms for subpoenas, the provision of information about infringement is, at least in England and Wales, a well-established form of relief in intellectual property matters, available even against those innocent of any wrongdoing, as in *Norwich Pharmacal v HM Customs & Excise Commissioners*,[48] even absent the express provisions in these new sections.

WIPO Copyright and Performances and Phonograms Treaties Implementation Act of 1998

4.40 The WIPO Copyright and Performances and Phonograms Treaties Implementation Act of 1998 introduced, by s 1203, civil remedies, and, by s 1204, criminal penalties for:

– violations regarding circumvention of technological measures (s 1201):
  – circumvention of access control technology for protected works (s 1201(a)(1));
  – trafficking in access control technology for protected works (s 1201(a)(2));
  – trafficking in technology that protects a right of a copyright owner (s 1201(b));
– providing false, or removing or altering, copyright management information (s 1202):
  – trafficking in technology that circumvents access (s 1202(a)(2));

---

47 Eg on 7 August 2003 subpoenas issued in the District of Columbia US District Court against two universities based in Massachusetts were quashed by the Massachusetts US District Court.

48 [1974] RPC 101 (House of Lords).

–   trafficking in technology that circumvents 'copying' etc (s 1202(b)).

4.41   It can thus be seen that s 1201 can broadly be said to implement Article 11 of the WCT and Article 18 of the WPPT, so corresponding to Article 6 of the Directive in the European Union, and s 1202 to implement Article 12 of the WCT and Article 19 of the WPPT, so corresponding to Article 7 of the Directive. Unlike Article 6 of the Directive, however, s 1201 draws a distinction between access control technologies (s 1201(a)) and copy control technologies (s 1201(b)), and indeed does not render the circumvention of copy control technology, as opposed to access control technology, illegal, but is concerned, as to copy control technology, only with 'trafficking' – namely the provision of means to circumvent such technology. In contrast, Article 6(3) of the Directive makes no such distinction, and expressly includes both access control and copy control within the scope of 'effective technological measures' the subject of Article 6(1) and (2). However, the s 1201(a) implementation, as to the circumvention of access control technology, despite being subject to exceptions for certain activities such as reverse engineering of computer programs and a mechanism for excepting whole classes of copyright work from its ambit, has been the source of considerable controversy, particularly as to the use sought to be made of it in impeding the activities of competitors.[49]

4.42   A challenge to the constitutionality of s 1201 failed in *Universal City Studios v Corley*.[50] The action concerned the 'DeCSS' computer program, which decrypted the Content Scramble System (CSS) that prevents copying of DVDs. It was held that posting such program on a website together with links to other websites with such postings constituted trafficking in a device which circumvented access control technology contrary to s 1201(a)(2)).

4.43   Section 1201(b) was in issue in the notorious criminal prosecution of the Russian programmer Dmitry Sklyarov and his employer Elcomsoft for providing a program which was alleged to circumvent the technical protection on Adobe's eBooks so allowing people to copy and view eBooks in Adobe's eBook format in other formats and on multiple computers without using Adobe's eBook Reader program. The prosecution was launched whilst Sklyarov was visiting the United States in 2001, although the prosecution was later dropped as against him personally. In May 2002 a constitutional challenge to the provision was rejected, but in December 2002 a jury returned a verdict finding Elcom not guilty, but, as a jury verdict, no reasons for this were given.

4.44   Implementation of s 1201(a)(1) was deferred for 2 years for the US Copyright Office to make rules excluding certain classes of copyright work from the ambit of the section after determining to what extent exceptions needed to be made to it if users of copyright works were, or were likely to be, adversely affected by the prohibition imposed by the section in their ability to make non-infringing use of a particular class of copyright work. Thereafter, such rulemaking takes place every 3 years, the second

---

49   For a regularly updated, albeit partisan, critique of s 1201 with an extensive listing of the controversies which have arisen under it, see 'Unintended Consequences: Five Years under the DMCA', published by the Electronic Frontier Foundation: www.eff.org. The site also provides an invaluable research resource by posting the various submissions filed and judgments entered in the litigation in this area that it follows.

50   273 F 3d 429, 60 USPQ 2d 1953 (US CA (2nd Cir), 2001).

round of rulemaking having concluded in October 2003.[51] This mechanism can thus be seen broadly to correspond to the exercise envisaged by Article 6(4) of the Directive, although given that s 1201 does not render the mere circumvention of copy control, as opposed to access control, or the trafficking in copy control circumvention means, illegal the demands on such rulemaking might be expected to be more limited than those under Article 6(4). However, two of the four classes of currently excluded copyright work under s 1201(a)(1) are computer programs, and, in the European Union, Article 6 of the Directive does not apply to these. Instead, as also discussed above, protection of anti-circumvention measures for computer programs in the European Union takes place by virtue of Article 7(1)(c) of the Computer Program Directive, but which has been in force for over a decade, without, it would appear, occasioning controversy.[52]

4.45 An impression of the controversies over the use of s 1201(a) in impeding the activities of competitors is provided by *The Chamberlain Group, Inc v Skylink Technologies, Inc* and *Lexmark International, Inc v Static Control Components, Inc.* The former action concerned Skylink's distribution of a universal remote transmitter, which could activate certain garage door openers manufactured by Chamberlain. Chamberlain alleged that Skylink violated s 1201(a)(2) by circumventing a technological measure that controlled access to the computer program in Chamberlain's garage door openers. One of Skylink's motions for summary judgment was denied in August 2003 but another was granted in November 2003.[53] The latter action concerned Lexmark printer toner cartridges containing integrated circuits that reported the amount of toner left and generated a code without which the printer would not work. Such code was alleged to be a technological measure designed to

---

51 See http://www.copyright.gov/1201/ for full details. For the period 28 October 2000 through to 28 October 2003 the excluded classes were: (1) compilations consisting of lists of websites blocked by filtering software applications; and (2) literary works, including computer programs and databases, protected by access control mechanisms that fail to permit access because of malfunction, damage, or obsoleteness. For the period 28 October 2003 through to 28 October 2006 the excluded classes are: (1) compilations consisting of lists of internet locations blocked by commercially marketed filtering software applications that are intended to prevent access to domains, websites or portions of websites, but not including lists of internet locations blocked by software applications that operate exclusively to protect against damage to a computer or computer network or lists of internet locations blocked by software applications that operate exclusively to prevent receipt of e-mail; (2) computer programs protected by dongles that prevent access due to malfunction or damage and which are obsolete; (3) computer programs and video games distributed in formats that have become obsolete and which require the original media or hardware as a condition of access. A format shall be considered obsolete if the machine or system necessary to render perceptible a work stored in that format is no longer manufactured or is no longer reasonably available in the commercial marketplace; (4) literary works distributed in e-book format when all existing e-book editions of the work (including digital text editions made available by authorised entities) contain access controls that prevent the enabling of the e-book's read-aloud function and that prevent the enabling of screen readers to render the text into a specialised format.

52 Indeed, the activity as that found to be contrary to the long-standing s 296 of the CDPA 1988 in *Sony Computer Entertainment Inc v Owen* ([2002] EWHC 45, [2002] EMLR 34), before its replacement by the Regulations to more closely accord with Art 7(1)(c) of the Computer Program Directive, that of circumventing copy protection and region control technologies, is similar to that activity which Sony has been criticised in the United States for seeking to control by means of s 1201. See 'Unintended Consequences: Five Years under the DMCA' at n 49 above.

53 US District Court for Northern District of Illinois: 29 August 2003, 13 November 2003.

prevent access to the computer program, and thus emulating it in recycled and resold cartridges was contrary to s 1201. Moreover, it was alleged that the computer program had been copied, and a preliminary injunction was granted against Static in February 2003,[54] which is under appeal. Static also sought to exclude such cartridges from the scope of the section in the context of the most recent round of Copyright Office rulemaking under s 1201(a)(1), discussed above, but this was rejected by the Register of Copyrights on the basis that s 1201(f), by excluding reverse engineering of computer programs from the ambit of s 1201(a)(1), already addressed the legitimate concerns of cartridge remanufacturers.

INTERNATIONAL ENFORCEMENT AND REMEDIES

Introduction

4.46 Copyright and related rights are national rights, and yet increasingly – and especially in the context of the internet – infringement of such rights can occur in multiple jurisdictions. This then raises the questions traditionally dealt with in the context of private international law, namely of what laws apply to such infringement, and what courts have jurisdiction to decide such matters.

4.47 Determining the correct applicable law is important because, even within Europe, there are considerable substantive differences in copyright law as between different countries.[55] The analysis can be complicated by the fact that such differences in substantive law can sometimes extend to the effective territorial scope of the right, as explained below. Determining what courts have jurisdiction is also important, even within Europe, as the procedural differences between different courts in different Member States may be considerable.

The territorial scope of national copyright laws

4.48 Copyright and other intellectual property rights present an especial challenge to private international law in that intellectual property may take the form either of non-property rights (which, like other torts, are not expressly territorial in their nature) such as unfair competition, or of property rights, which, like copyright and related rights, are generally territorial in nature. However, despite the inherently territorial nature of copyright and related rights, certain restricted acts, such as broadcasting, and now the new 'on-demand availability right', by their nature have the potential to take place at two separate locations. If the two separate locations are in two different jurisdictions this raises the question of which national copyright law applies to such acts. The problem, accentuated in an internet environment, can be seen as an instance of a more general one of cause and effect. Thus the cause may be in one jurisdiction, and the effect felt in another jurisdiction. In such a case, in which jurisdiction does infringement take place?

4.49 The matter has been the subject of considerable discussion in the context of broadcasting, particularly direct broadcasting by satellite, where reception can (as

---

54   253 F Supp 2d at 947 (ED Ky 2003).

55   See **5.36–5.37** for a discussion of some of the issues of European copyright law that remain still to be harmonised.

with the internet) take place in multiple jurisdictions. One can identify two different approaches to the problem:

– at the point of emission only (the 'Emission Theory');
– at both point of emission and point of reception (the 'Communication Theory' or 'Bogsch Theory'[56]).

4.50 In the context of direct broadcasting by satellite, UNESCO and WIPO advanced the communication theory, such that broadcasting took place both in the country of origination of the signal (the 'upleg' stage of transmission) and in the country or countries of reception (the 'downleg' stage of transmission). Austria, Canada, France, and Israel[57] have all followed the communication theory in the context of broadcasts. Adoption of this approach gives the rightholder a measure of flexibility, which it lacks under the emission theory. The debate has now arisen again in the context of the new 'on-demand availability' right. Neither the WIPO Treaties, nor Article 3 of the Directive, provide any guidance as to whether such right is infringed by an unauthorised act which only takes place at the place of origination, or is infringed by an unauthorised act which takes place at both that location and that of reception. The weight of academic thought on the issue is that the communication theory should apply.[58]

4.51 Throughout the European Union and the rest of the EEA, national laws have been modified for satellite broadcasting originating in such countries under the Satellite Broadcasting Directive, which mandates the application of the emission theory (expressed as the 'country of origin' principle) but only as to satellite broadcasts originating within the European Union, leaving national jurisdictions free to apply either the emission theory or the communication theory to other broadcasts.[59]

4.52 Under UK law, in the context of satellite broadcasting the CDPA 1988 has always adopted the 'emission theory' by virtue of s 6(4) of the CDPA 1988 and its predecessors, which have always specified that satellite broadcasting takes place at

---

56 So called after Dr Arpad Bogsch, the Director-General of WIPO, and who first suggested such an approach in 1985, at a UNESCO/WIPO meeting on the subject.

57 These cases, and the history of the communication theory, are discussed in Sterling *World Copyright Law* (Sweet & Maxwell, 2nd edn, 2003).

58 See, eg, Reinbothe and von Lewinski *The WIPO Treaties 1996* (Butterworths, 2002), at pp 108–109.

59 However, in contrast, the E-Commerce Directive applies within Europe the 'country of origin' principle to many information society services but expressly denies its application to intellectual property rights such as copyright and related rights.

the point of transmission.[60] The amendments made by the Regulations preserve this situation, but are silent as to the issue as applied to the exclusive right of 'communication to the public' under s 20 of the CDPA 1988 as amended, including, by s 20(2)(b), the 'on-demand availability right' of 'the making available to the public of the work by electronic transmission in such a way that members of the public may access it from a place and at a time individually chosen by them'. Thus, even though the emission theory, by definition, applies to broadcasts, this does not foreclose the possibility in the United Kingdom of arguing that the communication theory applies to the new on-demand availability right which is the subject of ss 20(2)(b) and 182CA of the CDPA 1988.

4.53 A further issue as to the territorial scope of infringement arises in relation to authorisation. Under UK law, while the various restricted acts such as reproduction, communication to the public (including the on-demand availability right and broadcasting), rental and distribution must, by definition, take place in the United Kingdom for them to infringe UK copyright, authorisation is not so limited. As confirmed in *Def Lepp Music v Stuart-Brown*,[61] no action can be brought in England for the alleged infringement of UK copyright by acts done outside the United Kingdom. The provision there interpreted is now s 16(1) of the CDPA 1988, by which (emphasis added) (as amended by Regulations):

'(1) The owner of copyright in a work has ... the exclusive right to do the following acts *in the United Kingdom* ...

(a)   to copy the work ...
(b)   to issue copies of the work to the public ...
(c)   to rent or lend the work to the public ...
(d)   to perform, show or play the work in public ...
(e)   to communicate the work to the public ...
(f)   to make an adaptation of the work or do any of the above in relation to an adaptation ...'

4.54 In contrast, however, as confirmed in *ABKCO Music & Records v Music Collection International*,[62] authorisation which takes place abroad, to do in the United Kingdom an act restricted by copyright, constitutes infringement by virtue of s 16(2) of the CDPA 1988, which provides that:

'(2)   Copyright in a work is infringed by a person who without the licence of the copyright owner does, or authorises another to do, any of the acts restricted by copyright.'

---

60   CDPA 1988, s 6(4) as originally enacted provided that ' ... the place from which a broadcast is made is, in the case of satellite transmission, the place from which the signals carrying the broadcast are transmitted to the satellite.' It was amended by the Copyright and Related Rights Regulations 1996, SI 1996/2967, as part of the UK implementation of the Satellite Broadcasting Directive, to provide that ' ... the place from which a broadcast is made is the place where, under the control and responsibility of the person making the broadcast, the programme carrying signals are introduced into an uninterrupted chain of communication (including, in the case of a satellite transmission, the chain leading to the satellite and down towards the earth).' The Regulations, consequential on the new definition of 'broadcast' elsewhere in s 6 of the CDPA 1988 to include certain types of internet transmission, amend ss 6(4) of the CDPA 1988 by inserting the word 'wireless' before 'broadcast' where it first appears.

61   [1986] RPC 273.

62   [1995] RPC 657.

The critical difference in the two sections lies in the absence in s 16(2) of the qualification 'in the United Kingdom' found in s 16(1) of the CDPA 1988.[63]

Determining the applicable law in copyright disputes

4.55 The Berne Convention would appear at first sight to address the question of the law to be applied to copyright disputes. Article 5(2) provides:

'... the extent of protection, as well as the means of redress afforded to the author to protect his rights, shall be governed exclusively by the laws of the country where protection is claimed.'

4.56 However, interpretation of this provision is not straightforward, as what is meant by 'the country where protection is claimed'? Is it the country where the action is brought, or the country whose copyright law is alleged to be infringed? The French Supreme Court has considered this matter in *Société Informatique Service Réalisation Organisation (Sisro) v Société de Droit Néerlandais en Liquidation Ampersand Software BV et al.*[64] Here the action was against two software companies, not based in France, for copyright infringement in the United Kingdom, the Netherlands and Sweden. The Supreme Court held that the law to be applied was not the law of the country of origin or of the court invoked, but rather the law of the country in whose territory the infringement occurred.

4.57 In the United Kingdom, a similar approach was taken in *Pearce v Ove Arup*,[65] in which an English court (which had jurisdiction in the matter by virtue of the Brussels Convention, as explained below) held that Dutch law should be applied to an allegation of infringement of Dutch copyright where the alleged infringing act took

---

63 In a similar way, as the definition of the restricted acts under the UK sui generis right in databases under reg 16(1) of the Copyright and Rights in Databases Regulations 1997 provides that ' ... a person infringes database right in database if, without the consent of the owner of the right, he extracts or re-utilises all or a substantial part of the contents of the database' lacks the qualification 'in the United Kingdom', there would appear to be no need that such act take place in the United Kingdom to infringe. Thus Laddie, Prescott and Vittoria, *Modern Law of Copyright and Designs* (Butterworths, 2000), at para 34A.30 observe: 'Applying [the ABCKO] reasoning to the [1997 Regulations], it becomes apparent that an act such as "re-utilisation" (meaning making the content available to the public by any means) can indeed found liability although done abroad, provided the consequences – availability to the public in this country – are sustained in the UK'.

64 Cour de Cassation, 5 March 2002, IIC 6/2003, p 701.

65 *Pearce v Ove Arup Partnership Ltd (Jurisdiction)* [2000] Ch 403, [2000] 3 WLR 332, [1999] 1 All ER 769, [1999] FSR 525 (Court of Appeal). The Court of Appeal did, however, observe that under Art 3(2) of the Berne Convention the question was not 'in respect of which country is the protection claimed' and so 'the protection is claimed in the country in which the proceedings are brought'. Such apparent inconsistency may be explained by such discussion taking place not in the context of applicable law but in the context of jurisdiction and the relationship between the Berne Convention and the Brussels Convention (discussed further below), as is apparent from its conclusion that 'What Article 5(2) does ... is to leave it to the courts of the country in which the proceedings are brought to decide whether the claim for protection should be upheld. It does not seek to confer jurisdiction on the courts of one country to the exclusion of any other.'

place in the Netherlands.[66] The position in the United Kingdom has now been further clarified by s 11 of the Private International Law (Miscellaneous Provisions) Act 1995 (postdating the circumstances which gave rise to the dispute in *Pearce v Ove Arup*) which now provides that:

> 'The general rule is that the applicable law is the law of the country in which the events constituting the tort or delict in question occur.'

4.58 More recently, the European Commission has initiated discussion on a 'Rome II' directive, which would harmonise the applicable law within the Community for 'non-contractual obligations'. This term must include intellectual property rights but it is evident that the draft originally circulated, as with so much activity in the field of private international law, had been prepared with no thought whatsoever of intellectual property rights. Thus the European Commission consultation paper of May 2002 on a Preliminary Draft Proposal for a Council Regulation on the law applicable to non-contractual relations had suggested in Article 3 a provision, which did not distinguish between intellectual property infringement and other torts:

> '1 The law applicable to a non-contractual obligation arising out of a tort or delict shall be the law of the country in which the loss is sustained, *irrespective of the country or countries in which the harmful event occurred* and irrespective of the country in which the indirect consequences of the harmful event are sustained ... ' [emphasis added]

4.59 Quite what this would have meant in the context of intellectual property is hard to envisage, but the version now published[67] recognises, in its accompanying Explanatory Memorandum, 'that the general rule contained in Article 3(1) does not appear to be compatible with the specific requirements in the field of intellectual property', and specifically addresses in Article 8 the issue of intellectual property, adopting language which is reminiscent of the Berne Convention:

> '1 The law applicable to a non-contractual obligation arising from infringement of intellectual property right shall be the law of the country for which protection is sought.'

This, however, would improve on the language of the Berne Convention as the expression 'the country for which protection is sought' is more clearly expressed than the 'the country where protection is claimed'.

Jurisdiction and enforcement

4.60 In questions of enforcement and jurisdiction, from an English law perspective, it is necessary to distinguish between the situation as between the United Kingdom and the rest of Europe (defined more specifically below), and the situation as between the United Kingdom and the rest of the world. Within Europe traditional private international law considerations, such as those of 'forum conveniens', have been

---

66 Although when the matter came to be heard on the merits in *Pearce v Ove Arup Partnership Ltd (Copying)* [2002] ECDR CN2 (Chancery Division) the trial judge did not feel it necessary to consider any of the expert evidence as to Dutch law addressing the ways in which Dutch law might have been said to differ from English law as to the degree of copying required for infringement to take place, as he held that there had been no copying anyway.

67 Proposal for a Regulation of the European Parliament and the Council on the law applicable to non-contractual obligations ('Rome II'): COM (2003) 427 final, Brussels, 22 July 2003.

supplanted by an exhaustive and exclusive set of rules for determining the proper jurisdiction for disputes to be adjudicated. Other than as between European countries, traditional private international law considerations still apply.[68]

4.61 Thus within Europe, the issue of which courts have jurisdiction, together with the related issue of enforcing a judgment of one court in another, is governed by the three measures which are in similar terms, at least insofar as they relate to intellectual property: the Brussels Convention,[69] the Lugano Convention[70] and the Brussels Regulation.[71] The Brussels Regulation sets out a hierarchy of rules for establishing jurisdiction and provisions under which other courts either in some circumstances must, or in others may, decline jurisdiction.[72] The rules for establishing jurisdiction relevant to the infringement of copyright and related rights are set out in Articles 2, 5(3) and 6(1) of the Brussels Regulation (the numbering of the corresponding provision in the Brussels Convention is the same). The primary rule, set out in Article 2, is that one must sue the defendant in its country of domicile:

'1(1) Subject to this Regulation, persons domiciled in a Member State shall, whatever their nationality, be sued in the courts of that Member State.
(2) Persons who are not nationals of the Member State in which they are domiciled shall be governed by the rules of jurisdiction applicable to nationals of that State.'

---

68 In England, the issue of 'forum conveniens' has not been addressed in relation to attempts to adjudicate copyright disputes arising outside Europe in the United Kingdom, because of certain preliminary impediments which used to be thought to exist as to English courts hearing intellectual property disputes concerning foreign territorial rights, such as copyright and related rights, in the form of the 'double actionability' rule and the *Mocambique* rule, as in *Tyburn Productions v Conan Doyle* [1990] 3 WLR 167. The 'double actionability' rule, but not the *Mocambique* rule, was repealed by s 10 of the Private International Law (Miscellaneous Provisions) Act 1995, but the scope in consequence of this for English courts to adjudicate on copyright disputes arising outside Europe has yet to be tested. However, in *Pearce v Ove Arup* the Court of Appeal, which held that the *Mocambique* rule did not, as a result of the Brussels Convention, require the English court to refuse to entertain a claim in respect of the alleged infringement of Dutch copyright, expressed some doubt as to whether, irrespective of the Brussels Convention, the *Mocambique* rule provided support for the proposition that a claim for breach of a foreign statutory intellectual property right could not be entertained by an English court.

69 The Brussels Convention still applies as between Denmark and other members of the European Union, but as between all other members of the European Union, including the United Kingdom, has been replaced as from May 2002 by the Brussels Regulation.

70 The Lugano Convention applies as between Poland, members of EFTA (including Switzerland, even though it is not a member of the EEA), Switzerland and the Member States of the European Union, but, as from EU enlargement in May 2004, the Brussels Regulation will replace it, as to Poland, on its becoming part of the European Union.

71 Council Regulation 2001/44/EC of 22 December 2000 on jurisdiction and the recognition and enforcement of judgments in civil and commercial matters. This applies as between all the members of the European Union except Denmark as from May 2002.

72 An added complication under the Brussels Regulation and the Brussels and Lugano Conventions, which need not be considered in the case of copyright and related rights, as these are not registered, occurs in relation to registered intellectual property rights such as patents, trade marks and registered designs, as there are special rules as to those courts which can adjudicate on the validity of such rights.

4.62 However, there are two significant qualifications to this. First, by Article 5(3), one may sue the defendant in the country where the harmful event occurred, although doing so is likely to limit the extent of the relief that can be claimed to that country:[73]

> '5 A person domiciled in a Member State may, in another Member State, be sued:
>
> . . .
>
> (3) in matters relating to tort, *delict* or *quasi-delict*, in the courts for the place where the harmful event occurred or may occur.'

4.63 Secondly, by Article 6(1), the defendant may be sued jointly with other defendants in the country where one defendant is domiciled, provided that the claims are 'so closely connected that it is expedient to hear . . . them together . . . ':

> '6   A person domiciled in a Member State may also be sued:
>
> (1) where he is one of a number of defendants, in the courts for the place where any one of them is domiciled, provided the claims are so closely connected that it is expedient to hear and determine them together to avoid the risk of irreconcilable judgments resulting from separate proceedings.'

4.64 Careful choice of co-defendants may by virtue of Articles 2 and 6(1) taken together provide considerable scope for a claimant to 'forum shop' within Europe by identifying a suitable co-defendant in the jurisdiction in which the claimant wishes to proceed, so that jurisdiction is established as against that defendant on an Article 2 basis and as against the other co-defendants, which may be based in jurisdictions which may be less favoured by the claimant, on an Article 6(1) basis. Thus in *Pearce v Ove Arup*, jurisdiction of the English courts over an alleged infringement which took place in the Netherlands (and had therefore to be determined under Dutch law as the applicable law, as explained above) was founded by a combination of Article 2 and Article 6(1) of the Brussels Convention,[74] despite some defendants being domiciled in the Netherlands and others in England.

4.65 The Brussels Regulation has two Articles as to declining jurisdiction where another court in Europe is already seized of a dispute, one which national courts must apply, and the other which they may apply. Article 27 (corresponding to Article 21 of the Brussels Convention) obliges a court to stay proceedings, and ultimately to decline jurisdiction where proceedings involve the same cause of action and are between the same parties:

> '1. Where proceedings involving the same cause of action and between the same parties are brought in the courts of different Member States, any court other than the court first seized shall of its own motion stay its proceedings until such time as the jurisdiction of the court first seized is established.

---

73 *Sheville v Press Alliance* [1995] 2 AC 18, [1995] 2 WLR 499, [1995] All ER (EC) 289, [1995] EMLR 543 (ECJ). See also *IBS Technologies (PVT) Ltd v APM Technologies SA (Jurisdiction)* (unreported) 7 April 2003 (Michael Briggs QC, Chancery Division).

74 The action had first been brought in England, where jurisdiction was established because although the third and first defendants were domiciled in the Netherlands, and the act complained of took place in the Netherlands (so that the applicable law was that of the Netherlands), the first defendant was domiciled in England. The result, under the rules of the Brussels Convention (which applied at the time, but has since been replaced by the Brussels Regulation, which as to this is in similar terms) was that no action could then be brought in the Netherlands.

2. Where the jurisdiction of the court first seized is established, any court other than the court first seized shall decline jurisdiction in favour of that court.'

4.66 However, Article 28 (corresponding to Article 21 of the Brussels Convention) permits, but does not oblige, a court to stay proceedings and to decline jurisdiction where the earlier proceedings are 'related':

'1. Where related actions are pending in the courts of different Member States, any court other than the court first seised may stay its proceedings.

2. Where these actions are pending at first instance, any court other than the court first seised may also, on the application of one of the parties, decline jurisdiction if the court first seised has jurisdiction over the actions in question and its law permits the consolidation thereof.

3. For the purposes of this Article, actions are deemed to be related where they are so closely connected that it is expedient to hear and determine them together to avoid the risk of irreconcilable judgments resulting from separate proceedings.'

4.67 However, these provisions do not preclude applications for interim relief, such as an interim injunction, as by Article 31 (corresponding to Article 21 of the Brussels Convention:

'Application may be made to the courts of a Member State for such provisional, including protective, measures as may be available under the law of that State, even if, under this Regulation, the courts of another Member State have jurisdiction as to the substance of the matter.'

4.68 Closely related to the issue of jurisdiction is that of enforcement of judgments, which as with jurisdiction, is addressed wholly differently as within Europe and as between European countries and those outside. Within Europe, judgments of courts of other Member States are accorded full recognition under the Brussels Regulation and the corresponding provisions of the Brussels and Lugano Conventions. The effect of Articles 33 and 36 of the Brussels Regulation is that a judgment from another Member State must be recognised without any special procedure and may under no circumstances be reviewed as to its substance. There are very few grounds on which recognition can be challenged, as set out in Articles 34 and 35 of the Brussels Regulation.

4.69 Outside Europe the situation as to the recognition of foreign judgements is very different. It will vary as between different European countries and the non-European country concerned. Thus the United Kingdom enjoys the benefit of certain bilateral agreements with non-European countries, which permit of reciprocal enforcement of money judgments.[75]

4.70 Attempts are being made to transfer the approach adopted under the Brussels Convention, the Lugano Convention and the Brussels Regulation to a wider international level. Such work has been undertaken under the auspices of the Hague Conference on private international law.[76] In June 2001 it discussed in Diplomatic Session a draft of a 'Convention on Jurisdiction and Foreign Judgments in Civil and

---

75 The Administration of Justice Act 1920, relating to a number of countries with historical links with the United Kingdom (but not Australia, Canada, India or Pakistan), and the Foreign Judgments (Reciprocal Enforcement) Act 1933, which now applies to very few countries, the most important of which is Israel.

76 A standing body concerned with matters of private international law: see www.hcch.net.

Commercial Matters' but there was lack of consensus as to a number of issues, including those as to copyright and other intellectual property rights, in the wake of which the Hague Conference has undertaken further consultations, and has now set itself for the time being in this area less ambitious tasks including a 'Convention of Exclusive Choice of Court Agreements'.[77] Such issues were also discussed at the WIPO Forum on Private International Law and Intellectual Property in Geneva in January 2001,[78] where a 'Draft Convention on Jurisdiction and Recognition of Judgments in Intellectual Property Matters', adapted from the October 1999 text of the Hague Conference draft, but directed to intellectual property, was tabled.

---

77   See http://www.hcch.net/e/workprog/jdgm.html for the progress of this aspect of the work of the Hague Conference.

78   See http://wipo.int/pil-forum/en/ for the papers there submitted.

Chapter 5

RESIDUAL AND EMERGING CONCERNS

TRANSIENT COPYING

Introduction

5.1   Various service providers which run communications networks, such as internet service providers (ISPs) and telecommunications service providers (Telcos) have long expressed concern at their potential liability for tortious activities, including matters such as copyright infringement, conducted over their networks by third parties, but of which they have no knowledge, and over which they have no control. They have thus lobbied extensively to secure various 'safe havens' from such liability.

5.2   The results of these lobbying activities litter the statute books. In the United States they have resulted in the safe harbours under the Online Copyright Liability Limitation Act, also discussed in Chapter 4. In Europe they have resulted in two measures: the safe harbours provided under the E-Commerce Directive which largely, as to copyright and related rights, correspond to those set out in the Online Copyright Liability Limitation Act, and also the mandatory exception provided by Article 5(1) of the Copyright Directive. Ironically, these measures may never have been needed in the first place, and the compromises made in securing them may have imposed potential burdens on service providers which would not otherwise have existed – for example, by providing for service providers to respond to subpoenas, as attempted in *RIAA v Verizon* (discussed in Chapter 4), or by providing for a free-standing injunctive right against service providers, as provided under the Copyright and Related Rights Regulations 2003 '(the Regulations')' as new s 97A and 191JA of the CDPA 1988, discussed below.

5.3   As to whether these measures were ever needed in the first place, as discussed below, in relation to the mandatory exception for transient copying, the Agreed Statement concerning Article 8 of the WCT makes clear the understanding that 'the mere provision of physical facilities for enabling or making a communication does not in itself amount to a communication within the meaning of [the WCT] or the Berne Convention'. As to the restricted act of reproduction (as, for example, discussed by Laddie, Prescott and Vittoria[1]), mere 'passive reproduction' or 'involuntary copying' (for example, by receipt of an unsolicited fax message) does not infringe copyright and thus a service provider on the internet ought not to be regarded as infringing copyright by the mere storage of a work on its server.

---

1   Laddie, Prescott and Vittoria *Modern Law of Copyright and Designs* (Butterworths, 2000), at paras 14.13 and 14.14.

5.4 Such a proposition was accepted in *Sony Music Entertainment (UK) Ltd and Others v Easyinternetcafé Limited*[2] as correct when applied to an ISP, but was held not to apply on the particular facts of the case so as to provide a defence for the defendant 'internet café' which allowed its customers to make a CD-R copy of material that they had stored in their private file area. Here a customer of an 'internet café' could ask employees of the internet café to copy onto CD-R material already stored in the customer's private file area after the customer had used the internet. However, it was held that the defendant could not avail itself of the 'involuntary copying' defence as the 'only material which is available [in this case] for this defence is that the defendant chooses to keep the files of an individual customer confidential allegedly by directing that the employees cannot see them unless the customer consents'.

Safe harbour under E-Commerce Directive

5.5 Article 3.3 of the E-Commerce Directive and the Annex to it exclude from the 'country of origin' principles established by Articles 3.1 and 3.2 for information society services within the European Union, inter alia:

> 'Copyright, neighbouring rights, rights referred to in Directive 87/54/EEC[3] and Directive 96/9/EC[4] as well as industrial property rights'.

However, despite this deliberate omission from its scope the E-Commerce Directive does have considerable significance for copyright and related rights. Such significance arises by virtue of the defences offered by Articles 12 to 14 of the E-Commerce Directive which provide a limited 'safe harbour' in respect of a wide range of potential liabilities of service providers, in respect of online activity, for:

- 'mere conduit' (Art 12);
- 'caching' (Art 13);
- 'hosting' (Art 14).

5.6 The general application of such defences can be contrasted with the copyright specific nature of the corresponding ones in the United States under the Online Copyright Infringement Liability Limitation Act (a part of the Digital Millennium Copyright Act 1998). Although there are certain differences of definition, the equivalence between each of these types of activity and the first three the subject of the Online Copyright Infringement Liability Limitation Act is readily apparent:

Online Copyright Infringement Liability Act section	Online Copyright Infringement Liability Act expression	Electronic Commerce Directive section	Electronic Commerce Directive expression
Section 512(a)	transitory digital network communications	Section 13	mere conduit
Section 512(b)	system caching	Section 14	caching

---

2   [2003] EWHC 62 (Ch), [2003] FSR 48, [2003] ECDR 27, [2003] IP&T 1059.

3   Namely semiconductor topography rights.

4   Namely the sui generis database right established under the Database Directive.

Online Copyright Infringement Liability Act section	Online Copyright Infringement Liability Act expression	Electronic Commerce Directive section	Electronic Commerce Directive expression
Section 512(c)	information residing on systems or networks at direction of users	Section 15	hosting
Section 512(d)	information location tools		

5.7 Apart from the safe harbour for 'mere conduit', the safe harbours under the E-Commerce Directive are subject to 'Notice and Takedown' procedures, by which the service provider can no longer avail itself of the defence if it fails to remove or block infringing material once notified of it, although the E-Commerce Directive, unlike the Online Copyright Infringement Liability Limitation Act, gives no guidance as to what might constitute adequate notice. Each of these three Articles, as to each such defence, provides that it 'shall not affect the possibility for a Court or administrative authority, in accordance with Member States' legal systems, to require the service provider to terminate or prevent an infringement'. However, the E-Commerce Directive does not mandate the establishment of any underlying right which would enable such a court to make such an order, and indeed Article 15 makes it clear that there is no general obligation on service providers to monitor the information they transmit or store.

5.8 Implementation of the E-Commerce Directive in the United Kingdom by the Electronic Commerce (EC Directive) Regulations 2002[5] adopted, as to these provisions, the rare (for the United Kingdom) approach of 'copy-out' and, as can be seen from the tabulation, in which the relevant provisions are set out, regs 17, 18 and 19 follow Articles 12.1, 13.1 and 14.1 almost to the word. Regulation 20 largely reflects Articles 12.3, 13.2 and 14.3. Regulation 21 is concerned with the effect of regs 17, 18 and 19 on the burden of proof in criminal proceedings and reg 22 provides certain guidance, lacking in the E-Commerce Directive, as to what might constitute adequate notice under the 'Notice and Takedown' provisions of regs 18 and 19:

---

5   SI 2002/2013. For the full background to the UK implementation of the E-Commerce Directive (which proved to be not entirely straightforward, but for other reasons than those provisions here discussed), see: *http://www2.dti.gov.uk/industries/ecommunications/electronic_commerce_directive_0031ec.html#cons_pdf*. Electronic Commerce (EC Directive) Regulations 2002 (SI 2002/2013) also apply to the Copyright (Visually Impaired Persons) Act 2002 and to the amendments to the CDPA 1988 made by the Regulations by virtue of the Electronic Commerce (EC Directive) (Extension) Regulations 2003 (SI 2003/115) and the Electronic Commerce (EC Directive) (Extension) (No 2) Regulations 2003 (SI 2003/2500).

	E-Commerce Directive	**Electronic Commerce (EC Directive) Regulations 2002**
'Mere conduit'	**12**–(1) Where an information society service is provided that consists of the transmission in a communication network of information provided by a recipient of the service or the provision of access to a communication network, Member States shall ensure that the service provider is not liable for the information transmitted, on condition that the provider – (a) does not initiate the transmission; (b) does not select the receiver of the transmission; and (c) does not select or modify the information contained in the transmission. (2) The acts of transmission and of provision of access referred to in paragraph 1 include the automatic, intermediate and transient storage of the information transmitted in so far as this takes place for the sole purpose of carrying out the transmission in the communication network, and provided that the information is not stored for any period longer than is reasonably necessary for the transmission. (3) This article shall not affect the possibility for a court or administrative authority, in accordance with Member States' legal systems, of requiring the service provider to terminate or prevent an infringement.	**17**–(1) Where an information society service is provided which consists of the transmission in a communication network of information provided by a recipient of the service or the provision of access to a communication network, the service provider (if he otherwise would) shall not be liable for damages or for any other pecuniary remedy or for any criminal sanction as a result of that transmission where the service provider – (a) did not initiate the transmission; (b) did not select the receiver of the transmission; and (c) did not select or modify the information contained in the transmission. (2) The acts of transmission and of provision of access referred to in paragraph (1) include the automatic, intermediate and transient storage of the information transmitted where: (a) this takes place for the sole purpose of carrying out the transmission in the communication network, and (b) the information is not stored for any period longer than is reasonably necessary for the transmission.

	E-Commerce Directive	**Electronic Commerce (EC Directive) Regulations 2002**
Caching	13–(1) Where an information society service is provided that consists of the transmission in a communication network of information provided by a recipient of the service, Member States shall ensure that the service provider is not liable for the automatic, intermediate and temporary storage of that information, performed for the sole purpose of making more efficient the information's onward transmission to other recipients of the service upon their request, on condition that: (a) the provider does not modify the information; (b) the provider complies with conditions on access to the information; (c) the provider complies with rules regarding the updating of the information, specified in a manner widely recognised and used by industry; (d) the provider does not interfere with the lawful use of technology, widely recognised and used by industry, to obtain data on the use of the information; and (e) the provider acts expeditiously to remove or to disable access to the information it has stored upon obtaining actual knowledge of the fact that the information at the initial source of the transmission has been removed from the network, or access to it has been disabled, or that a court or an administrative authority has ordered such removal or disablement. (3) This article shall not affect the possibility for a court or administrative authority, in accordance with Member States' legal systems, of requiring the service provider to terminate or prevent an infringement.	18 Where an information society service is provided which consists of the transmission in a communication network of information provided by a recipient of the service, the service provider (if he otherwise would) shall not be liable for damages or for any other pecuniary remedy or for any criminal sanction as a result of that transmission where – (a) the information is the subject of automatic, intermediate and temporary storage where that storage is for the sole purpose of making more efficient onward transmission of the information to other recipients of the service upon their request, and (b) the service provider – (i) does not modify the information; (ii) complies with conditions on access to the information; (iii) complies with any rules regarding the updating of the information, specified in a manner widely recognised and used by industry; (iv) does not interfere with the lawful use of technology, widely recognised and used by industry, to obtain data on the use of the information; and (v) acts expeditiously to remove or to disable access to the information he has stored upon obtaining actual knowledge of the fact that the information at the initial source of the transmission has been removed from the network, or access to it has been disabled, or that a court or an administrative authority has ordered such removal or disablement.

	E-Commerce Directive	**Electronic Commerce (EC Directive) Regulations 2002**
Hosting	**14**–(1) Where an information society service is provided which consists of the storage of information provided by a recipient of the service, Member States shall ensure that the service provider is not liable for the information stored at the request of a recipient of the service on condition that:	**19** Where an information society service is provided which consists of the storage of information provided by a recipient of the service, the service provider (if he otherwise would) shall not be liable for damages or for any other pecuniary remedy or for any criminal sanction as a result of that storage where –
	(a) the provider does not have actual knowledge of illegal activity or information and, as regards claims for damages, is not aware of facts or circumstances from which the illegal activity or information is apparent; or	(a) the service provider – (i) does not have actual knowledge of unlawful activity or information and, where a claim for damages is made, is not aware of facts or circumstances from which it would have been apparent to the service provider that the activity or information was unlawful; or
	(b) the provider, upon obtaining such knowledge or awareness, acts expeditiously to remove or to disable access to the information. (2) Paragraph 1 shall not apply when the recipient of the service is acting under the authority or the control of the provider. (3) This article shall not affect the possibility for a court or administrative authority, in accordance with Member States' legal systems, of requiring the service provider to terminate or prevent an infringement, nor does it affect the possibility for Member States of establishing procedures governing the removal or disabling of access to information.	(ii) upon obtaining such knowledge or awareness, acts expeditiously to remove or to disable access to the information, and (b) the recipient of the service was not acting under the authority or the control of the service provider.

E-Commerce Directive	Electronic Commerce (EC Directive) Regulations 2002
No general obligation to monitor **15**–(1) Member States shall not impose a general obligation on providers, when providing the services covered by Articles 12, 13 and 14, to monitor the information which they transmit or store, nor a general obligation actively to seek facts or circumstances indicating illegal activity. (2) Member States may establish obligations for information society providers, promptly to inform the competent authorities of alleged illegal activities undertaken or information provided by recipients of their service or obligations to communicate to the competent authorities, at their request, information enabling the identification of recipients of their service with whom they have storage requirements.	**Protection of rights** **20**–(1) Nothing in regulations 17, 18 and 19 shall – (a) prevent a person agreeing different contractual terms; or (b) affect the rights of any party to apply to a court for relief to prevent or stop infringement of any rights. (2) Any power of an administrative authority to prevent or stop infringement of any rights shall continue to apply notwithstanding regulations 17, 18 and 19.

	Notice for the purposes of actual knowledge
	22 In determining whether a service provider has actual knowledge for the purposes of regulations 18(b)(v) and 19(a)(i), a court shall take into account all matters which appear to it in the particular circumstances to be relevant and, among other things, shall have regard to –
	(a) whether a service provider has received a notice through a means of contact made available in accordance with regulation 6(1)(c), and
	(b) the extent to which any notice includes –
	  (i) the full name and address of the sender of the notice;
	  (ii) details of the location of the information in question; and
	  (iii) details of the unlawful nature of the activity or information in question.

Mandatory exception in the Copyright Directive for transient copying

5.9 Service providers, however, did not consider the protection that the provisions of the E-Commerce Directive gave them to be adequate, and during the passage of the Copyright Directive pressed for a further exception, the mandatory exception provided by Article 5(1) of the Directive. This provides:[6]

> '1. Temporary acts of reproduction referred to in Article 2, which are transient or incidental, which are an integral and essential part of a technological process and the sole purpose of which is to enable:
>
> (a)   a transmission in a network between third parties by an intermediary, or
> (b)   a lawful use
>
> of a work or other subject-matter to be made, and which have no independent economic significance, shall be exempted from the reproduction right provided for in Article 2.'

5.10 This is a mandatory provision, further explained at Recital (33) of the Directive, and has been included by the Regulations in the UK implementation of the Directive as s 28A of the CDPA 1988, in virtually the same form as it is set out in the Directive. Section 28A of the CDPA 1988 is, however, on its face wider than the exception mandated by the Directive in that it does not purport to distinguish between the restricted act of reproduction and the new restricted act established under Article 3 of the Directive (the 'on-demand availability right'), which is presumably also subject to the exception under UK law. This may not be of great significance as the Agreed Statement as to Article 8 of the WCT suggests that activities such as those the subject of Article 5(1) of the Directive do not fall within the scope of the 'on-demand availability right' established under Article 8 of the WCT (and Article 3 of the Directive):[7]

> 'It is understood that the mere provision of physical facilities for enabling or making a communication does not in itself amount to a communication within the meaning of this Treaty or the Berne Convention.'

5.11 Article 5(1) of the Directive, however, has no basis in the WIPO Treaties. Several observations can be made about its scope.

–   It applies only to reproduction, and not to other restricted acts.
–   To apply, the act involved must comply with *all* of the following requirements of:
    –   being temporary;
    –   being transient or incidental;

---

6   There is an error in the OJEC version of this provision as originally printed at OJ L 167, 22.6.2001, p 10. The correction is set out at OJ L 6, 10.1.2002, p 70.

7   There is, however, no Agreed Statement corresponding to that as to Art 8 of the WCT, as to Arts 10 and 14 of the WPPT, in relation to the 'on-demand availability right' for performances fixed in phonograms or phonograms.

- being an integral ... part of a technological process;
- being an ... essential part of a technological process;
- having the sole purpose of either:
  - (a) a transmission in a network between third parties by an intermediary, or
  - (b) a lawful use;
- having no independent economic significance;
- being compliant with the 'three-step' test of Article 5(5).

This would suggest that in its final form Article 5(1) of the Directive is so tightly drawn that its effect on rightholders ought to be limited. However, it does not, unlike the provisions in the E-Commerce Directive, simply provide service providers with a defence. Instead, it wholly excludes certain types of reproduction from the scope of protection by copyright and related rights, to the possible benefit of wrongdoers using the services offered by such service providers, which wrongdoers would be likely otherwise to remain liable for the involuntary copying by service providers which they occasion. Instead, liability of such wrongdoers must now be founded on the other infringing acts that they undertake.

Free-standing right in the Regulations to secure injunctions against service providers

5.12 Partially recognising the potential problems for rightholders caused by Article 5(1) of the Directive, Article 8(3) of the Directive requires that 'rightholders are in a position to apply for an injunction against intermediaries whose services are used by a third party to infringe a copyright or related right'. However, it does not explain how this is to be done, particularly as Article 5(1) had excluded from the scope of the restricted act of reproduction the legal basis for doing so.

5.13 It had originally not been proposed in the United Kingdom to make any specific provision implementing Article 8(3) but, in response to concerns expressed by rightholders, the Regulations now amend the CDPA 1988 to afford to the owners of copyright and related rights a free-standing right (in ss 97A and 191JA of the CDPA 1988) to secure an injunction against a 'service provider', 'where that service provider has actual knowledge of another person using their service to infringe [copyright/a performer's property right]'.

5.14 This new standalone right of action is notable in that it does not require that the service provider itself undertakes any infringing act. Moreover, it is unspecific as to what activities the injunction that can thereby be secured is directed. What is clear, however, is that the new right of action does not of itself confer any right to damages. Further, although unlike the subpoena provisions in the United States in the Online Copyright Infringement Act, discussed in Chapter 4, the new right of action does not provide in terms for subpoenas, the provision of information about infringement is, at least in England and Wales, a well-established form of injunctive relief in intellectual property matters, available even against those innocent of any wrongdoing, as in *Norwich Pharmacal v HM Customs & Excise Commissioners*,[8] and so would be expected to be a form of relief available under this new right of action.

---

8   [1974] RPC 101 (House of Lords).

5.15   The considerable flexibility of the new standalone right of action may perhaps prove to be one of the most important aspects of the Regulations in terms of conferring a tangible benefit to rightholders in their fight against internet piracy. However, there would have been no basis for conferring such a right had not service providers so vociferously and effectively campaigned for defences to, and exceptions from, copyright infringement for their activities, which probably never infringed copyright in the first place.

FILE-SHARING AND P2P NETWORKS

The nature of the problem

5.16   Given the high profile accorded in recent years to the issue of file-sharing and peer-to-peer ('P2P') networks (such as originally Napster, and more recently second generation diffused distribution models such as that employed by Grokster, StreamCast and KaZaa) by the recording industry, in that such networks allow internet users to 'swap' recordings (generally compressed to MP3 format), and the high profile litigation concerning such networks which has taken place in the United States, one might expect that the Directive, and thus the Regulations, had some specific relevance to this issue. Such, however, is not the case, and indeed the Directive has permitted the Regulations in the United Kingdom to take an approach which, far from harmonising, serves only to perpetuate the potentially different approaches to this issue as between Member States of the European Union. Before discussing the situation in Europe and the United Kingdom it is convenient to consider the situation in the United States, as it is in the United States where the issues associated with file-sharing and P2P networks have been most fully ventilated in the courts.

Situation in the United States

5.17   The issue of file-sharing was first addressed in *A&M Records Inc v Napster Inc*,[9] where a preliminary injunction was granted against Napster, which was largely upheld on appeal. As with other file-sharing cases,[10] there was no central database of recordings under the control of the defendant. The central server and the associated software distributed to users that indexed the MP3 files on users' computers did no more than enable users of the service to identify other users with MP3 files on their own computers that the first user wanted and then to download from such other user such MP3 files. The central server under the control of Napster was in effect no more than a 'signpost'. File transfer took place directly between users once they had been put in contact.

5.18   There was no serious issue that the activities of Napster users did not constitute reproduction by the users of the system, and the main issues at the end of the day were not only the question of the scope of the generalised US approach to exceptions and

---

9   54 USPQ 2d 1746 (ND Calif, 2000); 239 F 3d 1004 (9th Cir, 2001).

10   But in contradistinction to cases such as *UMG Recordings, Inc v MP3.com, Inc* 92 F Supp 2d 349, 54 USPQ 2d 349 (SD NY, 2000), where the defendant itself stored digital copies of recordings (compressed to MP3 format) on its own server, for downloading over the internet to subscribers to its service.

reservations from copyright in its 'fair use' defence, but also the issue of authorisation. Napster's argument, that its users were engaged in fair use of the copied material, failed. Its activities were held to have 'a deleterious effect on the present and future digital download market'. Moreover, its argument that the 'sampling' and 'space-shifting' aspects of its users' activities constituted fair use also failed, the latter because although 'time-shifting' and 'space-shifting' had been held in other cases to be fair uses,[11] in those cases 'the methods of shifting ... did not also simultaneously involve distribution of the copyrighted material to the general public; the time or space-shifting of copyrighted material exposed the material only to the original user.' Napster's plea that it was not liable for contributory infringement also failed, its 'actual, specific knowledge of direct infringement' rendering the *Sony* decision (where Sony had been held by the Supreme Court not liable for contributory infringement by supplying videocassette recorders, knowing that one of the uses to which they could be put was to reproduce copyright works) of limited assistance to Napster.

5.19   The issue of 'fair use' has featured less in subsequent cases, so the decision as to this in *Napster* would appear to be generally well accepted, but that of authorisation is being explored in further file-sharing cases, some of which present significantly different fact situations to that in *Napster*. A different Court of Appeal in *Re: Aimster Copyright Litigation, Appeal of John Deep*[12] observed that it disagreed with the Court of Appeal in *Napster* 'in suggesting that actual knowledge of specific infringing uses was a sufficient condition for deeming a facilitator a contributory infringer', but still upheld the grant of a preliminary injunction against the defendant's 'Aimster' file-sharing service. The same Court of Appeal as heard the appeal in *Napster* is now due to hear further argument on the issue of authorisation, but against the rather different fact situation of 'second generation' file-sharing networks, in *Metro-Goldwyn Mayer Studios et al v Grokster Ltd et al*,[13] where the District Court at first instance granted motions for summary judgment in favour of the defendants on the issue of contributory infringement, noting:

> 'Plaintiffs appear reluctant to acknowledge a seminal distinction between Grokster/ StreamCast and Napster: neither Grokster nor StreamCast provides the "site and facilities" for discrete infringement ... Neither StreamCast nor Grokster facilitates the exchange of files between users in the way Napster did. Users connect to the respective network, select which files to share, send and receive searches, and download files, all with no material involvement of the Defendants. If either Defendant closed their doors and deactivated all computers within their control, users of their products could still continue sharing files with little or no interruption ... '

This case reflects the increasing difficulty, as file-sharing networks become more disseminated and less centralised, of finding a defendant that can be said to be authorising. As a result of such difficulties, rightholders have now turned their attention on individual users of such networks, as discussed in the context of the Online Copyright Liability Limitation Act and *RIAA v Verizon* in Chapter 4.

---

11   Respectively *Sony Corp v Universal City Studios, Inc* 464 US 417, 104 S Ct 774 (1984) and *RIAA v Diamond Multimedia Sys, Inc* 180 F 3d 1072, 1079 (9th Cir, 1999).

12   30 June 2003 (7th Cir, 2003).

13   25 April 2003 (CD Calif, 2003).

Situation under the Directive in the European Union

5.20   Applying these principles to Europe, there can be, as in the United States, no question that file-sharing activities involve infringement of the restricted acts of reproduction (and also of the on-demand availability right). As in the United States, consideration must be given to both the issue of contributory infringement or authorisation, and that of the scope of the exception for private copying, as if the scope of the latter is such as to legitimise the file-swapping activities of P2P network users then those 'behind' such networks can hardly be liable for enabling, or even for encouraging, an activity that is itself legitimate.

5.21   The issue of contributory infringement or authorisation – which as can be seen from the above discussion is emerging as the critical one in the litigation to have taken place in the United States – has, however, not been harmonised by the Directive or by any other EU legislative measure to date.[14]

5.22   The Directive does, however, purport to harmonise the exception and reservation for private copying, by Article 5(2)(b), which provides:

> '5(2) Member States may provide for exceptions or limitations to the reproduction right provided for in Article 2 in the following cases:
> . . .
> (b)   in respect of reproductions on any medium made by a natural person for private use and for ends that are neither directly nor indirectly commercial, on condition that the rightholders receive fair compensation which takes account of the application or non-application of technological measures referred to in Article 6 to the work or subject matter concerned'.

5.23   Recitals (35), (38) and (39) of the Directive are relevant to this exception, which in most countries throughout Europe (but not the United Kingdom) is implemented by an already existing exception for private copying (generally introduced in the days of analogue copying onto tape) coupled with a levy on recording media and, in some cases, equipment, which is distributed to rightholders. Even where the exception is coupled with such a levy this ought not serve to legitimise the activities of the users of file-sharing systems, as the copying in which they participate can hardly be said to be 'private' in that such copying will take place with total strangers who also use the file-sharing system. Any other interpretation would be likely in any event to be inconsistent with Article 5(5) of the Directive to which all exceptions, including that under Article 5(2)(b), are subject. The 'three-step test' that Article 5(5) applies would be expected to come to similar conclusions as the analysis undertaken by the US courts in *Napster*, and which would seem not to have been challenged seriously in subsequent litigation.

Situation under the Regulations in the United Kingdom

5.24   The issue of private copying has occasioned little problem for the UK authorities in implementing the Directive. This is despite the United Kingdom's special position in implementing Article 5(2)(b) because, unlike most other countries

---

14   Thus decisions such as that of the Dutch Supreme Court in *BUMA/Stemra v KaZaA* of 19 December 2003, allowing KaZaA's appeal on contributory infringement grounds, may be of more limited significance in other European jurisdictions than might at first sight appear to be the case.

in Europe, it lacks a generalised private copying exception and an associated levy on recording media or equipment. Although in the consultation leading up to the CDPA 1988 such an exception and levy was discussed, it was abandoned in the face of consumer and press lobbying, which characterised this as a tax. To this day it is regarded as politically unacceptable to introduce a levy into the United Kingdom. Instead, the only form of private copying exception relevant to this issue is a limited 'time-shifting' exception, in s 70 of the CDPA 1988, which, as amended by the Regulations, provides, in subs (1):

> **'70 Recording for the purposes of time-shifting**
> (1) The making in domestic premises for private and domestic use of a recording of a broadcast solely for the purpose of enabling it to be viewed or listened to at a more convenient time does not infringe any copyright in the broadcast or in any work included in it.'

5.25   In view of the limited nature of this 'time-shifting' exception it should have no serious relevance to the issues raised by file-sharing systems under English law. Thus from an English law perspective there can be little doubt that the individuals participating in file-sharing copying infringe, and the only live legal issue is whether those 'behind' the file-sharing network, by enabling the infringing activity to take place, can be said thereby to have 'authorised' it so as to be liable for it under English law. Here one might expect an English court to take a similar view on authorisation as the US court in *Napster*, as discussed above, which found the situation different to that in *Sony v Universal City Studios*.[15] Thus an English court might well feel that the continuing element of potential control that Napster, on the facts of such case, could exercise made it a very different case to *CBS Songs v Amstrad*,[16] in which the House of Lords came to a similar conclusion as the United States Supreme Court in *Sony v Universal City Studios* and found that the sale of double-headed cassette recorders, although these were used mainly to infringe copyright, did not constitute any authorisation so to do. However, the issue of authorisation becomes more difficult with the more disseminated, and less centrally controlled, 'second generation' file-sharing networks that have now replaced the 'first generation' Napster service.

5.26   In summary, the Regulations do nothing to change the situation in which the United Kingdom is a country where private, but nonetheless infringing, copying is rife (one need only look at the stacks of hundreds of blank recordable CD-Rs for sale in any consumer electronics store) but where, unlike other countries in Europe, rightholders receive no compensation for such private copying. The view of the UK authorities would seem now to be to look to such levies as a transitional palliative pending the industry achieving the 'Holy Grail' of copy protection, whereupon the moral, if not legal, legitimacy which such levies currently accord private copying would become an irrelevant embarrassment that would be swept away. This may well be an over-optimistic view.

5.27   Perhaps of greater immediate relevance to the issue of file-sharing in the United Kingdom is the new free-standing right introduced by the Regulations (in ss 97A and 191JA of the CDPA 1988, discussed above) to secure an injunction against a 'service provider', and which will facilitate attempts by rightholders to identify and

---

15   464 US 417 (1984).

16   [1988] AC 1013 (House of Lords).

so to proceed against those individuals who are the most active in making infringing copies available to others over file-sharing networks.

INCONSISTENCIES LEFT BY THE DIRECTIVE

Introduction

5.28   Despite its extensive scope, as outlined below, the Directive has failed fully to harmonise the law of copyright and related rights in the European Union. Such failure has two causes implicit in the Directive, expanded on below:

– continued application of other legal provisions;
– limited optionality of provisions as to exceptions and reservations, and the uncertain nature of the scope and effect of such optionality.

Moreover, there still remain certain aspects of the law of copyright and related rights which remain to be harmonised throughout the European Union – such as moral rights, identifying the first owner of copyright, copyright contracts and what constitutes authorisation. There also remain numerous related rights of differing sorts throughout Europe, which have not been harmonised – from a UK perspective one can identify the rights in a typographical arrangement and in computer-generated works (both characterised as 'copyright' in the CDPA 1988) as such rights.

5.29   This is despite the extensive scope of the Copyright Directive, which scope can be seen from the following, much simplified, tabulation of those areas in which this and its preceding Directives have harmonised copyright law:

	Reproduction	Communication to the public of works, by wire or wireless means, including 'on-demand availability'[17]	Distribution	Rental and Lending
Copyright in Computer Programs	Computer Program Directive	Computer Directive	Computer Program Directive	Computer Program Directive
Copyright in Databases	Database Directive	Database Directive	Database Directive	Database Directive Copyright Directive
Copyright other than in Computer Programs and Databases	Copyright Directive	Satellite Broadcasting Directive Copyright Directive	Copyright Directive	Rental Lending and Related Rights Directive

For those related rights harmonised at a European level, a similar much simplified tabulation can be prepared:

---

17   Ie the making available to the public of works in such a way that members of the public may access these works from a place and at a time individually chosen by them.

	Repro- duction[18]	Broadcasting and communication to the public	'On-demand availability'[19]	Distribution	Rental and Lending
Related Rights – Phonograms	[Rental Lending and Related Rights Directive] Copyright Directive	Rental Lending and Related Rights Directive Satellite Broadcasting Directive	Copyright Directive	Rental Lending and Related Rights Directive	Rental Lending and Related Rights Directive
Related Rights – Performance Fixations	[Rental Lending and Related Rights Directive] Copyright Directive	Rental Lending and Related Rights Directive Satellite Broadcasting Directive	Copyright Directive	Rental Lending and Related Rights Directive	Rental Lending and Related Rights Directive
Related Rights – Broadcast Fixations	[Rental Lending and Related Rights Directive] Copyright Directive	Rental Lending and Related Rights Directive Satellite Broadcasting Directive	Copyright Directive	Rental Lending and Related Rights Directive	–
Related Rights – Film Fixations	[Rental Lending and Related Rights Directive] Copyright Directive	Rental Lending and Related Rights Directive Satellite Broadcasting Directive	Copyright Directive	Rental Lending and Related Rights Directive	Rental Lending and Related Rights Directive

5.30 As will be apparent from the above tabulation, the relationship between the restricted acts set out in Article 8 of the Rental, Lending and Related Rights Directive (entitled 'broadcasting and communication to the public') and the new restricted act under Article 3 of the Directive, that of 'making available to the public of works in such a way that members of the public may access these works from a place and at a time individually chosen by them' (the 'on-demand availability right'), is not addressed in the Directive.

---

18 The brackets around the Rental Lending and Related Rights Directive in the 'reproduction' column of the tabulation reflect the repeal by the Copyright Directive of the provisions of Art 7 of the Rental Lending and Related Rights Directive as to the restricted act of reproduction when applied to related rights, and its replacement by Art 2 of the Copyright Directive.

19 Ie the making available to the public of works in such a way that members of the public may access these works from a place and at a time individually chosen by them.

Continued application of other legal provisions

5.31   Article 1(2) of the Directive provides:

'2. Except in the cases referred to in Article 11, this Directive shall leave intact and shall in no way affect existing Community provisions relating to:
(a)   the legal protection of computer programs;
(b)   rental right, lending right and certain rights related to copyright in the field of intellectual property;
(c)   copyright and related rights applicable to broadcasting of programmes by satellite and cable retransmission;
(d)   the term of protection of copyright and certain related rights;
(e)   the legal protection of databases.'

Article 11 of the Directive is of limited application, amending only the Rental, Lending and Related Rights Directive and the Harmonisation of Term Directive. It amends the former by deleting its provisions as to the restricted act of reproduction (which are thus replaced by those in Article 2 of the Directive) and by adding the 'three-step test' to its provisions as to exceptions and reservations. It amends the latter by modifying slightly the term of the related rights held by the producers of phonograms. Thus, apart from these small modifications of these two other Directives effected by Article 11, the Directive retains any inconsistencies in approach as between it and the five Directives here listed.

5.32   In the field of copyright (meant in the strict sense as the rights the subject of the Berne Convention and the WCT) such inconsistencies arise by reason of paras (a) and (e) of this Article, leaving three different regimes applying to copyright in the strict sense, in the European Union, namely that in relation to computer programs, that in relation to databases, and that in relation to other works than computer programs and databases. The major differences between these can be summarised by the following tabulation:

	Computer programs	Databases in which copyright subsists by virtue of selection and arrangement	Other copyright works than computer programs and databases
Subsistence	Specific provision	Specific provision	Specific provision only as to photographs under the Harmonisation of Term Directive
Restricted acts	Extra restricted act of translation, adaptation, arrangement		

	Computer programs	Databases in which copyright subsists by virtue of selection and arrangement	Other copyright works than computer programs and databases
Exceptions and reservations	Computer Program Directive, Arts 5 and 6, all where undertaken by a lawful user: – acts necessary for use in accordance with intended purpose, including error correction – making of backup copy – observation study and testing functioning – decompilation	Database Directive, Art 6	Copyright Directive, Art 5
Legal protection of technological protection	Computer Program Directive, Art 7(3)	Copyright Directive, Art 6	Copyright Directive, Art 6

Such differences are reflected in the UK implementation of the Directive by the Regulations, as discussed in Chapter 4. In the field of related rights, the consequence of the continued application of other legal provisions is most felt in relation to exceptions and reservations, and so is discussed below.

Failure of harmonisation resulting from permitted exceptions and reservations

5.33   The UK implementation effected by Regulations, discussed in Chapter 4, demonstrates how limited is the harmonising effect of the Directive on the exceptions and reservations to which it applies, in that as little change as possible has been made to the structure of exceptions and reservations in the CDPA 1988, and that certain of the amendments to it have been justified on the basis of combining certain of the exceptions and reservations set out in Article 5(2) and (3) of the Directive. The considerable latitude given by the Directive in the manner of national implementation is further emphasised by the approach of the Regulations in retaining the time-shifting exception of s 70 of the CDPA 1988 without any accompanying levy, as discussed earlier in this chapter, maintaining the difference in approach as between the United Kingdom and most other countries in Europe.

5.34   Moreover, by virtue of the provisions as to the continued application of other legal provisions, discussed above, the harmonisation in respect of exceptions and reservations achieved by the Directive (and reflected in the Regulations) is inevitably limited as the following, differing, regimes apply to exceptions and reservations from copyright and related rights.

–   Copyright:
    –   computer programs: Computer Program Directive, Articles 5 and 6;
    –   databases in which copyright subsists: Database Directive, Article 6;
    –   other copyright works (in the sense meant by the Berne Convention and the WCT): Copyright Directive, Article 5;
–   Related rights (in performances, phonograms, film fixations and broadcasts):
    –   from restricted acts of fixation, broadcasting and communication to the public and distribution: Rental Lending and Related Rights Directive, Article 10;
    –   from restricted acts of reproduction and 'on-demand availability': Copyright Directive, Article 5.

5.35   However, in that in all of these areas a measure of (albeit occasionally inconsistent) harmonisation has been achieved by one Directive or another, the European Court of Justice, on a reference under Article 234 from national courts, has the scope to provide guidance as to the appropriate interpretation of all such measures, unless it takes the view that these provide national legislations and courts with a measure of discretion with which it should not interfere.[20]

ISSUES FOR THE FUTURE

Inconsistencies and lacunae in European law of copyright and related rights

5.36   As discussed above, the piecemeal nature of the legislation to date in Europe in the field of copyright and related rights has left a number of inconsistencies, which the Commission may well seek to address in further legislation. Moreover, the harmonisation of copyright and related rights effected to date in Europe has not been complete, and a number of significant areas remain still to be harmonised. Not only has this been in areas, such as exceptions and reservations, where the harmonisation has on its face been incomplete, but also in other areas which have not even been addressed in the harmonising measures, such as the area of moral rights for performers, discussed in Chapter 4, and, of particular relevance to the issue of file-sharing discussed earlier in this chapter, that of what constitutes 'authorisation' to infringe copyright. Other areas include first ownership of copyright, which has only been addressed for computer programs, or contracts assigning copyright.

5.37   All the EU copyright and related rights measures have involved *harmonisation,* and none have proposed the establishment of unitary copyright protection in the Community. This is in contrast, for example, to trade marks and designs, where harmonisation of national intellectual property rights has been accompanied by the

---

20   See, eg, the approach of the ECJ in Case C-60/98, *Butterfly Music Srl v Carosello Edizioni Musicale e Discografiche Srl* [2000] 1 CMLR 587, [1999] EMLR 847 and also in Case 230/98, *Entidad de Gestion de Derechos de los Productores Audiovisuals (EGEDA) v Hosteleria Astrurianos SA* [2000] EMLR 523, in both of which, for differing reasons, it was content to leave issues resulting from harmonising legislation in the field of copyright and related rights to the national legislations and the national courts, respectively.

establishment of a single, unitary, Community trade mark system which functions in parallel with the harmonised ones under national laws. Unitary protection is a less easy option for copyright and related rights because, unlike registered designs and registered trade marks, copyright and related rights automatically subsist in all the Member States of the European Union (as well as in virtually every other country of the world) independent of registration. In relation to copyright, this occurs by virtue of the Berne Convention and TRIPs. The result of copyright and related rights automatically subsisting on a national basis within the European Union is that there is no mechanism for choosing whether to seek protection on an EU-wide rather than on a national basis. This situation can be expected to continue until such time in the distant future as political development and further harmonisation of national copyright and related rights laws permits separate national copyright and related rights systems in the European Union to be abandoned in favour of, or supplemented by, a unitary EU system.

Wider international issues

5.38   It is not only within a European context that further development of the law of copyright and related rights can be expected. As already discussed in Chapter 4, new international conventions, paralleling the WIPO Treaties, as to the rights of broadcasters and of audiovisual performers, are under discussion within WIPO. In Chapter 4 it was also observed that the Hague Conference has shelved, for the time being, its bold proposal for an international convention on jurisdiction and enforcement of judgments. However, it is only a matter of time before such a proposal is once again tabled.

5.39   Other issues in copyright and related rights at an international level may also demand resolution. As also discussed in Chapter 4, in relation to applicable law, the issue of whether the new 'on-line availability right' is infringed only at the point of emission, or at both the points of emission and of reception, has also to be resolved.

5.40   Pressure can also be expected for extending the term of protection of certain related rights beyond the fixation plus 50 years now set out in the WPPT for the related rights that are subject to it and increasingly accepted as an international standard for other related rights (as, for example, under the Rental Lending and Related Rights Directive in the European Union). This is a consequence of the extension of the term of certain such rights in the United States under the Copyright Term Extension Act 1998, which was in turn in part a response by the United States to the Harmonisation of Term Directive in Europe, which had harmonised copyright term upwards to life plus 70 years and the term of related rights at fixation plus 50 years. Under the Copyright Term Extension Act 1998 (which was unsuccessfully challenged in *Eldred v Ashcroft*[21]) a 20-year term extension was granted for all works not yet in the public domain, with the effect that, subject to special provisions for works published before 1978, the term of copyright in the United States was extended to life plus 70 years, and that of 'works for hire' (including phonograms) to the lesser of creation plus 120 years or publication plus 95 years. Thus rightholders can be expected to seek similar extended protection in the European Union for certain related rights, such as those in phonograms.

---

21   123 S Ct 769 (2003).

Appendix 1

DIRECTIVE 2001/29/EC OF THE EUROPEAN PARLIAMENT AND OF THE COUNCIL
of 22 May 2001
on the harmonisation of certain aspects of copyright and related rights in the information society

THE EUROPEAN PARLIAMENT AND THE COUNCIL OF THE EUROPEAN UNION,

Having regard to the Treaty establishing the European Community, and in particular Articles 47(2), 55 and 95 thereof,

Having regard to the proposal from the Commission[1],

Having regard to the opinion of the Economic and Social Committee[2],

Acting in accordance with the procedure laid down in Article 251 of the Treaty[3],

Whereas:

(1)　The Treaty provides for the establishment of an internal market and the institution of a system ensuring that competition in the internal market is not distorted. Harmonisation of the laws of the Member States on copyright and related rights contributes to the achievement of these objectives.

(2)　The European Council, meeting at Corfu on 24 and 25 June 1994, stressed the need to create a general and flexible legal framework at Community level in order to foster the development of the information society in Europe. This requires, *inter alia*, the existence of an internal market for new products and services. Important Community legislation to ensure such a regulatory framework is already in place or its adoption is well under way. Copyright and related rights play an important role in this context as they protect and stimulate the development and marketing of new products and services and the creation and exploitation of their creative content.

(3)　The proposed harmonisation will help to implement the four freedoms of the internal market and relates to compliance with the fundamental principles of law and especially of property, including intellectual property, and freedom of expression and the public interest.

1　OJ C 108, 7.4.1998, p 6 and OJ C 180, 25.6.1999, p 6.

2　OJ C 407, 28.12.1998, p 30.

3　Opinion of the European Parliament of 10 February 1999 (OJ C 150, 28.5.1999, p 171), Council Common Position of 28 September 2000 (OJ C 344, 1.12.2000, p 1) and Decision of the European Parliament of 14 February 2001 (not yet published in the Official Journal). Council Decision of 9 April 2001.

(4) A harmonised legal framework on copyright and related rights, through increased legal certainty and while providing for a high level of protection of intellectual property, will foster substantial investment in creativity and innovation, including network infrastructure, and lead in turn to growth and increased competitiveness of European industry, both in the area of content provision and information technology and more generally across a wide range of industrial and cultural sectors. This will safeguard employment and encourage new job creation.

(5) Technological development has multiplied and diversified the vectors for creation, production and exploitation. While no new concepts for the protection of intellectual property are needed, the current law on copyright and related rights should be adapted and supplemented to respond adequately to economic realities such as new forms of exploitation.

(6) Without harmonisation at Community level, legislative activities at national level which have already been initiated in a number of Member States in order to respond to the technological challenges might result in significant differences in protection and thereby in restrictions on the free movement of services and products incorporating, or based on, intellectual property, leading to a refragmentation of the internal market and legislative inconsistency. The impact of such legislative differences and uncertainties will become more significant with the further development of the information society, which has already greatly increased transborder exploitation of intellectual property. This development will and should further increase. Significant legal differences and uncertainties in protection may hinder economies of scale for new products and services containing copyright and related rights.

(7) The Community legal framework for the protection of copyright and related rights must, therefore, also be adapted and supplemented as far as is necessary for the smooth functioning of the internal market. To that end, those national provisions on copyright and related rights which vary considerably from one Member State to another or which cause legal uncertainties hindering the smooth functioning of the internal market and the proper development of the information society in Europe should be adjusted, and inconsistent national responses to the technological developments should be avoided, whilst differences not adversely affecting the functioning of the internal market need not be removed or prevented.

(8) The various social, societal and cultural implications of the information society require that account be taken of the specific features of the content of products and services.

(9) Any harmonisation of copyright and related rights must take as a basis a high level of protection, since such rights are crucial to intellectual creation. Their protection helps to ensure the maintenance and development of creativity in the interests of authors, performers, producers, consumers, culture, industry and the public at large. Intellectual property has therefore been recognised as an integral part of property.

(10) If authors or performers are to continue their creative and artistic work, they have to receive an appropriate reward for the use of their work, as must producers in order to be able to finance this work. The investment required to produce products such as phonograms, films or multimedia products, and services such as 'on-demand' services, is considerable. Adequate legal protection of intellectual property rights is necessary in order to guarantee the availability of such a reward and provide the opportunity for satisfactory returns on this investment.

(11) A rigorous, effective system for the protection of copyright and related rights is one of the main ways of ensuring that European cultural creativity and production receive the necessary resources and of safeguarding the independence and dignity of artistic creators and performers.

(12) Adequate protection of copyright works and subject-matter of related rights is also of great importance from a cultural standpoint. Article 151 of the Treaty requires the Community to take cultural aspects into account in its action.

(13) A common search for, and consistent application at European level of, technical measures to protect works and other subject-matter and to provide the necessary information on rights are essential insofar as the ultimate aim of these measures is to give effect to the principles and guarantees laid down in law.

(14) This Directive should seek to promote learning and culture by protecting works and other subject-matter while permitting exceptions or limitations in the public interest for the purpose of education and teaching.

(15) The Diplomatic Conference held under the auspices of the World Intellectual Property Organisation (WIPO) in December 1996 led to the adoption of two new Treaties, the 'WIPO Copyright Treaty' and the 'WIPO Performances and Phonograms Treaty', dealing respectively with the protection of authors and the protection of performers and phonogram producers. Those Treaties update the international protection for copyright and related rights significantly, not least with regard to the so-called 'digital agenda', and improve the means to fight piracy world-wide. The Community and a majority of Member States have already signed the Treaties and the process of making arrangements for the ratification of the Treaties by the Community and the Member States is under way. This Directive also serves to implement a number of the new international obligations.

(16) Liability for activities in the network environment concerns not only copyright and related rights but also other areas, such as defamation, misleading advertising, or infringement of trademarks, and is addressed horizontally in Directive 2000/31/EC of the European Parliament and of the Council of 8 June 2000 on certain legal aspects of information society services, in particular electronic commerce, in the internal market ('Directive on electronic commerce')[4], which clarifies and harmonises various legal issues relating to information society services including electronic commerce. This Directive should be implemented within a timescale similar to that for the implementation of the Directive on electronic commerce, since that Directive provides a harmonised framework of principles and provisions relevant *inter alia* to important parts of this Directive. This Directive is without prejudice to provisions relating to liability in that Directive.

(17) It is necessary, especially in the light of the requirements arising out of the digital environment, to ensure that collecting societies achieve a higher level of rationalisation and transparency with regard to compliance with competition rules.

(18) This Directive is without prejudice to the arrangements in the Member States concerning the management of rights such as extended collective licences.

(19) The moral rights of rightholders should be exercised according to the legislation of the Member States and the provisions of the Berne Convention for the Protection of Literary and Artistic Works, of the WIPO Copyright Treaty and of the WIPO Performances and Phonograms Treaty. Such moral rights remain outside the scope of this Directive.

---

4   OJ L 178, 17.7.2000, p 1.

(20) This Directive is based on principles and rules already laid down in the Directives currently in force in this area, in particular Directives 91/250/EEC[5], 92/100/EEC[6], 93/83/EEC[7], 93/98/EEC[8] and 96/9/EC[9], and it develops those principles and rules and places them in the context of the information society. The provisions of this Directive should be without prejudice to the provisions of those Directives, unless otherwise provided in this Directive.

(21) This Directive should define the scope of the acts covered by the reproduction right with regard to the different beneficiaries. This should be done in conformity with the acquis communautaire. A broad definition of these acts is needed to ensure legal certainty within the internal market.

(22) The objective of proper support for the dissemination of culture must not be achieved by sacrificing strict protection of rights or by tolerating illegal forms of distribution of counterfeited or pirated works.

(23) This Directive should harmonise further the author's right of communication to the public. This right should be understood in a broad sense covering all communication to the public not present at the place where the communication originates. This right should cover any such transmission or retransmission of a work to the public by wire or wireless means, including broadcasting. This right should not cover any other acts.

(24) The right to make available to the public subject-matter referred to in Article 3(2) should be understood as covering all acts of making available such subject-matter to members of the public not present at the place where the act of making available originates, and as not covering any other acts.

(25) The legal uncertainty regarding the nature and the level of protection of acts of on-demand transmission of copyright works and subject-matter protected by related rights over networks should be overcome by providing for harmonised protection at Community level. It should be made clear that all rightholders recognised by this Directive should have an exclusive right to make available to the public copyright works or any other subject-matter by way of interactive on-demand transmissions. Such interactive on-demand transmissions are characterised by the fact that members of the public may access them from a place and at a time individually chosen by them.

(26) With regard to the making available in on-demand services by broadcasters of their radio or television productions incorporating music from commercial phonograms as an integral part thereof, collective licensing arrangements are to be encouraged in order to facilitate the clearance of the rights concerned.

---

5   Council Directive 91/250/EEC of 14 May 1991 on the legal protection of computer programs (OJ L 122, 17.5.1991, p 42). Directive as amended by Directive 93/98/EEC.

6   Council Directive 92/100/EEC of 19 November 1992 on rental right and lending right and on certain rights related to copyright in the field of intellectual property (OJ L 346, 27.11.1992, p 61). Directive as amended by Directive 93/98/EEC.

7   Council Directive 93/83/EEC of 27 September 1993 on the coordination of certain rules concerning copyright and rights related to copyright applicable to satellite broadcasting and cable retransmission (OJ L 248, 6.10.1993, p 15).

8   Council Directive 93/98/EEC of 29 October 1993 harmonising the term of protection of copyright and certain related rights (OJ L 290, 24.11.1993, p 9).

9   Directive 96/9/EC of the European Parliament and of the Council of 11 March 1996 on the legal protection of databases (OJ L 77, 27.3.1996, p 20).

(27) The mere provision of physical facilities for enabling or making a communication does not in itself amount to communication within the meaning of this Directive.

(28) Copyright protection under this Directive includes the exclusive right to control distribution of the work incorporated in a tangible article. The first sale in the Community of the original of a work or copies thereof by the rightholder or with his consent exhausts the right to control resale of that object in the Community. This right should not be exhausted in respect of the original or of copies thereof sold by the rightholder or with his consent outside the Community. Rental and lending rights for authors have been established in Directive 92/100/EEC. The distribution right provided for in this Directive is without prejudice to the provisions relating to the rental and lending rights contained in Chapter I of that Directive.

(29) The question of exhaustion does not arise in the case of services and on-line services in particular. This also applies with regard to a material copy of a work or other subject-matter made by a user of such a service with the consent of the rightholder. Therefore, the same applies to rental and lending of the original and copies of works or other subject-matter which are services by nature. Unlike CD-ROM or CD-I, where the intellectual property is incorporated in a material medium, namely an item of goods, every on-line service is in fact an act which should be subject to authorisation where the copyright or related right so provides.

(30) The rights referred to in this Directive may be transferred, assigned or subject to the granting of contractual licences, without prejudice to the relevant national legislation on copyright and related rights.

(31) A fair balance of rights and interests between the different categories of rightholders, as well as between the different categories of rightholders and users of protected subject-matter must be safeguarded. The existing exceptions and limitations to the rights as set out by the Member States have to be reassessed in the light of the new electronic environment. Existing differences in the exceptions and limitations to certain restricted acts have direct negative effects on the functioning of the internal market of copyright and related rights. Such differences could well become more pronounced in view of the further development of transborder exploitation of works and cross-border activities. In order to ensure the proper functioning of the internal market, such exceptions and limitations should be defined more harmoniously. The degree of their harmonisation should be based on their impact on the smooth functioning of the internal market.

(32) This Directive provides for an exhaustive enumeration of exceptions and limitations to the reproduction right and the right of communication to the public. Some exceptions or limitations only apply to the reproduction right, where appropriate. This list takes due account of the different legal traditions in Member States, while, at the same time, aiming to ensure a functioning internal market. Member States should arrive at a coherent application of these exceptions and limitations, which will be assessed when reviewing implementing legislation in the future.

(33) The exclusive right of reproduction should be subject to an exception to allow certain acts of temporary reproduction, which are transient or incidental reproductions, forming an integral and essential part of a technological process and carried out for the sole purpose of enabling either efficient transmission in a network between third parties by an intermediary, or a lawful use of a work or other subject-matter to be made. The acts of reproduction concerned should have no separate economic value on their own. To the extent that they meet these conditions, this exception should include acts which enable browsing as well as acts of caching to take place, including those which enable transmission systems to function efficiently, provided that the intermediary does not

modify the information and does not interfere with the lawful use of technology, widely recognised and used by industry, to obtain data on the use of the information. A use should be considered lawful where it is authorised by the rightholder or not restricted by law.

(34) Member States should be given the option of providing for certain exceptions or limitations for cases such as educational and scientific purposes, for the benefit of public institutions such as libraries and archives, for purposes of news reporting, for quotations, for use by people with disabilities, for public security uses and for uses in administrative and judicial proceedings.

(35) In certain cases of exceptions or limitations, rightholders should receive fair compensation to compensate them adequately for the use made of their protected works or other subject-matter. When determining the form, detailed arrangements and possible level of such fair compensation, account should be taken of the particular circumstances of each case. When evaluating these circumstances, a valuable criterion would be the possible harm to the rightholders resulting from the act in question. In cases where rightholders have already received payment in some other form, for instance as part of a licence fee, no specific or separate payment may be due. The level of fair compensation should take full account of the degree of use of technological protection measures referred to in this Directive. In certain situations where the prejudice to the rightholder would be minimal, no obligation for payment may arise.

(36) The Member States may provide for fair compensation for rightholders also when applying the optional provisions on exceptions or limitations which do not require such compensation.

(37) Existing national schemes on reprography, where they exist, do not create major barriers to the internal market. Member States should be allowed to provide for an exception or limitation in respect of reprography.

(38) Member States should be allowed to provide for an exception or limitation to the reproduction right for certain types of reproduction of audio, visual and audio-visual material for private use, accompanied by fair compensation. This may include the introduction or continuation of remuneration schemes to compensate for the prejudice to rightholders. Although differences between those remuneration schemes affect the functioning of the internal market, those differences, with respect to analogue private reproduction, should not have a significant impact on the development of the information society. Digital private copying is likely to be more widespread and have a greater economic impact. Due account should therefore be taken of the differences between digital and analogue private copying and a distinction should be made in certain respects between them.

(39) When applying the exception or limitation on private copying, Member States should take due account of technological and economic developments, in particular with respect to digital private copying and remuneration schemes, when effective technological protection measures are available. Such exceptions or limitations should not inhibit the use of technological measures or their enforcement against circumvention.

(40) Member States may provide for an exception or limitation for the benefit of certain non-profit making establishments, such as publicly accessible libraries and equivalent institutions, as well as archives. However, this should be limited to certain special cases covered by the reproduction right. Such an exception or limitation should not cover uses made in the context of on-line delivery of protected works or other subject-matter. This Directive should be without prejudice to the Member States' option to derogate from the

exclusive public lending right in accordance with Article 5 of Directive 92/100/EEC. Therefore, specific contracts or licences should be promoted which, without creating imbalances, favour such establishments and the disseminative purposes they serve.

(41) When applying the exception or limitation in respect of ephemeral recordings made by broadcasting organisations it is understood that a broadcaster's own facilities include those of a person acting on behalf of and under the responsibility of the broadcasting organisation.

(42) When applying the exception or limitation for non-commercial educational and scientific research purposes, including distance learning, the non-commercial nature of the activity in question should be determined by that activity as such. The organisational structure and the means of funding of the establishment concerned are not the decisive factors in this respect.

(43) It is in any case important for the Member States to adopt all necessary measures to facilitate access to works by persons suffering from a disability which constitutes an obstacle to the use of the works themselves, and to pay particular attention to accessible formats.

(44) When applying the exceptions and limitations provided for in this Directive, they should be exercised in accordance with international obligations. Such exceptions and limitations may not be applied in a way which prejudices the legitimate interests of the rightholder or which conflicts with the normal exploitation of his work or other subject-matter. The provision of such exceptions or limitations by Member States should, in particular, duly reflect the increased economic impact that such exceptions or limitations may have in the context of the new electronic environment. Therefore, the scope of certain exceptions or limitations may have to be even more limited when it comes to certain new uses of copyright works and other subject-matter.

(45) The exceptions and limitations referred to in Article 5(2), (3) and (4) should not, however, prevent the definition of contractual relations designed to ensure fair compensation for the rightholders insofar as permitted by national law.

(46) Recourse to mediation could help users and rightholders to settle disputes. The Commission, in cooperation with the Member States within the Contact Committee, should undertake a study to consider new legal ways of settling disputes concerning copyright and related rights.

(47) Technological development will allow rightholders to make use of technological measures designed to prevent or restrict acts not authorised by the rightholders of any copyright, rights related to copyright or the *sui generis* right in databases. The danger, however, exists that illegal activities might be carried out in order to enable or facilitate the circumvention of the technical protection provided by these measures. In order to avoid fragmented legal approaches that could potentially hinder the functioning of the internal market, there is a need to provide for harmonised legal protection against circumvention of effective technological measures and against provision of devices and products or services to this effect.

(48) Such legal protection should be provided in respect of technological measures that effectively restrict acts not authorised by the rightholders of any copyright, rights related to copyright or the *sui generis* right in databases without, however, preventing the normal operation of electronic equipment and its technological development. Such legal protection implies no obligation to design devices, products, components or services to

correspond to technological measures, so long as such device, product, component or service does not otherwise fall under the prohibition of Article 6. Such legal protection should respect proportionality and should not prohibit those devices or activities which have a commercially significant purpose or use other than to circumvent the technical protection. In particular, this protection should not hinder research into cryptography.

(49) The legal protection of technological measures is without prejudice to the application of any national provisions which may prohibit the private possession of devices, products or components for the circumvention of technological measures.

(50) Such a harmonised legal protection does not affect the specific provisions on protection provided for by Directive 91/250/EEC. In particular, it should not apply to the protection of technological measures used in connection with computer programs, which is exclusively addressed in that Directive. It should neither inhibit nor prevent the development or use of any means of circumventing a technological measure that is necessary to enable acts to be undertaken in accordance with the terms of Article 5(3) or Article 6 of Directive 91/250/EEC. Articles 5 and 6 of that Directive exclusively determine exceptions to the exclusive rights applicable to computer programs.

(51) The legal protection of technological measures applies without prejudice to public policy, as reflected in Article 5, or public security. Member States should promote voluntary measures taken by rightholders, including the conclusion and implementation of agreements between rightholders and other parties concerned, to accommodate achieving the objectives of certain exceptions or limitations provided for in national law in accordance with this Directive. In the absence of such voluntary measures or agreements within a reasonable period of time, Member States should take appropriate measures to ensure that rightholders provide beneficiaries of such exceptions or limitations with appropriate means of benefiting from them, by modifying an implemented technological measure or by other means. However, in order to prevent abuse of such measures taken by rightholders, including within the framework of agreements, or taken by a Member State, any technological measures applied in implementation of such measures should enjoy legal protection.

(52) When implementing an exception or limitation for private copying in accordance with Article 5(2)(b), Member States should likewise promote the use of voluntary measures to accommodate achieving the objectives of such exception or limitation. If, within a reasonable period of time, no such voluntary measures to make reproduction for private use possible have been taken, Member States may take measures to enable beneficiaries of the exception or limitation concerned to benefit from it. Voluntary measures taken by rightholders, including agreements between rightholders and other parties concerned, as well as measures taken by Member States, do not prevent rightholders from using technological measures which are consistent with the exceptions or limitations on private copying in national law in accordance with Article 5(2)(b), taking account of the condition of fair compensation under that provision and the possible differentiation between various conditions of use in accordance with Article 5(5), such as controlling the number of reproductions. In order to prevent abuse of such measures, any technological measures applied in their implementation should enjoy legal protection.

(53) The protection of technological measures should ensure a secure environment for the provision of interactive on-demand services, in such a way that members of the public may access works or other subject-matter from a place and at a time individually chosen by them. Where such services are governed by contractual arrangements, the first and second subparagraphs of Article 6(4) should not apply. Non-interactive forms of online use should remain subject to those provisions.

(54) Important progress has been made in the international standardisation of technical systems of identification of works and protected subject-matter in digital format. In an increasingly networked environment, differences between technological measures could lead to an incompatibility of systems within the Community. Compatibility and interoperability of the different systems should be encouraged. It would be highly desirable to encourage the development of global systems.

(55) Technological development will facilitate the distribution of works, notably on networks, and this will entail the need for rightholders to identify better the work or other subject-matter, the author or any other rightholder, and to provide information about the terms and conditions of use of the work or other subject-matter in order to render easier the management of rights attached to them. Rightholders should be encouraged to use markings indicating, in addition to the information referred to above, *inter alia* their authorisation when putting works or other subject-matter on networks.

(56) There is, however, the danger that illegal activities might be carried out in order to remove or alter the electronic copyright-management information attached to it, or otherwise to distribute, import for distribution, broadcast, communicate to the public or make available to the public works or other protected subject-matter from which such information has been removed without authority. In order to avoid fragmented legal approaches that could potentially hinder the functioning of the internal market, there is a need to provide for harmonised legal protection against any of these activities.

(57) Any such rights-management information systems referred to above may, depending on their design, at the same time process personal data about the consumption patterns of protected subject-matter by individuals and allow for tracing of on-line behaviour. These technical means, in their technical functions, should incorporate privacy safeguards in accordance with Directive 95/46/EC of the European Parliament and of the Council of 24 October 1995 on the protection of individuals with regard to the processing of personal data and the free movement of such data[10].

(58) Member States should provide for effective sanctions and remedies for infringements of rights and obligations as set out in this Directive. They should take all the measures necessary to ensure that those sanctions and remedies are applied. The sanctions thus provided for should be effective, proportionate and dissuasive and should include the possibility of seeking damages and/or injunctive relief and, where appropriate, of applying for seizure of infringing material.

(59) In the digital environment, in particular, the services of intermediaries may increasingly be used by third parties for infringing activities. In many cases such intermediaries are best placed to bring such infringing activities to an end. Therefore, without prejudice to any other sanctions and remedies available, rightholders should have the possibility of applying for an injunction against an intermediary who carries a third party's infringement of a protected work or other subject-matter in a network. This possibility should be available even where the acts carried out by the intermediary are exempted under Article 5. The conditions and modalities relating to such injunctions should be left to the national law of the Member States.

(60) The protection provided under this Directive should be without prejudice to national or Community legal provisions in other areas, such as industrial property, data protection, conditional access, access to public documents, and the rule of media exploitation chronology, which may affect the protection of copyright or related rights.

---

10 OJ L 281, 23.11.1995, p 31.

(61) In order to comply with the WIPO Performances and Phonograms Treaty, Directives 92/100/EEC and 93/98/EEC should be amended,

HAVE ADOPTED THIS DIRECTIVE:

CHAPTER I

OBJECTIVE AND SCOPE

Article 1

Scope

1. This Directive concerns the legal protection of copyright and related rights in the framework of the internal market, with particular emphasis on the information society.

2. Except in the cases referred to in Article 11, this Directive shall leave intact and shall in no way affect existing Community provisions relating to:

(a) the legal protection of computer programs;
(b) rental right, lending right and certain rights related to copyright in the field of intellectual property;
(c) copyright and related rights applicable to broadcasting of programmes by satellite and cable retransmission;
(d) the term of protection of copyright and certain related rights;
(e) the legal protection of databases.

CHAPTER II

RIGHTS AND EXCEPTIONS

Article 2

Reproduction right

Member States shall provide for the exclusive right to authorise or prohibit direct or indirect, temporary or permanent reproduction by any means and in any form, in whole or in part:

(a) for authors, of their works;
(b) for performers, of fixations of their performances;
(c) for phonogram producers, of their phonograms;
(d) for the producers of the first fixations of films, in respect of the original and copies of their films;
(e) for broadcasting organisations, of fixations of their broadcasts, whether those broadcasts are transmitted by wire or over the air, including by cable or satellite.

Article 3

Right of communication to the public of works and right of making available to the public other subject-matter

1. Member States shall provide authors with the exclusive right to authorise or prohibit any communication to the public of their works, by wire or wireless means, including the making available to the public of their works in such a way that members of the public may access them from a place and at a time individually chosen by them.

2.   Member States shall provide for the exclusive right to authorise or prohibit the making available to the public, by wire or wireless means, in such a way that members of the public may access them from a place and at a time individually chosen by them:

(a)   for performers, of fixations of their performances;
(b)   for phonogram producers, of their phonograms;
(c)   for the producers of the first fixations of films, of the original and copies of their films;
(d)   for broadcasting organisations, of fixations of their broadcasts, whether these broadcasts are transmitted by wire or over the air, including by cable or satellite.

3.   The rights referred to in paragraphs 1 and 2 shall not be exhausted by any act of communication to the public or making available to the public as set out in this Article.

Article 4

Distribution right

1.   Member States shall provide for authors, in respect of the original of their works or of copies thereof, the exclusive right to authorise or prohibit any form of distribution to the public by sale or otherwise.

2.   The distribution right shall not be exhausted within the Community in respect of the original or copies of the work, except where the first sale or other transfer of ownership in the Community of that object is made by the rightholder or with his consent.

Article 5

Exceptions and limitations

1.   Temporary acts of reproduction referred to in Article 2, which are transient or incidental [and] an integral and essential part of a technological process and whose sole purpose is to enable:

(a)   a transmission in a network between third parties by an intermediary, or
(b)   a lawful use

of a work or other subject-matter to be made, and which have no independent economic significance, shall be exempted from the reproduction right provided for in Article 2.

2.   Member States may provide for exceptions or limitations to the reproduction right provided for in Article 2 in the following cases:

(a)   in respect of reproductions on paper or any similar medium, effected by the use of any kind of photographic technique or by some other process having similar effects, with the exception of sheet music, provided that the rightholders receive fair compensation;
(b)   in respect of reproductions on any medium made by a natural person for private use and for ends that are neither directly nor indirectly commercial, on condition that the rightholders receive fair compensation which takes account of the application or non-application of technological measures referred to in Article 6 to the work or subject-matter concerned;
(c)   in respect of specific acts of reproduction made by publicly accessible libraries, educational establishments or museums, or by archives, which are not for direct or indirect economic or commercial advantage;
(d)   in respect of ephemeral recordings of works made by broadcasting organisations by means of their own facilities and for their own broadcasts; the preservation of these recordings in official archives may, on the grounds of their exceptional documentary character, be permitted;

(e) in respect of reproductions of broadcasts made by social institutions pursuing non-commercial purposes, such as hospitals or prisons, on condition that the rightholders receive fair compensation.

3. Member States may provide for exceptions or limitations to the rights provided for in Articles 2 and 3 in the following cases:

(a) use for the sole purpose of illustration for teaching or scientific research, as long as the source, including the author's name, is indicated, unless this turns out to be impossible and to the extent justified by the non-commercial purpose to be achieved;

(b) uses, for the benefit of people with a disability, which are directly related to the disability and of a non-commercial nature, to the extent required by the specific disability;

(c) reproduction by the press, communication to the public or making available of published articles on current economic, political or religious topics or of broadcast works or other subject-matter of the same character, in cases where such use is not expressly reserved, and as long as the source, including the author's name, is indicated, or use of works or other subject-matter in connection with the reporting of current events, to the extent justified by the informatory purpose and as long as the source, including the author's name, is indicated, unless this turns out to be impossible;

(d) quotations for purposes such as criticism or review, provided that they relate to a work or other subject-matter which has already been lawfully made available to the public, that, unless this turns out to be impossible, the source, including the author's name, is indicated, and that their use is in accordance with fair practice, and to the extent required by the specific purpose;

(e) use for the purposes of public security or to ensure the proper performance or reporting of administrative, parliamentary or judicial proceedings;

(f) use of political speeches as well as extracts of public lectures or similar works or subject-matter to the extent justified by the informatory purpose and provided that the source, including the author's name, is indicated, except where this turns out to be impossible;

(g) use during religious celebrations or official celebrations organised by a public authority;

(h) use of works, such as works of architecture or sculpture, made to be located permanently in public places;

(i) incidental inclusion of a work or other subject-matter in other material;

(j) use for the purpose of advertising the public exhibition or sale of artistic works, to the extent necessary to promote the event, excluding any other commercial use;

(k) use for the purpose of caricature, parody or pastiche;

(l) use in connection with the demonstration or repair of equipment;

(m) use of an artistic work in the form of a building or a drawing or plan of a building for the purposes of reconstructing the building;

(n) use by communication or making available, for the purpose of research or private study, to individual members of the public by dedicated terminals on the premises of establishments referred to in paragraph 2(c) of works and other subject-matter not subject to purchase or licensing terms which are contained in their collections;

(o) use in certain other cases of minor importance where exceptions or limitations already exist under national law, provided that they only concern analogue uses and do not affect the free circulation of goods and services within the Community, without prejudice to the other exceptions and limitations contained in this Article.

4. Where the Member States may provide for an exception or limitation to the right of reproduction pursuant to paragraphs 2 and 3, they may provide similarly for an exception or limitation to the right of distribution as referred to in Article 4 to the extent justified by the purpose of the authorised act of reproduction.

5. The exceptions and limitations provided for in paragraphs 1, 2, 3 and 4 shall only be applied in certain special cases which do not conflict with a normal exploitation of the work or other subject-matter and do not unreasonably prejudice the legitimate interests of the rightholder.

CHAPTER III

PROTECTION OF TECHNOLOGICAL MEASURES AND RIGHTS-MANAGEMENT INFORMATION

Article 6

Obligations as to technological measures

1. Member States shall provide adequate legal protection against the circumvention of any effective technological measures, which the person concerned carries out in the knowledge, or with reasonable grounds to know, that he or she is pursuing that objective.

2. Member States shall provide adequate legal protection against the manufacture, import, distribution, sale, rental, advertisement for sale or rental, or possession for commercial purposes of devices, products or components or the provision of services which:

(a)   are promoted, advertised or marketed for the purpose of circumvention of, or
(b)   have only a limited commercially significant purpose or use other than to circumvent, or
(c)   are primarily designed, produced, adapted or performed for the purpose of enabling or facilitating the circumvention of,

any effective technological measures.

3. For the purposes of this Directive, the expression 'technological measures' means any technology, device or component that, in the normal course of its operation, is designed to prevent or restrict acts, in respect of works or other subject-matter, which are not authorised by the rightholder of any copyright or any right related to copyright as provided for by law or the *sui generis* right provided for in Chapter III of Directive 96/9/EC. Technological measures shall be deemed 'effective' where the use of a protected work or other subject-matter is controlled by the rightholders through application of an access control or protection process, such as encryption, scrambling or other transformation of the work or other subject-matter or a copy control mechanism, which achieves the protection objective.

4. Notwithstanding the legal protection provided for in paragraph 1, in the absence of voluntary measures taken by rightholders, including agreements between rightholders and other parties concerned, Member States shall take appropriate measures to ensure that rightholders make available to the beneficiary of an exception or limitation provided for in national law in accordance with Article 5(2)(a), (2)(c), (2)(d), (2)(e), (3)(a), (3)(b) or (3)(e) the means of benefiting from that exception or limitation, to the extent necessary to benefit from that exception or limitation and where that beneficiary has legal access to the protected work or subject-matter concerned.

A Member State may also take such measures in respect of a beneficiary of an exception or limitation provided for in accordance with Article 5(2)(b), unless reproduction for private use has already been made possible by rightholders to the extent necessary to benefit from the exception or limitation concerned and in accordance with the provisions of Article 5(2)(b) and (5), without preventing rightholders from adopting adequate measures regarding the number of reproductions in accordance with these provisions.

The technological measures applied voluntarily by rightholders, including those applied in implementation of voluntary agreements, and technological measures applied in implementation of the measures taken by Member States, shall enjoy the legal protection provided for in paragraph 1.

The provisions of the first and second subparagraphs shall not apply to works or other subject-matter made available to the public on agreed contractual terms in such a way that members of the public may access them from a place and at a time individually chosen by them.

When this Article is applied in the context of Directives 92/100/EEC and 96/9/EC, this paragraph shall apply *mutatis mutandis.*

Article 7

Obligations concerning rights-management information

1.   Member States shall provide for adequate legal protection against any person knowingly performing without authority any of the following acts:

   (a)   the removal or alteration of any electronic rights-management information;
   (b)   the distribution, importation for distribution, broadcasting, communication or making available to the public of works or other subject-matter protected under this Directive or under Chapter III of Directive 96/9/EC from which electronic rights-management information has been removed or altered without authority,

if such person knows, or has reasonable grounds to know, that by so doing he is inducing, enabling, facilitating or concealing an infringement of any copyright or any rights related to copyright as provided by law, or of the *sui generis* right provided for in Chapter III of Directive 96/9/EC.

2.   For the purposes of this Directive, the expression 'rights-management information' means any information provided by rightholders which identifies the work or other subject-matter referred to in this Directive or covered by the *sui generis* right provided for in Chapter III of Directive 96/9/EC, the author or any other rightholder, or information about the terms and conditions of use of the work or other subject-matter, and any numbers or codes that represent such information.

The first subparagraph shall apply when any of these items of information is associated with a copy of, or appears in connection with the communication to the public of, a work or other subject matter referred to in this Directive or covered by the *sui generis* right provided for in Chapter III of Directive 96/9/EC.

CHAPTER IV

COMMON PROVISIONS

Article 8

Sanctions and remedies

1.   Member States shall provide appropriate sanctions and remedies in respect of infringements of the rights and obligations set out in this Directive and shall take all the measures necessary to ensure that those sanctions and remedies are applied. The sanctions thus provided for shall be effective, proportionate and dissuasive.

2.   Each Member State shall take the measures necessary to ensure that rightholders whose interests are affected by an infringing activity carried out on its territory can bring an action for damages and/or apply for an injunction and, where appropriate, for the seizure of infringing material as well as of devices, products or components referred to in Article 6(2).

3.   Member States shall ensure that rightholders are in a position to apply for an injunction against intermediaries whose services are used by a third party to infringe a copyright or related right.

Article 9

Continued application of other legal provisions

This Directive shall be without prejudice to provisions concerning in particular patent rights, trade marks, design rights, utility models, topographies of semi-conductor products, type faces, conditional access, access to cable of broadcasting services, protection of national treasures, legal deposit requirements, laws on restrictive practices and unfair competition, trade secrets, security, confidentiality, data protection and privacy, access to public documents, the law of contract.

Article 10

Application over time

1.   The provisions of this Directive shall apply in respect of all works and other subject-matter referred to in this Directive which are, on 22 December 2002, protected by the Member States' legislation in the field of copyright and related rights, or which meet the criteria for protection under the provisions of this Directive or the provisions referred to in Article 1(2).

2.   This Directive shall apply without prejudice to any acts concluded and rights acquired before 22 December 2002.

Article 11

Technical adaptations

1.   Directive 92/100/EEC is hereby amended as follows:

(a)   Article 7 shall be deleted;
(b)   Article 10(3) shall be replaced by the following:

'3.   The limitations shall only be applied in certain special cases which do not conflict with a normal exploitation of the subject-matter and do not unreasonably prejudice the legitimate interests of the rightholder.'

2.   Article 3(2) of Directive 93/98/EEC shall be replaced by the following:

'2.   The rights of producers of phonograms shall expire 50 years after the fixation is made. However, if the phonogram has been lawfully published within this period, the said rights shall expire 50 years from the date of the first lawful publication. If no lawful publication has taken place within the period mentioned in the first sentence, and if the phonogram has been lawfully communicated to the public within this period, the said rights shall expire 50 years from the date of the first lawful communication to the public.

However, where through the expiry of the term of protection granted pursuant to this paragraph in its version before amendment by Directive 2001/29/EC of the European Parliament and of the Council of 22 May 2001 on the harmonisation of certain aspects of copyright and related rights in the information society* the rights of producers of phonograms are no longer protected on 22 December 2002, this paragraph shall not have the effect of protecting those rights anew.

---

* OJ L 167, 22.6.2001, p 10.'

Article 12

Final provisions

1.   Not later than 22 December 2004 and every three years thereafter, the Commission shall submit to the European Parliament, the Council and the Economic and Social Committee a report on the application of this Directive, in which, *inter alia*, on the basis of specific information supplied by the Member States, it shall examine in particular the application of Articles 5, 6 and 8 in the light of the development of the digital market. In the case of Article 6, it shall examine in particular whether that Article confers a sufficient level of protection and whether acts which are permitted by law are being adversely affected by the use of effective technological measures. Where necessary, in particular to ensure the functioning of the internal market pursuant to Article 14 of the Treaty, it shall submit proposals for amendments to this Directive.

2.   Protection of rights related to copyright under this Directive shall leave intact and shall in no way affect the protection of copyright.

3.   A contact committee is hereby established. It shall be composed of representatives of the competent authorities of the Member States. It shall be chaired by a representative of the Commission and shall meet either on the initiative of the chairman or at the request of the delegation of a Member State.

4.   The tasks of the committee shall be as follows:

   (a)   to examine the impact of this Directive on the functioning of the internal market, and to highlight any difficulties;
   (b)   to organise consultations on all questions deriving from the application of this Directive;
   (c)   to facilitate the exchange of information on relevant developments in legislation and case-law, as well as relevant economic, social, cultural and technological developments;
   (d)   to act as a forum for the assessment of the digital market in works and other items, including private copying and the use of technological measures.

Article 13

Implementation

1.   Member States shall bring into force the laws, regulations and administrative provisions necessary to comply with this Directive before 22 December 2002. They shall forthwith inform the Commission thereof.

When Member States adopt these measures, they shall contain a reference to this Directive or shall be accompanied by such reference on the occasion of their official publication. The methods of making such reference shall be laid down by Member States.

2.   Member States shall communicate to the Commission the text of the provisions of domestic law which they adopt in the field governed by this Directive.

Article 14

Entry into force

This Directive shall enter into force on the day of its publication in the *Official Journal of the European Communities*.

Article 15

Addressees

This Directive is addressed to the Member States.

Appendix 2

COPYRIGHT, DESIGNS AND PATENTS ACT 1988, showing sections amended by the Copyright and Related Rights Regulations 2003

1988 c 48

PART I

COPYRIGHT

Chapter I

Subsistence, ownership and duration of copyright

Introductory

1   Copyright and copyright works

(1) Copyright is a property right which subsists in accordance with this Part in the following descriptions of work –

  (a)   original literary, dramatic, musical or artistic works,
  (b)   sound recordings, films [or broadcasts], and
  (c)   the typographical arrangement of published editions.

(2) In this Part 'copyright work' means a work of any of those descriptions in which copyright subsists.

(3) Copyright does not subsist in a work unless the requirements of this Part with respect to qualification for copyright protection are met (see section 153 and the provisions referred to there).

Amendments: Words in square brackets substituted: SI 2003/2498, regs 3, 5(2).

6   Broadcasts

[(1) In this Part a 'broadcast' means an electronic transmission of visual images, sounds or other information which –

  (a)   is transmitted for simultaneous reception by members of the public and is capable of being lawfully received by them, or
  (b)   is transmitted at a time determined solely by the person making the transmission for presentation to members of the public,

and which is not excepted by subsection (1A); and references to broadcasting shall be construed accordingly.

(1A) Excepted from the definition of 'broadcast' is any internet transmission unless it is –

(a)   a transmission taking place simultaneously on the internet and by other means,

(b)   a concurrent transmission of a live event, or

(c)   a transmission of recorded moving images or sounds forming part of a programme service offered by the person responsible for making the transmission, being a service in which programmes are transmitted at scheduled times determined by that person.]

(2) An encrypted transmission shall be regarded as capable of being lawfully received by members of the public only if decoding equipment has been made available to members of the public by or with the authority of the person making the transmission or the person providing the contents of the transmission.

(3) References in this Part to the person making a broadcast [or a transmission which is a broadcast] are –

(a)   to the person transmitting the programme, if he has responsibility to any extent for its contents, and

(b)   to any person providing the programme who makes with the person transmitting it the arrangements necessary for its transmission; and references in this Part to a programme, in the context of broadcasting, are to any item included in a broadcast.

(4) For the purposes of this Part, the place from which a [wireless] broadcast is made is the place where, under the control and responsibility of the person making the broadcast, the programme-carrying signals are introduced into an uninterrupted chain of communication (including, in the case of a satellite transmission, the chain leading to the satellite and down towards the earth).

(4A) Subsections (3) and (4) have effect subject to section 6A (safeguards in case of certain satellite broadcasts).

(5) References in this Part to the reception of a broadcast include reception of a broadcast relayed by means of a telecommunications system.

[(5A) The relaying of a broadcast by reception and immediate re-transmission shall be regarded for the purposes of this Part as a separate act of broadcasting from the making of the broadcast which is so re-transmitted.]

(6) Copyright does not subsist in a broadcast which infringes, or to the extent that it infringes, the copyright in another broadcast . . . .

Amendments: Subsections (1), (1A) substituted, words in square brackets substituted, and sub-s (5A) inserted by SI 2003/2498, regs 3, 4. Words omitted repealed by SI 2003/2498, reg 2(2), Sch 2.

6A   Safeguards in relation to certain satellite broadcasts

(1) This section applies where the place from which a broadcast by way of satellite transmission is made is located in a country other than an EEA State and the law of that country fails to provide at least the following level of protection –

(a)   exclusive rights in relation to [wireless] broadcasting equivalent to those conferred by section 20 ([infringement by communication to the public]) on the authors of literary, dramatic, musical and artistic works, films and broadcasts;

(b)   a right in relation to live [wireless] broadcasting equivalent to that conferred on a performer by section 182(1)(b) (consent required for live broadcast of performance); and

(c)   a right for authors of sound recordings and performers to share in a single equitable remuneration in respect of the [wireless] broadcasting of sound recordings.

(2) Where the place from which the programme-carrying signals are transmitted to the satellite ('the uplink station') is located in an EEA State –

(a) that place shall be treated as the place from which the broadcast is made, and

(b) the person operating the uplink station shall be treated as the person making the broadcast.

(3) Where the uplink station is not located in an EEA State but a person who is established in an EEA State has commissioned the making of the broadcast –

(a) that person shall be treated as the person making the broadcast, and

(b) the place in which he has his principal establishment in the European Economic Area shall be treated as the place from which the broadcast is made.

Amendments: Words in square brackets inserted or substituted: SI 2003/2498, regs 3, 5(3).

7   ...

Amendment: Section repealed by SI 2003/2498, regs 2(2), 3, 5(1), Sch 2.

Authorship and ownership of copyright

9   Authorship of work

(1) In this Part 'author', in relation to a work, means the person who creates it.

(2) That person shall be taken to be –

(aa) in the case of a sound recording, the producer;

(ab) in the case of a film, the producer and the principal director;

(b) in the case of a broadcast, the person making the broadcast (see section 6(3)) or, in the case of a broadcast which relays another broadcast by reception and immediate re-transmission, the person making that other broadcast;

(c)   ...

(d) in the case of the typographical arrangement of a published edition, the publisher.

(3) In the case of a literary, dramatic, musical or artistic work which is computer-generated, the author shall be taken to be the person by whom the arrangements necessary for the creation of the work are undertaken.

(4) For the purposes of this Part a work is of 'unknown authorship' if the identity of the author is unknown or, in the case of a work of joint authorship, if the identity of none of the authors is known.

(5) For the purposes of this Part the identity of an author shall be regarded as unknown if it is not possible for a person to ascertain his identity by reasonable inquiry; but if his identity is once known it shall not subsequently be regarded as unknown.

Amendments: Subsection (2)(c) repealed by SI 2003/2498, regs 2(2), 3, 5(4), Sch 2.

Duration of copyright

12   Duration of copyright in literary, dramatic, musical or artistic work

(1) The following provisions have effect with respect to the duration of copyright in a literary, dramatic, musical or artistic work.

(2) Copyright expires at the end of the period of 70 years from the end of the calendar year in which the author dies, subject as follows.

(3) If the work is of unknown authorship, copyright expires –

    (a) at the end of the period of 70 years from the end of the calendar year in which the work was made, or

    (b) if during that period the work is made available to the public, at the end of the period of 70 years from the end of the calendar year in which it is first so made available, subject as follows.

(4) Subsection (2) applies if the identity of the author becomes known before the end of the period specified in paragraph (a) or (b) of subsection (3).

(5) For the purposes of subsection (3) making available to the public includes –

    (a) in the case of a literary, dramatic or musical work –
        (i)   performance in public, or
        [(ii) communication to the public;]
    (b) in the case of an artistic work –
        (i)   exhibition in public,
        (ii) a film including the work being shown in public, or
        [(iii) communication to the public;]

but in determining generally for the purposes of that subsection whether a work has been made available to the public no account shall be taken of any unauthorised act.

(6) Where the country of origin of the work is not an EEA state and the author of the work is not a national of an EEA state, the duration of copyright is that to which the work is entitled in the country of origin, provided that does not exceed the period which would apply under subsections (2) to (5).

(7) If the work is computer-generated the above provisions do not apply and copyright expires at the end of the period of 50 years from the end of the calendar year in which the work was made.

(8) The provisions of this section are adapted as follows in relation to a work of joint authorship –

    (a) the reference in subsection (2) to the death of the author shall be construed –
        (i)   if the identity of all the authors is known, as a reference to the death of the last of them to die, and
        (ii) if the identity of one or more of the authors is known and the identity of one or more others is not, as a reference to the death of the last whose identity is known;
    (b) the reference in subsection (4) to the identity of the author becoming known shall be construed as a reference to the identity of any of the authors becoming known;
    (c) the reference in subsection (6) to the author not being a national of an EEA state shall be construed as a reference to none of the authors being a national of an EEA state.

(9) This section does not apply to Crown copyright or Parliamentary copyright (see sections 163 to 166B) or to copyright which subsists by virtue of section 168 (copyright of certain international organisations).

Amendment: Paragraphs substituted by SI 2003/2498, reg 2(1), Sch 1, Pt 1, paras 1, 4.

13A   Duration of copyright in sound recordings

(1) The following provisions have effect with respect to the duration of copyright in a sound recording.

[(2) Subject to subsections (4) and (5), copyright expires –

  (a) at the end of the period of 50 years from the end of the calendar year in which the recording is made, or
  (b) if during that period the recording is published, 50 years from the end of the calendar year in which it is first published, or
  (c) if during that period the recording is not published but is made available to the public by being played in public or communicated to the public, 50 years from the end of the calendar year in which it is first so made available,

but in determining whether a sound recording has been published, played in public or communicated to the public, no account shall be taken of any unauthorised act.]

(3) ...

(4) Where the author of a sound recording is not a national of an EEA state, the duration of copyright is that to which the sound recording is entitled in the country of which the author is a national, provided that does not exceed the period which would apply under [subsection (2)].

(5) If or to the extent that the application of subsection (4) would be at variance with an international obligation to which the United Kingdom became subject prior to 29th October 1993, the duration of copyright shall be as specified in [subsection (2)].

Amendments: Subsection (2) substituted, sub-s (3) repealed, and words in square brackets substituted: SI 2003/2498, regs 3, 29.

13B   Duration of copyright in films

(1) The following provisions have effect with respect to the duration of copyright in a film.

(2) Copyright expires at the end of the period of 70 years from the end of the calendar year in which the death occurs of the last to die of the following persons –

  (a) the principal director,
  (b) the author of the screenplay,
  (c) the author of the dialogue, or
  (d) the composer of music specially created for and used in the film;

subject as follows.

(3) If the identity of one or more of the persons referred to in subsection (2)(a) to (d) is known and the identity of one or more others is not, the reference in that subsection to the death of the last of them to die shall be construed as a reference to the death of the last whose identity is known.

(4) If the identity of the persons referred to in subsection (2)(a) to (d) is unknown, copyright expires at –

  (a) the end of the period of 70 years from the end of the calendar year in which the film was made, or
  (b) if during that period the film is made available to the public, at the end of the period of 70 years from the end of the calendar year in which it is first so made available.

(5) Subsections (2) and (3) apply if the identity of any of those persons becomes known before the end of the period specified in paragraph (a) or (b) of subsection (4).

(6) For the purposes of subsection (4) making available to the public includes –

(a)   showing in public, or
[(b) communicating to the public;]

but in determining generally for the purposes of that subsection whether a film has been made available to the public no account shall be taken of any unauthorised act.

(7) Where the country of origin is not an EEA state and the author of the film is not a national of an EEA state, the duration of copyright is that to which the work is entitled in the country of origin, provided that does not exceed the period which would apply under subsections (2) to (6).

(8) In relation to a film of which there are joint authors, the reference in subsection (7) to the author not being a national of an EEA state shall be construed as a reference to none of the authors being a national of an EEA state.

(9) If in any case there is no person falling within paragraphs (a) to (d) of subsection (2), the above provisions do not apply and copyright expires at the end of the period of 50 years from the end of the calendar year in which the film was made.

(10) For the purposes of this section the identity of any of the persons referred to in subsection (2)(a) to (d) shall be regarded as unknown if it is not possible for a person to ascertain his identity by reasonable inquiry; but if the identity of any such person is once known it shall not subsequently be regarded as unknown.

Amendment: Paragraph substituted: SI 2003/2498, reg 2(1), Sch 1, Pt 1, paras 1, 4(3).

Chapter II

Rights of Copyright Owner

The acts restricted by copyright

16   The acts restricted by copyright in a work

(1) The owner of the copyright in a work has, in accordance with the following provisions of this Chapter, the exclusive right to do the following acts in the United Kingdom –

(a)   to copy the work (see section 17);
(b)   to issue copies of the work to the public (see section 18);
(ba) to rent or lend the work to the public (see section 18A);
(c)   to perform, show or play the work in public (see section 19);
[(d) to communicate the work to the public (see section 20);]
(e)   to make an adaptation of the work or do any of the above in relation to an adaptation (see section 21);

and those acts are referred to in this Part as the 'acts restricted by the copyright'.

(2) Copyright in a work is infringed by a person who without the licence of the copyright owner does, or authorises another to do, any of the acts restricted by the copyright.

(3) References in this Part to the doing of an act restricted by the copyright in a work are to the doing of it –

(a)   in relation to the work as a whole or any substantial part of it, and
(b)   either directly or indirectly;

and it is immaterial whether any intervening acts themselves infringe copyright.

(4) This Chapter has effect subject to –

(a)   the provisions of Chapter III (acts permitted in relation to copyright works), and
(b)   the provisions of Chapter VII (provisions with respect to copyright licensing).

Amendment: Paragraph substituted: SI 2003/2498, regs 3, 6(2).

17   Infringement of copyright by copying

(1) The copying of the work is an act restricted by the copyright in every description of copyright work; and references in this Part to copying and copies shall be construed as follows.

(2) Copying in relation to a literary, dramatic, musical or artistic work means reproducing the work in any material form. This includes storing the work in any medium by electronic means.

(3) In relation to an artistic work copying includes the making of a copy in three dimensions of a two-dimensional work and the making of a copy in two dimensions of a three-dimensional work.

(4) Copying in relation to a film [or broadcast] includes making a photograph of the whole or any substantial part of any image forming part of the film [or broadcast].

(5) Copying in relation to the typographical arrangement of a published edition means making a facsimile copy of the arrangement.

(6) Copying in relation to any description of work includes the making of copies which are transient or are incidental to some other use of the work.

Amendments: Words in square brackets substituted: SI 2003/2498, regs 2(1), 3, 5(5), Sch 1, Pt 1, paras 1, 3(a).

18A   Infringement by rental or lending of work to the public

(1) The rental or lending of copies of the work to the public is an act restricted by the copyright in –

(a)   a literary, dramatic or musical work,
(b)   an artistic work, other than –
    (i)   a work of architecture in the form of a building or a model for a building, or
    (ii)   a work of applied art, or
(c)   a film or a sound recording.

(2) In this Part, subject to the following provisions of this section –

(a)   'rental' means making a copy of the work available for use, on terms that it will or may be returned, for direct or indirect economic or commercial advantage, and
(b)   'lending' means making a copy of the work available for use, on terms that it will be or may be returned, otherwise than for direct or indirect economic or commercial advantage, through an establishment which is accessible to the public.

(3) The expressions 'rental' and 'lending' do not include –

(a)   making available for the purpose of public performance, playing or showing in public [or communication to the public];
(b)   making available for the purpose of exhibition in public; or

(c) making available for on-the-spot reference use.

(4) The expression 'lending' does not include making available between establishments which are accessible to the public.

(5) Where lending by an establishment accessible to the pubic gives rise to a payment the amount of which does not go beyond what is necessary to cover the operating costs of the estalbishment, there is no direct or indirect economic or commercial advantage for the purposes of this section.

(6) References in this Part to the rental or lending of copies of a work include the rental or lending of the original.

Amendment: Words in square brackets substituted: SI 2003/2498, reg 2(1), Sch 1, para 1, 6(2)(a).

19   Infringement by performance, showing or playing of work in public

(1) The performance of the work in public is an act restricted by the copyright in a literary, dramatic or musical work.

(2) In this Part 'performance', in relation to a work –

   (a) includes delivery in the case of lectures, addresses, speeches and sermons, and
   (b) in general, includes any mode of visual or acoustic presentation, including presentation by means of a sound recording, film [or broadcast] of the work.

(3) The playing or showing of the work in public is an act restricted by the copyright in a sound recording, film [or broadcast].

(4) Where copyright in a work is infringed by its being performed, played or shown in public by means of apparatus for receiving visual images or sounds conveyed by electronic means, the person by whom the visual images or sounds are sent, and in the case of a performance the performers, shall not be regarded as responsible for the infringement.

Amendment: Words in square brackets substituted: SI 2003/2498, reg 2(1), Sch 1, Pt 1, paras 1, 3.

[20   Infringement by communication to the public]

[(1) The communication to the public of the work is an act restricted by the copyright in –

   (a) a literary, dramatic, musical or artistic work,
   (b) a sound recording or film, or
   (c) a broadcast.

(2) References in this Part to communication to the public are to communication to the public by electronic transmission, and in relation to a work include –

   (a) the broadcasting of the work;
   (b) the making available to the public of the work by electronic transmission in such a way that members of the public may access it from a place and at a time individually chosen by them.]

Amendment: Section substituted: SI 2003/2498, regs 3, 6(1).

24   Secondary infringement: providing means for making infringing copies

(1) Copyright in a work is infringed by a person who, without the licence of the copyright owner –

(a) makes,

(b) imports into the United Kingdom,

(c) possesses in the course of a business, or

(d) sells or lets for hire, or offers or exposes for sale or hire,

an article specifically designed or adapted for making copies of that work, knowing or having reason to believe that it is to be used to make infringing copies.

(2) Copyright in a work is infringed by a person who without the licence of the copyright owner transmits the work by means of a telecommunications system (otherwise than by [communication to the public]), knowing or having reason to believe that infringing copies of the work will be made by means of the reception of the transmission in the United Kingdom or elsewhere.

Amendment: Words in square brackets substituted: SI 2003/2498, reg 2(1), Sch 1, Pt 1, paras 1, 5(a).

Infringing copies

27 Meaning of 'infringing copy'

(1) In this Part 'infringing copy', in relation to a copyright work, shall be construed in accordance with this section.

(2) An article is an infringing copy if its making constituted an infringement of the copyright in the work in question.

(3) An article is also an infringing copy if –

(a) it has been or is proposed to be imported into the United Kingdom, and

(b) its making in the United Kingdom would have constituted an infringement of the copyright in the work in question, or a breach of an exclusive licence agreement relating to that work.

(4) Where in any proceedings the question arises whether an article is an infringing copy and it is shown –

(a) that the article is a copy of the work, and

(b) that copyright subsists in the work or has subsisted at any time,

it shall be presumed until the contrary is proved that the article was made at a time when copyright subsisted in the work.

(5) Nothing in subsection (3) shall be construed as applying to an article which may lawfully be imported into the United Kingdom by virtue of any enforceable Community right within the meaning of section 2(1) of the European Communities Act 1972.

(6) In this Part 'infringing copy' includes a copy falling to be treated as an infringing copy by virtue of any of the following provisions –

section 31A(6) and (9) (making a single accessible copy for personal use),

section 31B(9) and (10) (multiple copies for visually impaired persons),

section 31C(2) (intermediate copies held by approved bodies),

section 32(5) (copies made for purposes of instruction or examination),

section 35(3) (recordings made by educational establishments for educational purposes),

section 36(5) (reprographic copying by educational establishments for purposes of instruction), section 37(3)(b) (copies made by librarian or archivist in reliance on false declaration),

section 56(2) (further copies, adaptations, &c of work in electronic form retained on transfer of principal copy),

section 63(2) (copies made for purpose of advertising artistic work for sale),

section 68(4) (copies made for purpose of broadcast ...),

[section 70(2) (recording for the purposes of time-shifting),

section 71(2) (photographs of broadcasts), or]

any provision of an order under section 141 (statutory licence for certain reprographic copying by educational establishments).

Amendments: Entries substituted in subs (6) relating to ss 70 and 71, and words repealed: SI 2003/ 2498, regs 2(2), 3, 20(3), Sch 2.

General

[28A   Making of temporary copies]

[Copyright in a literary work, other than a computer program or a database, or in a dramatic, musical or artistic work, the typographical arrangement of a published edition, a sound recording or a film, is not infringed by the making of a temporary copy which is transient or incidental, which is an integral and essential part of a technological process and the sole purpose of which is to enable –

(a)   a transmission of the work in a network between third parties by an intermediary; or
(b)   a lawful use of the work;

and which has no independent economic significance.]

Amendment: Section inserted: SI 2003/2498, regs 3, 8(1).

29   Research and private study

[(1) Fair dealing with a literary, dramatic, musical or artistic work for the purposes of research for a non-commercial purpose does not infringe any copyright in the work provided that it is accompanied by a sufficient acknowledgement.]

[(1B) No acknowledgement is required in connection with fair dealing for the purposes mentioned in subsection (1) where this would be impossible for reasons of practicality or otherwise.

(1C) Fair dealing with a literary, dramatic, musical or artistic work for the purposes of private study does not infringe any copyright in the work.]

(2) Fair dealing with the typographical arrangement of a published edition for the purposes [of research or private study] does not infringe any copyright in the arrangement.

(3) Copying by a person other than the researcher or student himself is not fair dealing if –

(a)   in the case of a librarian, or a person acting on behalf of a librarian, he does anything which regulations under section 40 would not permit to be done under section 38 or 39 (articles or parts of published works: restriction on multiple copies of same material), or

(b) in any other case, the person doing the copying knows or has reason to believe that it will result in copies of substantially the same material being provided to more than one person at substantially the same time and for substantially the same purpose.

(4) It is not fair dealing –

(a) to convert a computer program expressed in a low level language into a version expressed in a higher level language, or
(b) incidentally in the course of so converting the program, to copy it,

(these acts being permitted if done in accordance with section 50B (decompilation)).

[(4A) It is not fair dealing to observe, study or test the functioning of a computer program in order to determine the ideas and principles which underlie any element of the program (these acts being permitted if done in accordance with section 50BA (observing, studying and testing)).]

[(5) . . .]

Amendments: Subsections substituted, inserted or repealed, and words in square brackets substituted: SI 2003/2498, regs 3, 9 and Sch 2.

30 Criticism, review and news reporting

(1) Fair dealing with a work for the purpose of criticism or review, of that or another work or of a performance of a work, does not infringe any copyright in the work provided that it is accompanied by a sufficient acknowledgement [and provided that the work has been made available to the public].

[(1A) For the purposes of subsection (1) a work has been made available to the public if it has been made available by any means, including –

(a) the issue of copies to the public;
(b) making the work available by means of an electronic retrieval system;
(c) the rental or lending of copies of the work to the public;
(d) the performance, exhibition, playing or showing of the work in public;
(e) the communication to the public of the work,

but in determining generally for the purposes of that subsection whether a work has been made available to the public no account shall be taken of any unauthorised act.]

(2) Fair dealing with a work (other than a photograph) for the purpose of reporting current events does not infringe any copyright in the work provided that (subject to subsection (3)) it is accompanied by a sufficient acknowledgement.

(3) No acknowledgement is required in connection with the reporting of current events by means of a sound recording, film [or broadcast where this would be impossible for reasons of practicality or otherwise].

Amendments: Subsection inserted and words inserted or substituted: SI 2003/2498, regs 3, 10.

31 Incidental inclusion of copyright material

(1) Copyright in a work is not infringed by its incidental inclusion in an artistic work, sound recording, film [or broadcast].

(2) Nor is the copyright infringed by the issue to the public of copies, or the playing, showing [or communication to the public], of anything whose making was, by virtue of subsection (1), not an infringement of the copyright.

(3) A musical work, words spoken or sung with music, or so much of a sound recording [or broadcast] as includes a musical work or such words, shall not be regarded as incidentally included in another work if it is deliberately included.

Amendments: Words in square brackets substituted: SI 2003/2498, reg 2(1), Sch 1, Pt 1, paras 1, 3, 6.

Education

32   Things done for purposes of instruction or examination

[(1) Copyright in a literary, dramatic, musical or artistic work is not infringed by its being copied in the course of instruction or of preparation for instruction, provided the copying –

    (a) is done by a person giving or receiving instruction,
    (b) is not done by means of a reprographic process, and
    (c) is accompanied by a sufficient acknowledgement,

and provided that the instruction is for a non-commercial purpose.

(2) Copyright in a sound recording, film or broadcast is not infringed by its being copied by making a film or film sound-track in the course of instruction, or of preparation for instruction, in the making of films or film sound-tracks, provided the copying –

    (a) is done by a person giving or receiving instruction, and
    (b) is accompanied by a sufficient acknowledgement,

and provided that the instruction is for a non-commercial purpose.

(2A) Copyright in a literary, dramatic, musical or artistic work which has been made available to the public is not infringed by its being copied in the course of instruction or of preparation for instruction, provided the copying –

    (a) is fair dealing with the work,
    (b) is done by a person giving or receiving instruction,
    (c) is not done by means of a reprographic process, and
    (d) is accompanied by a sufficient acknowledgement.

(2B) The provisions of section 30(1A) (works made available to the public) apply for the purposes of subsection (2A) as they apply for the purposes of section 30(1).]

(3) Copyright is not infringed by anything done for the purposes of an examination by way of setting the questions, communicating the questions to the candidates or answering the questions[, provided that the questions are accompanied by a sufficient acknowledgement].

[(3A) No acknowledgement is required in connection with copying as mentioned in subsection (1), (2) or (2A), or in connection with anything done for the purposes mentioned in subsection (3), where this would be impossible for reasons of practicality or otherwise.]

(4) Subsection (3) does not extend to the making of a reprographic copy of a musical work for use by an examination candidate in performing the work.

(5) Where a copy which would otherwise be an infringing copy is made in accordance with this section but is subsequently dealt with, it shall be treated as an infringing copy for the purpose of that dealing, and if that dealing infringes copyright for all subsequent purposes.

[For this purpose 'dealt with' means –

(a) sold or let for hire, offered or exposed for sale or hire; or

(b) communicated to the public, unless that communication, by virtue of subsection (3), is not an infringement of copyright.]

Amendments: Subsections substituted or inserted, and words in square brackets inserted or substituted: SI 2003/2498, regs 3, 11.

34   Performing, playing or showing work in course of activities of educational establishment

(1) The performance of a literary, dramatic or musical work before an audience consisting of teachers and pupils at an educational establishment and other persons directly connected with the activities of the establishment –

(a) by a teacher or pupil in the course of the activities of the establishment, or

(b) at the establishment by any person for the purposes of instruction,

is not a public performance for the purposes of infringement of copyright.

(2) The playing or showing of a sound recording, film [or broadcast] before such an audience at an educational establishment for the purposes of instruction is not a playing or showing of the work in public for the purposes of infringement of copyright.

(3) A person is not for this purpose directly connected with the activities of the educational establishment simply because he is the parent of a pupil at the establishment.

Amendment: Words in square brackets substituted: SI 2003/2498, reg 2(1), Sch 1, Pt 1, paras 1, 3(1)(f).

35   Recording by educational establishments of broadcasts ...

(1) A recording of a broadcast ..., or a copy of such a recording, may be made by or on behalf of an educational establishment for the educational purposes of that establishment without thereby infringing the copyright in the broadcast ..., or in any work included in it[, provided that it is accompanied by a sufficient acknowledgement of the broadcast and that the educational purposes are non-commercial].

[(1A) Copyright is not infringed where a recording of a broadcast or a copy of such a recording, whose making was by virtue of subsection (1) not an infringement of copyright, is communicated to the public by a person situated within the premises of an educational establishment provided that the communication cannot be received by any person situated outside the premises of that establishment.]

(2) This section does not apply if or to the extent that there is a licensing scheme certified for the purposes of this section under section 143 providing for the grant of licences.

(3) Where a copy which would otherwise be an infringing copy is made in accordance with this section but is subsequently dealt with, it shall be treated as an infringing copy for the purposes of that dealing, and if that dealing infringes copyright for all subsequent purposes. For this purpose 'dealt with' means sold or let for hire[, offered or exposed for sale or hire, or communicated from within the premises of an educational establishment to any person situated outside those premises].

Amendments: Subsection inserted and words inserted or repealed: SI 2003/2498, regs 2(2), 3, 12, Sch 2.

36 Reprographic copying by educational establishments of passages from published works

(1) Reprographic copies of passages from published literary, dramatic or musical works may, to the extent permitted by this section, be made by or on behalf of an educational establishment for the purposes of instruction without infringing any copyright in the work, [provided that they are accompanied by a sufficient acknowledgement and the instruction is for a non-commercial purpose].

[(1A) No acknowledgement is required in connection with the making of copies as mentioned in subsection (1) where this would be impossible for reasons of practicality or otherwise.

(1B) Reprographic copies of passages from published editions may, to the extent permitted by this section, be made by or on behalf of an educational establishment for the purposes of instruction without infringing any copyright in the typographical arrangement of the edition.]

(2) Not more than one per cent of any work may be copied by or on behalf of an establishment by virtue of this section in any quarter, that is, in any period 1st January to 31st March, 1st April to 30th June, 1st July to 30th September or 1st October to 31st December.

(3) Copying is not authorised by this section if, or to the extent that, licences are available authorising the copying in question and the person making the copies knew or ought to have been aware of that fact.

(4) The terms of a licence granted to an educational establishment authorising the reprographic copying for the purposes of instruction of passages from published . . . works are of no effect so far as they purport to restrict the proportion of a work which may be copied (whether on payment or free of charge) to less than that which would be permitted under this section.

(5) Where a copy which would otherwise be an infringing copy is made in accordance with this section but is subsequently dealt with, it shall be treated as an infringing copy for the purposes of that dealing, and if that dealing infringes copyright for all subsequent purposes.

For this purpose 'dealt with' means sold or let for hire[, offered or exposed for sale or hire or communicated to the public].

Amendments: Subsections (1A) and (1B) inserted and words in square brackets substituted: SI 2003/2498, regs 3, 13. Words omitted repealed: SI 2003/2498, reg 2(2), Sch 2.

38 Copying by librarians: articles in periodicals

(1) The librarian of a prescribed library may, if the prescribed conditions are complied with, make and supply a copy of an article in a periodical without infringing any copyright in the text, in any illustrations accompanying the text or in the typographical arrangement.

(2) The prescribed conditions shall include the following –

[(a) that copies are supplied only to persons satisfying the librarian that they require them for the purposes of –
(i) research for a non-commercial purpose, or
(ii) private study,
and will not use them for any other purpose;]
(b) that no person is furnished with more than one copy of the same article or with copies of more than one article contained in the same issue of a periodical; and
(c) that persons to whom copies are supplied are required to pay for them a sum not less than the cost (including a contribution to the general expenses of the library) attributable to their production.

Amendment: Paragraph substituted: SI 2003/2498, regs 3, 14(1).

39   Copying by librarians: parts of published works

(1) The librarian of a prescribed library may, if the prescribed conditions are complied with, make and supply from a published edition a copy of part of a literary, dramatic or musical work (other than an article in a periodical) without infringing any copyright in the work, in any illustrations accompanying the work or in the typographical arrangement.

(2) The prescribed conditions shall include the following –

   [(a) that copies are supplied only to persons satisfying the librarian that they require them for the purposes of –
      (i)   research for a non-commercial purpose, or
      (ii)   private study,
      and will not use them for any other purpose;]
   (b) that no person is furnished with more than one copy of the same material or with a copy of more than a reasonable proportion of any work; and
   (c) that person to whom copies are supplied are required to pay for them a sum not less than the cost (including a contribution to the general expenses of the library) attributable to their production.

Amendment: Paragraph substituted: SI 2003/2498, regs 3, 14(1).

43   Copying by librarians or archivists: certain unpublished works

(1) The librarian or archivist of a prescribed library or archive may, if the prescribed conditions are complied with, make and supply a copy of the whole or part of a literary, dramatic or musical work from a document in the library or archive without infringing any copyright in the work or any illustrations accompanying it.

(2) This section does not apply if –

   (a) the work had been published before the document was deposited in the library or archive, or
   (b) the copyright owner has prohibited copying of the work,

and at the time the copy is made the librarian or archivist making it is, or ought to be, aware of that fact.

(3) The prescribed conditions shall include the following –

   [(a) that copies are supplied only to persons satisfying the librarian or archivist that they require them for the purposes of –
      (i)   research for a non-commercial purpose, or
      (ii)   private study,
      and will not use them for any other purpose;]
   (b) that no person is furnished with more than one copy of the same material; and
   (c) that persons to whom copies are supplied are required to pay for them a sum not less than the cost (including a contribution to the general expenses of the library or archive) attributable to their production.

Amendment: Paragraph substituted: SI 2003/2498, regs 3, 14(2).

50A   Back up copies

(1) It is not an infringement of copyright for a lawful user of a copy of a computer program to make any back up copy of it which it is necessary for him to have for the purposes of his lawful use.

(2) For the purposes of this section and sections 50B[, 50BA] and 50C a person is a lawful user of a computer program if (whether under a licence to do any acts restricted by the copyright in the program or otherwise), he has a right to use the program.

(3) Where an act is permitted under this section, it is irrelevant whether or not there exists any term or condition in an agreement which purports to prohibit or restrict the act (such terms being, by virtue of section 296A, void).

Amendment: Words in square brackets inserted: SI 2003/2498, regs 3, 15(2).

[50BA   Observing, studying and testing of computer programs]

[(1) It is not an infringement of copyright for a lawful user of a copy of a computer program to observe, study or test the functioning of the program in order to determine the ideas and principles which underlie any element of the program if he does so while performing any of the acts of loading, displaying, running, transmitting or storing the program which he is entitled to do.

(2) Where an act is permitted under this section, it is irrelevant whether or not there exists any term or condition in an agreement which purports to prohibit or restrict the act (such terms being, by virtue of section 296A, void).]

Amendment: Section inserted: SI 2003/2498, regs 3, 15(1).

50C   Other acts permitted to lawful users

(1) It is not an infringement of copyright for a lawful user of a copy of a computer program to copy or adapt it, provided that the copying or adapting –

  (a) is necessary for his lawful use; and
  (b) is not prohibited under any term or condition of an agreement regulating the circumstances in which his use is lawful.

(2) It may, in particular, be necessary for the lawful use of a computer program to copy it or adapt it for the purpose of correcting errors in it.

(3) This section does not apply to any copying or adapting permitted under [section 50A, 50B or 50BA].

Amendment: Words in square brackets substituted: SI 2003/2498, regs 3, 15(3).

Designs

51   Design documents and models

(1) It is not an infringement of any copyright in a design document or model recording or embodying a design for anything other than an artistic work or a typeface to make an article to the design or to copy an article made to the design.

(2) Nor is it an infringement of the copyright to issue to the public, or include in a film [or communicate to the public], anything the making of which was, by virtue of subsection (1), not an infringement of that copyright.

(3) In this section –

'design' means the design of any aspect of the shape or configuration (whether internal or external) of the whole or part of an article, other than surface decoration; and

'design document' means any record of a design, whether in the form of a drawing, a written description, a photograph, data stored in a computer or otherwise.

Amendment: Words in square brackets substituted: SI 2003/2498, reg 2(1), Sch 1, Pt 1, paras 1, 8(3).

58 Use of notes or recordings of spoken words in certain cases

(1) Where a record of spoken words is made, in writing or otherwise, for the purpose –

(a) of reporting current events, or
(b) of [communicating to the public] the whole or part of the work,

it is not an infringement of any copyright in the words as a literary work to use the record or material taken from it (or to copy the record, or any such material, and use the copy) for that purpose, provided the following conditions are met.

(2) The conditions are that –

(a) the record is a direct record of the spoken words and is not taken from a previous record or from a broadcast ... ;
(b) the making of the record was not prohibited by the speaker and, where copyright already subsisted in the work, did not infringe copyright;
(c) the use made of the record or material taken from it is not of a kind prohibited by or on behalf of the speaker or copyright owner before the record was made; and
(d) the use is by or with the authority of a person who is lawfully in possession of the record.

Amendments: Words in square brackets substituted: SI 2003/2498, reg 2(1), Sch 1, Pt 1, paras 1, 12(a). Words omitted repealed: SI 2003/2498, reg 2(2), Sch 2.

59 Public reading or recitation

(1) The reading or recitation in public by one person of a reasonable extract from a published literary or dramatic work does not infringe any copyright in the work if it is accompanied by a sufficient acknowledgement.

(2) Copyright in a work is not infringed by the making of a sound recording, or the [communication to the public], of a reading or recitation which by virtue of subsection (1) does not infringe copyright in the work, provided that the recording [or communication to the public] consists mainly of material in relation to which it is not necessary to rely on that subsection.

Amendment: Words in square brackets substituted: SI 2003/2498, reg 2(1), Sch 1, Pt 1, paras 1, 5(b), 9(a).

61 Recordings of folksongs

(1) A sound recording of a performance of a song may be made for the purpose of including it in an archive maintained by a designated body without infringing any copyright in the words as a literary work or in the accompanying musical work, provided the conditions in subsection (2) below are met.

(2) The conditions are that –

(a) the words are unpublished and of unknown authorship at the time the recording is made, (b)　the making of the recording does not infringe any other copyright, and

(c)　its making is not prohibited by any performer.

(3) Copies of a sound recording made in reliance on subsection (1) and included in an archive maintained by a designated body may, if the prescribed conditions are met, be made and supplied by the archivist without infringing copyright in the recording or the works included in it.

(4) The prescribed conditions shall include the following –

[(a) that copies are only supplied to persons satisfying the archivist that they require them for the purposes of –
(i)　　research for a non-commercial purpose, or
(ii)　　private study,
and will not use them for any other purpose, and]

(b)　that no person is furnished with more than one copy of the same recording.

(5) In this section –

(a)　'designated' means designated for the purposes of this section by order of the Secretary of State, who shall not designate a body unless satisfied that it is not established or for profit,

(b)　'prescribed' means prescribed for the purposes of this section by order of the Secretary of State, and

(c)　references to the archivist include a person acting on his behalf.

(6) An order under this section shall be made by statutory instrument which shall be subject to annulment in pursuance of a resolution of either House of Parliament.

Amendment: Paragraph substituted: SI 2003/2498, regs 3, 16.

62　Representation of certain artistic works on public display

(1) This section applies to –

(a)　buildings, and

(b)　sculptures, models for buildings and works of artistic craftsmanship, if permanently situated in a public place or in premises open to the public.

(2) The copyright in such a work is not infringed by –

(a)　making a graphic work representing it,

(b)　making a photograph or film of it, or

(c)　[making a broadcast of] a visual image of it.

(3) Nor is the copyright infringed by the issue to the public of copies, or the [communication to the public], of anything whose making was, by virtue of this section, not an infringement of the copyright.

Amendments: Words in square brackets substituted: SI 2003/2498, reg 2(1), Sch 1, Pt 1, paras 1, 5(c), 14.

63　Advertisement of sale of artistic work

(1) It is not an infringement of copyright in an artistic work to copy it, or to issue copies to the public, for the purpose of advertising the sale of the work.

(2) Where a copy which would otherwise be an infringing copy is made in accordance with this section but is subsequently dealt with for any other purpose, it shall be treated as an infringing copy for the purposes of that dealing, and if that dealing infringes copyright for all subsequent purposes.

For this purpose 'dealt with' means sold or let for hire, offered or exposed for sale or hire, exhibited in public[, distributed or communicated to the public].

Amendment: Words in square brackets substituted: SI 2003/2498, regs 3, 17.

67 Playing of sound recordings for purposes of club, society, etc

(1) It is not an infringement of the copyright in a sound recording to play it as part of the activities of, or for the benefit of, a club, society or other organisation if the following conditions are met.

(2) The conditions are –

  (a) that the organisation is not established or conducted for profit and its main objects are charitable or are otherwise concerned with the advancement of religion, education or social welfare,

  [(b) that the sound recording is played by a person who is acting primarily and directly for the benefit of the organisation and who is not acting with a view to gain,

  (c) that the proceeds of any charge for admission to the place where the recording is to be heard are applied solely for the purposes of the organisation, and

  (d) that the proceeds from any goods or services sold by, or on behalf of, the organisation –

    (i) in the place where the sound recording is heard, and

    (ii) on the occasion when the sound recording is played,

    are applied solely for the purposes of the organisation].

Amendment: Paragraphs substituted: SI 2003/2498, regs 3, 18(1).

Miscellaneous: broadcasts ...

Amendment: Words omitted repealed: SI 2003/2498, reg 2(2), Sch 2.

69 Recording for purposes of supervision and control of broadcasts and [other services]

(1) Copyright is not infringed by the making or use by the British Broadcasting Corporation, for the purpose of maintaining supervision and control over programmes broadcast by them, of recordings of those programmes.

(2) Copyright is not infringed by anything done in pursuance of –

  (a) section 11(1), 95(1) or 167(1) of the Broadcasting Act 1990 or section 115(4) or (6), 116(5) or 117 of the Broadcasting Act 1996;

  (b) a condition which, by virtue of section 11(2) or 95(2) of the Broadcasting Act 1990 [by virtue of section 334(1) of the Communications Act 2003], is included in a licence granted under Part I or III of that Act or Part I or II of the Broadcasting Act 1996; or

  (c) a direction given under section 109(2) of the Broadcasting Act 1990 (power of Radio Authority to require production of recordings etc);

  (d) section 334(3) of the Communications Act 2003.

(3) Copyright is not infringed by –

(a) the use by the Independent Television Commission or the Radio Authority, in connection with the performance of any of their functions under the Broadcasting Act 1990 or the Broadcasting Act 1996, of any recording, script or transcript which is provided to them under or by virtue of any provision of those Acts; or

(b) the use by the Broadcasting Standards Commission, in connection with any complaint made to them under the Broadcasting Act 1996, of any recording or transcript requested or required to be provided to them, and so provided, under section 115(4) or (6) or 116(5) of that Act.

Amendment: Words in square brackets substituted: SI 2003/2498, reg 2(1), Sch 1, Pt 1, paras 1, 2(1).

70   Recording for purposes of time-shifting

[(1)] The making [in domestic premises] for private and domestic use of a recording of a broadcast ... solely for the purpose of enabling it to be viewed or listened to at a more convenient time does not infringe any copyright in the broadcast ... or in any work included in it.

[(2) Where a copy which would otherwise be an infringing copy is made in accordance with this section but is subsequently dealt with –

(a) it shall be treated as an infringing copy for the purposes of that dealing; and

(b) if that dealing infringes copyright, it shall be treated as an infringing copy for all subsequent purposes.

(3) In subsection (2), 'dealt with' means sold or let for hire, offered or exposed for sale or hire or communicated to the public.]

Amendment: Subsection (1) numbered, subsections (2) and (3) inserted, and words in square brackets inserted: SI 2003/2498, regs 3, 19. Words omitted repealed: SI 2003/2498, reg 2(2), Sch 2.

[71 Photographs of broadcasts]

[(1) The making in domestic premises for private and domestic use of a photograph of the whole or any part of an image forming part of a broadcast, or a copy of such a photograph, does not infringe any copyright in the broadcast or in any film included in it.

(2) Where a copy which would otherwise be an infringing copy is made in accordance with this section but is subsequently dealt with –

(a) it shall be treated as an infringing copy for the purposes of that dealing; and

(b) if that dealing infringes copyright, it shall be treated as an infringing copy for all subsequent purposes.

(3) In subsection (2), 'dealt with' means sold or let for hire, offered or exposed for sale or hire or communicated to the public.]

Amendment: Section substituted: SI 2003/2498, regs 3, 20(1).

72   Free public showing or playing of broadcast ...

(1) The showing or playing in public of a broadcast ... to an audience who have not paid for admission to the place where the broadcast ... is to be seen or heard does not infringe any copyright in –

[(a) the broadcast;

(b) any sound recording (except so far as it is an excepted sound recording) included in it; or

(c) any film included in it].

[(1A) For the purposes of this Part an 'excepted sound recording' is a sound recording –

(a) whose author is not the author of the broadcast in which it is included; and

(b) which is a recording of music with or without words spoken or sung.

(1B) Where by virtue of subsection (1) the copyright in a broadcast shown or played in public is not infringed, copyright in any excepted sound recording included in it is not infringed if the playing or showing of that broadcast in public –

(a) forms part of the activities of an organisation that is not established or conducted for profit; or

(b) is necessary for the purposes of –
    (i)   repairing equipment for the reception of broadcasts;
    (ii)   demonstrating that a repair to such equipment has been carried out; or
    (iii) demonstrating such equipment which is being sold or let for hire or offered or exposed for sale or hire.]

(2) The audience shall be treated as having paid for admission to a place –

(a) if they have paid for admission to a place of which that place forms part; or

(b) if goods or services are supplied at that place (or a place of which it forms part) –
    (i)   at prices which are substantially attributable to the facilities afforded for seeing or hearing the broadcast . . . , or
    (ii)   at prices exceeding those usually charged there and which are partly attributable to those facilities.

(3) The following shall not be regarded as having paid for admission to a place –

(a) persons admitted as residents or inmates of the place;

(b) persons admitted as members of a club or society where the payment is only for membership of the club or society and the provision of facilities for seeing or hearing broadcasts . . . is only incidental to the main purposes of the club or society.

(4) Where the making of the broadcast . . . was an infringement of the copyright in a sound recording or film, the fact that it was heard or seen in public by the reception of the broadcast . . . shall be taken into account in assessing the damages for that infringement.

Amendments: Words omitted repealed: SI 2003/2498, reg 2(2), Sch 2. Subsections (1A) and (1B) inserted and paragraphs substituted: SI 2003/2498, regs 3, 21(1).

73   Reception and re-transmission of [wireless broadcast by cable]

[(1) This section applies where a [wireless] broadcast made from a place in the United Kingdom is [received and immediately re-transmitted by cable].

(2) The copyright in the broadcast is not infringed –

(a) if the [re-transmission by cable] is in pursuance of a relevant requirement, or

(b) if and to the extent that the broadcast is made for reception in the area in which [it is re-transmitted by cable] and forms part of a qualifying service.

(3) The copyright in any work included in the broadcast is not infringed if and to the extent that the broadcast is made for reception in the area in which [it is re-transmitted by cable]; but where

the making of the broadcast was an infringement of the copyright in the work, the fact that the broadcast was re-transmitted [by cable] shall be taken into account in assessing the damages for that infringement.

(4) Where –

    (a)   the [re-transmission by cable] is in pursuance of a relevant requirement, but

    (b)   to any extent, the area in which the [re-transmission by cable takes place] ('the cable area') falls outside the area for reception in which the broadcast is made ('the broadcast area'),

the [re-transmission by cable] (to the extent that it is provided for so much of the cable area as falls outside the broadcast area) of any work included in the broadcast shall, subject to subsection (5), be treated as licensed by the owner of the copyright in the work, subject only to the payment to him by the person making the broadcast of such reasonable royalty or other payment in respect of the [re-transmission by cable of the broadcast] as may be agreed or determined in default of agreement by the Copyright Tribunal.

(5) Subsection (4) does not apply if, or to the extent that, the [re-transmission of the work by cable] is (apart from that subsection) licensed by the owner of the copyright in the work.

(6) In this section 'qualifying service' means, subject to subsection (8), any of the following services –

    (a)   a regional or national Channel 3 service,

    (b)   Channel 4, Channel 5 and S4C,

    (c)   the teletext service referred to in section 49(2) of the Broadcasting Act 1990,

    (d)   the service referred to in section 57(1A)(a) of that Act (power of S4C to provide digital service), and

    (e)   the television broadcasting services and teletext service of the British Broadcasting Corporation;

and expressions used in this subsection have the same meaning as in Part I of the Broadcasting Act 1990.

(7) In this section 'relevant requirement' means a requirement imposed under –

    (a)   section 78A of the Broadcasting Act 1990 (inclusion of certain services in local delivery services provided by digital means), or

    (b)   paragraph 4 of Part III of Schedule 12 to that Act (inclusion of certain services in diffusion services originally licensed under the Cable and Broadcasting Act 1984).

(8) The Secretary of State may by order amend subsection (6) so as to add any service to, or remove any service from, the definition of 'qualifying service'.

(9) The Secretary of State may also by order –

    (a)   provide that in specified cases subsection (3) is to apply in relation to broadcasts of a specified description which are not made as mentioned in that subsection, or

    (b)   exclude the application of that subsection in relation to broadcasts of a specified description made as mentioned in that subsection.

(10) Where the Secretary of State exercises the power conferred by subsection (9)(b) in relation to broadcasts of any description, the order may also provide for subsection (4) to apply, subject to such modifications as may be specified in the order, in relation to broadcasts of that description.

(11) An order under this section may contain such transitional provision as appears to the Secretary of State to be appropriate.

(12) An order under this section shall be made by statutory instrument which shall be subject to annulment in pursuance of a resolution of either House of Parliament.

[(13) In this section references to re-transmission by cable include the transmission of microwave energy between terrestrial fixed points.]

Amendments: Subsection (13) and words in square brackets substituted: SI 2003/2498, regs 3, 22(1).

73A   Royalty or other sum payable in pursuance of section 73(4)

(1) An application to settle the royalty or other sum payable in pursuance of subsection (4) of section 73 (reception and re-transmission of [wireless broadcast by cable]) may be made to the Copyright Tribunal by the copyright owner or the person making the broadcast.

(2) The Tribunal shall consider the matter and make such order as it may determine to be reasonable in the circumstances.

(3) Either party may subsequently apply to the Tribunal to vary the order, and the Tribunal shall consider the matter and make such order confirming or varying the original order as it may determine to be reasonable in the circumstances.

(4) An application under subsection (3) shall not, except with the special leave of the Tribunal, be made within twelve months from the date of the original order or of the order on a previous application under that subsection.

(5) An order under subsection (3) has effect from the date on which it is made or such later date as may be specified by the Tribunal.

Amendment: Words in square brackets substituted: SI 2003/2498, regs 3, 22(2).

74   Provision of sub-titled copies of broadcast ...

(1) A designated body may, for the purpose of providing people who are deaf or hard of hearing, or physically or mentally handicapped in other ways, with copies which are sub-titled or otherwise modified for their special needs, make copies of ... broadcasts ... and issue [or lend] copies to the public, without infringing any copyright in the broadcasts ... or works included in them.

(2) A 'designated body' means a body designated for the purposes of this section by order of the Secretary of State, who shall not designate a body unless he is satisfied that it is not established or conducted for profit.

(3) An order under this section shall be made by statutory instrument which shall be subject to annulment in pursuance of a resolution of either House of Parliament.

(4) This section does not apply if, or to the extent that, there is a licensing scheme certified for the purposes of this section under section 143 providing for the grant of licences.

Amendments: Words omitted repealed: SI 2003/2498, reg 2(2), Sch 2. Words in square brackets inserted: SI 2003/2498, regs 3, 23(1).

Chapter IV

Moral Rights

Right to be identified as author or director

77   Right to be identified as author or director

(1) The author of a copyright literary, dramatic, musical or artistic work, and the director of a copyright film, has the right to be identified as the author or director of the work in the circumstances mentioned in this section; but the right is not infringed unless it has been asserted in accordance with section 78.

(2) The author of a literary work (other than words intended to be sung or spoken with music) or a dramatic work has the right to be identified whenever –

(a) the work is published commercially, performed in public [or communicated to the public]; or

(b) copies of a film or sound recording including the work are issued to the public; and that right includes the right to be identified whenever any of those events occur in relation to an adaptation of the work as the author of the work from which the adaptation was made.

(3) The author of a musical work, or a literary work consisting of words intended to be sung or spoken with music, has the right to be identified whenever –

(a) the work is published commercially;

(b) copies of a sound recording of the work are issued to the public; or

(c) a film of which the sound-track includes the work is shown in public or copies of such a film are issued to the public; and that right includes the right to be identified whenever any of those events occur in relation to an adaptation of the work as the author of the work from which the adaptation was made.

(4) The author of an artistic work has the right to be identified whenever –

(a) the work is published commercially or exhibited in public, or a visual image of it is [communicated to the public];

(b) a film including a visual image of the work is shown in public or copies of such a film are issued to the public; or

(c) in the case of a work of architecture in the form of a building or a model for a building, a sculpture or a work of artistic craftsmanship, copies of a graphic work representing it, or of a photograph of it, are issued to the public.

(5) The author of a work of architecture in the form of a building also has the right to be identified on the building as constructed or, where more than one building is constructed to the design, on the first to be constructed.

(6) The director of a film has the right to be identified whenever the film is shown in public [or communicated to the public] or copies of the film are issued to the public.

(7) The right of the author or director under this section is –

(a) in the case of commercial publication or the issue to the public of copies of a film or sound recording, to be identified in or on each copy or, if that is not appropriate, in some other manner likely to bring his identity to the notice of a person acquiring a copy,

(b) in the case of identification on a building, to be identified by appropriate means visible to persons entering or approaching the building, and

(c)   in any other case, to be identified in a manner likely to bring his identity to the attention of a person seeing or hearing the performance, exhibition, showing [or communication to the public] in question; and the identification must in each case be clear and reasonably prominent.

(8) If the author or director in asserting his right to be identified specifies a pseudonym, initials or some other particular form of identification, that form shall be used; otherwise any reasonable form of identification may be used.

(9) This section has effect subject to section 79 (exceptions to right).

Amendment: Words in square brackets substituted: SI 2003/2498, reg 2(1), Sch 1, Pt 1, paras 1, 8, 9.

79   Exceptions to right

(1) The right conferred by section 77 (right to be identified as author or director) is subject to the following exceptions.

(2) The right does not apply in relation to the following descriptions of work –

(a)   a computer program;
(b)   the design of a typeface;
(c)   any computer-generated work.

(3) The right does not apply to anything done by or with the authority of the copyright owner where copyright in the work originally [vested in the author's or director's employer by virtue of section 11(2) (works produced in the course of employment)].

(4) The right is not infringed by an act which by virtue of any of the following provisions would not infringe copyright in the work –

(a)   section 30 (fair dealing for certain purposes), so far as it relates to the reporting of current events by means of a sound recording, film [or broadcast];
(b)   section 31 (incidental inclusion of work in an artistic work, sound recording, film [or broadcast]);
(c)   section 32(3) (examination questions);
(d)   section 45 (parliamentary and judicial proceedings);
(e)   section 46(1) or (2) (Royal Commissions and statutory inquiries);
(f)   section 51 (use of design documents and models);
(g)   section 52 (effect of exploitation of design derived from artistic work);
(h)   section 57 or 66A (acts permitted on assumptions as to expiry of copyright, etc).

(5) The right does not apply in relation to any work made for the purpose of reporting current events.

(6) The right does not apply in relation to the publication in –

(a)   a newspaper, magazine or similar periodical, or
(b)   an encyclopaedia, dictionary, yearbook or other collective work of reference, of a literary, dramatic, musical or artistic work made for the purposes of such publication or made available with the consent of the author for the purposes of such publication.

(7) The right does not apply in relation to –

(a)   a work in which Crown copyright or Parliamentary copyright subsists, or
(b)   a work in which copyright originally vested in an international organisation by virtue of section 168, unless the author or director has previously been identified as such in or on published copies of the work.

Amendment: Words in square brackets substituted: SI 2003/2498, reg 2(1), Sch 1, Pt 1, paras 1, 3, 18(1).

Right to object to derogatory treatment of work

80 Right to object to derogatory treatment of work

(1) The author of a copyright literary, dramatic, musical or artistic work, and the director of a copyright film, has the right in the circumstances mentioned in this section not to have his work subjected to derogatory treatment.

(2) For the purposes of this section –

(a) 'treatment' of a work means any addition to, deletion from or alteration to or adaptation of the work, other than –
  (i) a translation of a literary or dramatic work, or
  (ii) an arrangement or transcription of a musical work involving no more than a change of key or register; and
(b) the treatment of a work is derogatory if it amounts to distortion or mutilation of the work or is otherwise prejudicial to the honour or reputation of the author or director; and in the following provisions of this section references to a derogatory treatment of a work shall be construed accordingly.

(3) In the case of a literary, dramatic or musical work the right is infringed by a person who –

(a) publishes commercially, performs in public [or communicates to the public] a derogatory treatment of the work; or
(b) issues to the public copies of a film or sound recording of, or including, a derogatory treatment of the work.

(4) In the case of an artistic work the right is infringed by a person who –

(a) publishes commercially or exhibits in public a derogatory treatment of the work, [or communicates to the public] a visual image of a derogatory treatment of the work,
(b) shows in public a film including a visual image of a derogatory treatment of the work or issues to the public copies of such a film, or
(c) in the case of –
  (i) a work of architecture in the form of a model for a building,
  (ii) a sculpture, or
  (iii) a work of artistic craftsmanship,
  issues to the public copies of a graphic work representing, or of a photograph of, a derogatory treatment of the work.

(5) Subsection (4) does not apply to a work of architecture in the form of a building; but where the author of such a work is identified on the building and it is the subject of derogatory treatment he has the right to require the identification to be removed.

(6) In the case of a film, the right is infringed by a person who –

(a) shows in public [or communicates to the public] a derogatory treatment of the film; or
(b) issues to the public copies of a derogatory treatment of the film.

(7) The right conferred by this section extends to the treatment of parts of a work resulting from a previous treatment by a person other than the author or director, if those parts are attributed to, or are likely to be regarded as the work of, the author or director.

(8) This section has effect subject to sections 81 and 82 (exceptions to and qualifications of right).

Amendment: Words in square brackets substituted: SI 2003/2498, reg 2(1), Sch 1, Pt 1, paras 1, 10(1), 13(2).

82 Qualification of right in certain cases

(1) This section applies to –

   (a)   works in which copyright originally vested in the author's [or director's] employer by virtue of section 11(2) (works produced in course of employment) ... ,

   (b)   works in which Crown copyright or Parliamentary copyright subsists, and

   (c)   works in which copyright originally vested in an international organisation by virtue of section 168.

(2) The right conferred by section 80 (right to object to derogatory treatment of work) does not apply to anything done in relation to such a work by or with the authority of the copyright owner unless the author or director –

   (a)   is identified at the time of the relevant act, or

   (b)   has previously been identified in or on published copies of the work; and where in such a case the right does apply, it is not infringed if there is a sufficient disclaimer.

Amendment: Words in square brackets inserted: SI 2003/2498, reg 2(1), Sch 1, Pt 1, paras 1, 18(2). Words omitted repealed: SI 2003/2498, reg 2, Sch 1, Pt 1, paras 1, 18(2), Sch 2.

False attribution of work

84 False attribution of work

(1) A person has the right in the circumstances mentioned in this section –

   (a)   not to have a literary, dramatic, musical or artistic work falsely attributed to him as author, and

   (b)   not to have a film falsely attributed to him as director; and in this section an 'attribution', in relation to such a work, means a statement (express or implied) as to who is the author or director.

(2) The right is infringed by a person who –

   (a)   issues to the public copies of a work of any of those descriptions in or on which there is a false attribution, or

   (b)   exhibits in public an artistic work, or a copy of an artistic work, in or on which there is a false attribution.

(3) The right is also infringed by a person who –

   (a)   in the case of a literary, dramatic or musical work, performs the work in public [or communicates it to the public] as being the work of a person, or

   (b)   in the case of a film, shows it in public [or communicates it to the public] as being directed by a person, knowing or having reason to believe that the attribution is false.

(4) The right is also infringed by the issue to the public or public display of material containing a false attribution in connection with any of the acts mentioned in subsection (2) or (3).

(5) The right is also infringed by a person who in the course of a business –

(a) possesses or deals with a copy of a work of any of the descriptions mentioned in subsection (1) in or on which there is a false attribution, or

(b) in the case of an artistic work, possesses or deals with the work itself when there is a false attribution in or on it, knowing or having reason to believe that there is such an attribution and that it is false.

(6) In the case of an artistic work the right is also infringed by a person who in the course of a business –

(a) deals with a work which has been altered after the author parted with possession of it as being the unaltered work of the author, or

(b) deals with a copy of such a work as being a copy of the unaltered work of the author, knowing or having reason to believe that that is not the case.

(7) References in this section to dealing are to selling or letting for hire, offering or exposing for sale or hire, exhibiting in public, or distributing.

(8) This section applies where, contrary to the fact –

(a) a literary, dramatic or musical work is falsely represented as being an adaptation of the work of a person, or

(b) a copy of an artistic work is falsely represented as being a copy made by the author of the artistic work, as it applies where the work is falsely attributed to a person as author.

Amendment: Words in square brackets substituted: SI 2003/2498, reg 2(1), Sch 1, Pt 1, paras 1, 10(2).

Right to privacy of certain photographs and films

85 Right to privacy of certain photographs and films

(1) A person who for private and domestic purposes commissions the taking of a photograph or the making of a film has, where copyright subsists in the resulting work, the right not to have –

(a) copies of the work issued to the public,

(b) the work exhibited or shown in public, or

(c) the work [communicated to the public]; and, except as mentioned in subsection (2), a person who does or authorises the doing of any of those acts infringes that right.

(2) The right is not infringed by an act which by virtue of any of the following provisions would not infringe copyright in the work –

(a) section 31 (incidental inclusion of work in an artistic work, film [or broadcast]);

(b) section 45 (parliamentary and judicial proceedings);

(c) section 46 (Royal Commissions and statutory inquiries);

(d) section 50 (acts done under statutory authority);

(e) section 57 or 66A (acts permitted on assumptions as to expiry of copyright, etc).

Amendment: Words in square brackets substituted: SI 2003/2498, reg 2(1), Sch 1, Pt 1, paras 1, 3, 8(2)(b).

[97A Injunctions against service providers]

[(1) The High Court (in Scotland, the Court of Session) shall have power to grant an injunction against a service provider, where that service provider has actual knowledge of another person using their service to infringe copyright.

(2) In determining whether a service provider has actual knowledge for the purpose of this section, a court shall take into account all matters which appear to it in the particular circumstances to be relevant and, amongst other things, shall have regard to –

    (a) whether a service provider has received a notice through a means of contact made available in accordance with regulation 6(1)(c) of the Electronic Commerce (EC Directive) Regulations 2002 (SI 2002/2013); and

    (b) the extent to which any notice includes –
        (i)   the full name and address of the sender of the notice;
        (ii) details of the infringement in question.

(3) In this section 'service provider' has the meaning given to it by regulation 2 of the Electronic Commerce (EC Directive) Regulations 2002.]

Amendment: Section inserted: SI 2003/2498, regs 3, 27(1).

[101A   Certain infringements actionable by a non-exclusive licensee]

[(1) A non-exclusive licensee may bring an action for infringement of copyright if –

    (a) the infringing act was directly connected to a prior licensed act of the licensee; and
    (b) the licence –
        (i)   is in writing and is signed by or on behalf of the copyright owner; and
        (ii) expressly grants the non-exclusive licensee a right of action under this section.

(2) In an action brought under this section, the non-exclusive licensee shall have the same rights and remedies available to him as the copyright owner would have had if he had brought the action.

(3) The rights granted under this section are concurrent with those of the copyright owner and references in the relevant provisions of this Part to the copyright owner shall be construed accordingly.

(4) In an action brought by a non-exclusive licensee by virtue of this section a defendant may avail himself of any defence which would have been available to him if the action had been brought by the copyright owner.

(5) Subsections (1) to (4) of section 102 shall apply to a non-exclusive licensee who has a right of action by virtue of this section as it applies to an exclusive licensee.

(6) In this section a 'non-exclusive licensee' means the holder of a licence authorising the licensee to exercise a right which remains exercisable by the copyright owner.]

Amendment: Section inserted: SI 2003/2498, regs 3, 28.

105   Presumptions relevant to sound recordings and films

(1) In proceedings brought by virtue of this Chapter with respect to a sound recording, where copies of the recording as issued to the public bear a label or other mark stating –

    (a) that a named person was the owner of copyright in the recording at the date of issue of the copies, or
    (b) that the recording was first published in a specified year or in a specified country,

the label or mark shall be admissible as evidence of the facts stated and shall be presumed to be correct until the contrary is proved.

(2) In proceedings brought by virtue of this Chapter with respect to a film, where copies of the film as issued to the public bear a statement –

    (a) that a named person was the director or producer of the film,

  (aa) that a named person was the principal director, the author of the screenplay, the author of the dialogue or the composer of music specifically created for and used in the film,

    (b) that a named person was the owner of copyright in the film at the date of issue of the copies, or

    (c) that the film was first published in a specified year or in a specified country,

the statement shall be admissible as evidence of the facts stated and shall be presumed to be correct until the contrary is proved.

(3) In proceedings brought by virtue of this Chapter with respect to a computer program, where copies of the program are issued to the public in electronic form bearing a statement –

    (a) that a named person was the owner of copyright in the program at the date of issue of the copies, or

    (b) that the program was first published in a specified country or that copies of it were first issued to the public in electronic form in a specified year,

the statement shall be admissible as evidence of the facts stated and shall be presumed to be correct until the contrary is proved.

(4) The above presumptions apply equally in proceedings relating to an infringement alleged to have occurred before the date on which the copies were issued to the public.

(5) In proceedings brought by virtue of this Chapter with respect to a film, where the film as shown in public [or communicated to the public] bears a statement –

    (a) that a named person was the director or producer of the film, or

  (aa) that a named person was the principal director of the film, the author of the screenplay, the author of the dialogue or the composer of music specifically created for and used in the film, or,

    (b) that a named person was the owner of copyright in the film immediately after it was made,

the statement shall be admissible as evidence of the facts stated and shall be presumed to be correct until the contrary is proved.

This presumption applies equally in proceedings relating to an infringement alleged to have occurred before the date on which the film was shown in public [or communicated to the public].

(6) For the purposes of this section, a statement that a person was the director of a film shall be taken, unless a contrary indication appears, as meaning that he was the principal director of the film.

Amendment: Words in square brackets substituted: SI 2003/2498, reg 2(1), Sch 1, Pt 1, paras 1, 8(1)(c).

Offences

107   Criminal liability for making or dealing with infringing articles, etc

(1) A person commits an offence who, without the licence of the copyright owner –

    (a) makes for sale or hire, or

(b) imports into the United Kingdom otherwise than for his private and domestic use, or

(c) possesses in the course of a business with a view to committing any act infringing the copyright, or

(d) in the course of a business –
   (i) sells or lets for hire, or
   (ii) offers or exposes for sale or hire, or
   (iii) exhibits in public, or
   (iv) distributes, or

(e) distributes otherwise than in the course of a business to such an extent as to affect prejudicially the owner of the copyright,

an article which is, and which he knows or has reason to believe is, an infringing copy of a copyright work.

(2) A person commits an offence who –

(a) makes an article specifically designed or adapted for making copies of a particular copyright work, or

(b) has such an article in his possession,

knowing or having reason to believe that it is to be used to make infringing copies for sale or hire or for use in the course of a business.

[(2A) A person who infringes copyright in a work by communicating the work to the public –

(a) in the course of a business, or

(b) otherwise than in the course of a business to such an extent as to affect prejudicially the owner of the copyright,

commits an offence if he knows or has reason to believe that, by doing so, he is infringing copyright in that work.]

(3) Where copyright is infringed (otherwise than by reception of a [communication to the public]) –

(a) by the public performance of a literary, dramatic or musical work, or

(b) by the playing or showing in public of a sound recording or film,

any person who caused the work to be so performed, played or shown is guilty of an offence if he knew or had reason to believe that copyright would be infringed.

(4) A person guilty of an offence under subsection (1)(a), (b), (d)(iv) or (e) is liable –

(a) on summary conviction to imprisonment for a term not exceeding six months or a fine not exceeding the statutory maximum, or both;

(b) on conviction on indictment to a fine or imprisonment for a term not exceeding [ten] years, or both.

[(4A) A person guilty of an offence under subsection (2A) is liable –

(a) on summary conviction to imprisonment for a term not exceeding three months or a fine not exceeding the statutory maximum, or both;

(b) on conviction on indictment to a fine or imprisonment for a term not exceeding two years, or both.]

(5) A person guilty of any other offence under this section is liable on summary conviction to imprisonment for a term not exceeding six months or a fine not exceeding level 5 on the standard scale, or both.

(6) Sections 104 to 106 (presumptions as to various matters connected with copyright) do not apply to proceedings for an offence under this section; but without prejudice to their application in proceedings for an order under section 108 below.

Amendments: Subsections (2A) and (4A) inserted: SI 2003/2498, regs 3, 26(1). Words in square brackets substituted: SI 2003/2498, reg 2(1), Sch 1, Pt 1, paras 1, 9(2).

109   Search warrants

(1) Where a justice of the peace (in Scotland, a sheriff or justice of the peace) is satisfied by information on oath given by a constable (in Scotland, by evidence on oath) that there are reasonable grounds for believing –

(a)   that an offence under [section 107(1), (2) or (2A)] has been or is about to be committed in any premises, and
(b)   that evidence that such an offence has been or is about to be committed is in those premises,

he may issue a warrant authorising a constable to enter and search the premises, using such reasonable force as is necessary.

(2) The power conferred by subsection (1) does not, in England and Wales, extend to authorising a search for material of the kinds mentioned in section 9(2) of the Police and Criminal Evidence Act 1984 (certain classes of personal or confidential material).

(3) A warrant under this section –

(a)   may authorise persons to accompany any constable executing the warrant, and
(b)   remains in force for 28 days from the date of its issue.

(4) In executing a warrant issued under this section a constable may seize an article if he reasonably believes that it is evidence that any offence under [section 107(1), (2) or (2A)] has been or is about to be committed.

(5) In this section 'premises' includes land, buildings, fixed or moveable structures, vehicles, vessels, aircraft and hovercraft.

Amendment: Words in square brackets substituted: SI 2003/2498, regs 3, 26(2).

114A   Forfeiture of infringing copies, etc: England and Wales or Northern Ireland

(1) In England and Wales or Northern Ireland where there have come into the possession of any person in connection with the investigation or prosecution of a relevant offence –

(a)   infringing copies of a copyright work, or
(b)   articles specifically designed or adapted for making copies of a particular copyright work,

that person may apply under this section for an order for the forfeiture of the infringing copies or articles.

(2) For the purposes of this section 'relevant offence' means –

(a)   an offence under [section 107(1), (2) or (2A)] (criminal liability for making or dealing with infringing articles, etc),
(b)   an offence under the Trade Descriptions Act 1968 (c 29), or
(c)   an offence involving dishonesty or deception.

(3) An application under this section may be made –

(a) where proceedings have been brought in any court for a relevant offence relating to some or all of the infringing copies or articles, to that court, or

(b) where no application for the forfeiture of the infringing copies or articles has been made under paragraph (a), by way of complaint to a magistrates' court.

(4) On an application under this section, the court shall make an order for the forfeiture of any infringing copies or articles only if it is satisfied that a relevant offence has been committed in relation to the infringing copies or articles.

(5) A court may infer for the purposes of this section that such an offence has been committed in relation to any infringing copies or articles if it is satisfied that such an offence has been committed in relation to infringing copies or articles which are representative of the infringing copies or articles in question (whether by reason of being of the same design or part of the same consignment or batch or otherwise).

(6) Any person aggrieved by an order made under this section by a magistrates' court, or by a decision of such a court not to make such an order, may appeal against that order or decision –

(a) in England and Wales, to the Crown Court, or

(b) in Northern Ireland, to the county court.

(7) An order under this section may contain such provision as appears to the court to be appropriate for delaying the coming into force of the order pending the making and determination of any appeal (including any application under section 111 of the Magistrates' Courts Act 1980 (c 43) or Article 146 of the Magistrates' Courts (Northern Ireland) Order 1981 (SI 1981/1675 (NI 26)) (statement of case)).

(8) Subject to subsection (9), where any infringing copies or articles are forfeited under this section they shall be destroyed in accordance with such directions as the court may give.

(9) On making an order under this section the court may direct that the infringing copies or articles to which the order relates shall (instead of being destroyed) be forfeited to the owner of the copyright in question or dealt with in such other way as the court considers appropriate.

Amendment: Words in square brackets substituted: SI 2003/2498, regs 3, 26(2)(iii).

114B   Forfeiture of infringing copies, etc: Scotland

(1) In Scotland the court may make an order under this section for the forfeiture of any –

(a) infringing copies of a copyright work, or

(b) articles specifically designed or adapted for making copies of a particular copyright work.

(2) An order under this section may be made –

(a) on an application by the procurator-fiscal made in the manner specified in section 134 of the Criminal Procedure (Scotland) Act 1995 (c 46), or

(b) where a person is convicted of a relevant offence, in addition to any other penalty which the court may impose.

(3) On an application under subsection (2)(a), the court shall make an order for the forfeiture of any infringing copies or articles only if it is satisfied that a relevant offence has been committed in relation to the infringing copies or articles.

(4) The court may infer for the purposes of this section that such an offence has been committed in relation to any infringing copies or articles if it is satisfied that such an offence has been

committed in relation to infringing copies or articles which are representative of the infringing copies or articles in question (whether by reason of being of the same design or part of the same consignment or batch or otherwise).

(5) The procurator-fiscal making the application under subsection (2)(a) shall serve on any person appearing to him to be the owner of, or otherwise to have an interest in, the infringing copies or articles to which the application relates a copy of the application, together with a notice giving him the opportunity to appear at the hearing of the application to show cause why the infringing copies or articles should not be forfeited.

(6) Service under subsection (5) shall be carried out, and such service may be proved, in the manner specified for citation of an accused in summary proceedings under the Criminal Procedure (Scotland) Act 1995.

(7) Any person upon whom notice is served under subsection (5) and any other person claiming to be the owner of, or otherwise to have an interest in, infringing copies or articles to which an application under this section relates shall be entitled to appear at the hearing of the application to show cause why the infringing copies or articles should not be forfeited.

(8) The court shall not make an order following an application under subsection (2)(a) –

  (a) if any person on whom notice is served under subsection (5) does not appear, unless service of the notice on that person is proved, or
  (b) if no notice under subsection (5) has been served, unless the court is satisfied that in the circumstances it was reasonable not to serve such notice.

(9) Where an order for the forfeiture of any infringing copies or articles is made following an application under subsection (2)(a), any person who appeared, or was entitled to appear, to show cause why infringing copies or articles should not be forfeited may, within 21 days of the making of the order, appeal to the High Court by Bill of Suspension.

(10) Section 182(5)(a) to (e) of the Criminal Procedure (Scotland) Act 1995 (c 46) shall apply to an appeal under subsection (9) as it applies to a stated case under Part 2 of that Act.

(11) An order following an application under subsection (2)(a) shall not take effect –

  (a) until the end of the period of 21 days beginning with the day after the day on which the order is made, or
  (b) if an appeal is made under subsection (9) above within that period, until the appeal is determined or abandoned.

(12) An order under subsection (2)(b) shall not take effect –

  (a) until the end of the period within which an appeal against the order could be brought under the Criminal Procedure (Scotland) Act 1995, or
  (b) if an appeal is made within that period, until the appeal is determined or abandoned.

(13) Subject to subsection (14), infringing copies or articles forfeited under this section shall be destroyed in accordance with such directions as the court may give.

(14) On making an order under this section the court may direct that the infringing copies or articles to which the order relates shall (instead of being destroyed) be forfeited to the owner of the copyright in question or dealt with in such other way as the court considers appropriate.

(15) For the purposes of this section –

    'relevant offence' means an offence under [section 107(1), (2) or (2A)] (criminal liability for making or dealing with infringing articles, etc), or under the Trade Descriptions Act 1968 (c 29) or any offence involving dishonesty or deception;

'the court' means –

(a) in relation to an order made on an application under subsection (2)(a), the sheriff, and

(b) in relation to an order made under subsection (2)(b), the court which imposed the penalty.

Amendment: Words in square brackets substituted by SI 2003/2498, regs 3, 26(2)(iv).

References and applications with respect to licensing schemes

117   Licensing schemes to which following sections apply

Sections 118 to 123 (references and applications with respect to licensing schemes) apply to licensing schemes which are operated by licensing bodies and cover works of more than one author, so far as they relate to licences for –

(a) copying the work,

(b) rental or lending of copies of the work to the public,

(c) performing, showing or playing the work in public, or

[(d) communicating the work to the public;]

and references in those sections to a licensing scheme shall be construed accordingly.

Amendment: Paragraph (d) substituted: SI 2003/2498, reg 2(1), Sch 1, Pt 1, paras 1, 4(4).

120   Further reference of scheme to tribunal

(1) Where the Copyright Tribunal has on a previous reference of a licensing scheme under [section 118, 119 or 128A], or under this section, made an order with respect to the scheme, then, while the other remains in force –

(a) the operator of the scheme,

(b) a person claiming that he requires a licence in a case of the description to which the order applies, or

(c) an organisation claiming to be representative of such persons,

may refer the scheme again to the Tribunal so far as it relates to cases of that description.

(2) A licensing scheme shall not, except with the special leave of the Tribunal, be referred again to the Tribunal in respect of the same description of cases –

(a) within twelve months from the date of the order on the previous reference, or

(b) if the order was made so as to be in force for 15 months or less, until the last three months before the expiry of the order.

(3) A scheme which has been referred to the Tribunal under this section shall remain in operation until proceedings on the reference are concluded.

(4) The Tribunal shall consider the matter in dispute and make such order, either confirming, varying or further varying the scheme so far as it relates to cases of the description to which the reference relates, as the Tribunal may determine to be reasonable in the circumstances.

(5) The order may be made so as to be in force immediately or for such period as the Tribunal may determine.

Amendment: Words in square brackets substituted: SI 2003/2498, regs 3, 21(4).

References and applications with respect to licensing by licensing bodies

124   Licences to which following sections apply

Sections 125 to 128 (references and applications with respect to licensing by licensing bodies) apply to licences which are granted by a licensing body otherwise than in pursuance of a licensing scheme and cover works of more than one author, so far as they authorise –

    (a) copying the work,
    (b) rental or lending of copies of the work to the public,
    (c) performing, showing or playing the work in public, or
   [(d) communicating the work to the public;]

and references in those sections to a licence shall be construed accordingly.

Amendment: Paragraph (d) substituted: SI 2003/2498, reg 2(1), Sch 1, Pt 1, paras 1, 4(4).

127   Application for review of order as to licence

(1) Where the Copyright Tribunal has made an order under [section 125, 126 or 128B (where that order did not relate to a licensing scheme)], the licensing body or the person entitled to the benefit of the order may apply to the Tribunal to review its order.

(2) An application shall not be made, except with the special leave of the Tribunal –

    (a) within twelve months from the date of the order or of the decision on a previous application under this section, or
    (b) if the order was made so as to be in force for 15 months or less, or as a result of the decision on a previous application under this section is due to expire within 15 months of that decision, until the last three months before the expiry date.

(3) The Tribunal shall on an application for review confirm or vary its order as the Tribunal may determine to be reasonable in the circumstances.

Amendment: Words in square brackets substituted: SI 2003/2498, regs 3, 21(5).

[128A   Notification of licence or licensing scheme for excepted sound recordings]

[(1) This section only applies to a proposed licence or licensing scheme that will authorise the playing in public of excepted sound recordings included in broadcasts, in circumstances where by reason of the exclusion of excepted sound recordings from section 72(1), the playing in public of such recordings would otherwise infringe the copyright in them.

(2) A licensing body must notify the Secretary of State of the details of any proposed licence or licensing scheme for excepted sound recordings before it comes into operation.

(3) A licence or licensing scheme, which has been notified under subsection (2), may not be operated by the licensing body until 28 days have elapsed since that notification.

(4) Subject to subsection (5), the Secretary of State shall take into account the matters set out in subsection (6) and then either –

    (a) refer the licence or licensing scheme to the Copyright Tribunal for a determination of whether the licence or licensing scheme is reasonable in the circumstances, or
    (b) notify the licensing body that he does not intend to refer the licence or licensing scheme to the Tribunal.

(5) If the Secretary of State becomes aware –

   (a) that a licensing body has failed to notify him of a licence or licensing scheme under subsection (2) before it comes into operation; or

   (b) that a licence or licensing scheme has been operated within 28 days of a notification under subsection (2),

subsection (4) does not apply, but the Secretary of State may at any time refer the licence or licensing scheme to the Tribunal for a determination of whether the licence or licensing scheme is reasonable in the circumstances, or may notify the licensing body that he does not intend to refer it to the Tribunal.

(6) The matters referred to in subsection (4) are –

   (a) whether the terms and conditions of the proposed licence or licensing scheme have taken into account the factors set out in subsection (7);

   (b) any written representations received by the Secretary of State;

   (c) previous determinations of the Tribunal;

   (d) the availability of other schemes, or the granting of other licences, to other persons in similar circumstances, and the terms of those schemes or licences; and

   (e) the extent to which the licensing body has consulted any person who would be affected by the proposed licence or licensing scheme, or organisations representing such persons, and the steps, if any, it has taken as a result.

(7) The factors referred to in subsection (6) are –

   (a) the extent to which the broadcasts to be shown or played by a potential licensee in circumstances mentioned in subsection (1) are likely to include excepted sound recordings;

   (b) the size and the nature of the audience that a licence or licensing scheme would permit to hear the excepted sound recordings;

   (c) what commercial benefit a potential licensee is likely to obtain from playing the excepted sound recordings; and

   (d) the extent to which the owners of copyright in the excepted sound recordings will receive equitable remuneration, from sources other than the proposed licence or licensing scheme, for the inclusion of their recordings in the broadcasts to be shown or played in public by a potential licensee.

(8) A proposed licence or licensing scheme that must be notified to the Secretary of State under subsection (2) may only be referred to the Tribunal under section 118 or 125 before such notification takes place.

(9) A proposed licensing scheme that has been notified to the Secretary of State under subsection (2) may only be referred to the Tribunal under section 119 after the Secretary of State has notified the licensing body that he does not intend to refer the licensing scheme to the Tribunal.

(10) If a reference made to the Tribunal under section 118 or 125 is permitted under subsection (8) then –

   (a) the reference shall not be considered premature only because the licence or licensing scheme has not been notified to the Secretary of State under subsection (2); and

   (b) where the Tribunal decides to entertain the reference, subsection (2) to (5) shall not apply.

(11) Nothing in this section shall be taken to prejudice any right to make a reference or application to the Tribunal under sections 120 to 122, 126 or 127.

(12) This section applies to modifications to an existing licence or licensing scheme as it applies to a proposed licence or licensing scheme.

(13) In this section and in section 128B, any reference to a 'licence' means a licence granted by a licensing body otherwise than in pursuance of a licensing scheme and which covers works of more than one author.]

Amendment: Section inserted: SI 2003/2498, regs 3, 21(3).

[128B   References to the Tribunal by the Secretary of State under section 128A]

[(1) The Copyright Tribunal may make appropriate enquiries to establish whether a licence or licensing scheme referred to it by the Secretary of State under section 128A(4)(a) or (5) is reasonable in the circumstances.

(2) When considering the matter referred, and after concluding any such enquiries, the Tribunal shall take into account –

   (a) whether the terms and conditions of the proposed licence or licensing scheme have taken into account the factors set out in section 128A(7); and
   (b) any other factors it considers relevant,

and shall then make an order under subsection (3).

(3) The Tribunal shall make such order –

   (a) in the case of a licensing scheme, either confirming or varying the proposed scheme, either generally or so far as it relates to cases of any description; or
   (b) in the case of a licence, either confirming or varying the proposed licence, as the Tribunal may determine to be reasonable in the circumstances.

(4) The Tribunal may direct that the order, so far as it reduces the amount of charges payable, has effect from a date before that on which it is made.

If such a direction is made, any necessary repayments to a licensee shall be made in respect of charges already paid.

(5) The Tribunal may award simple interest on repayments, at such rate and for such period, ending not later than the date of the order, as it thinks fit.]

Amendment: Section inserted: SI 2003/2498, regs 3, 21(3).

132   Licences to reflect conditions imposed by promoters of events

(1) This section applies to references or applications under this Chapter in respect of licences relating to sound recordings, films [or broadcasts] which include, or are to include, any entertainment or other event.

(2) The Copyright Tribunal shall have regard to any conditions imposed by the promoters of the entertainment or other event; and, in particular, the Tribunal shall not hold a refusal or failure to grant a licence to be unreasonable if it could not have been granted consistently with those conditions.

(3) Nothing in this section shall require the Tribunal to have regard to any such conditions in so far as they –

   (a) purport to regulate the charges to be imposed in respect of the grant of licences, or
   (b) relate to payments to be made to the promoters of any event in consideration of the grant of facilities for making the recording, film [or broadcast].

Amendments: Words in square brackets substituted: SI 2003/2498, reg 2(1), Sch 1, Pt 1, paras 1, 3(1)(j), (2)(a).

133   Licences to reflect payments in respect of underlying rights

(1) In considering what charges should be paid for a licence –

    (a) on a reference or application under this Chapter relating to licences for the rental or lending of copies of a work, or

    (b) on an application under section 142 (royalty or other sum payable for lending of certain works),

the Copyright Tribunal shall take into account any reasonable payments which the owner of the copyright in the work is liable to make in consequence of the granting of the licence, or of the acts authorised by the licence, to owners of copyright in works included in that work.

(2) On any reference or application under this Chapter relating to licensing in respect of the copyright in sound recordings, films [or broadcasts], the Copyright Tribunal shall take into account, in considering what charges should be paid for a licence, any reasonable payments which the copyright owner is liable to make in consequence of the granting of the licence, or of the acts authorised by the licence, in respect of any performance included in the recording, film [or broadcast].

Amendments: Words in square brackets substituted: SI 2003/2498, reg 2(1), Sch 1, Pt 1, paras 1, 3(1)(k), (2)(b).

135A   Circumstances in which right available

(1) Section 135C applies to the inclusion in a broadcast ... of any sound recordings if –

    (a) a licence to include those recordings in the broadcast ... could be granted by a licensing body or such a body could procure the grant of a licence to do so,

    (b) the condition in subsection (2) or (3) applies, and

    (c) the person including those recordings in the broadcast ... has complied with section 135B.

(2) Where the person including the recordings in the broadcast ... does not hold a licence to do so, the condition is that the licensing body refuses to grant, or procure the grant of, such a licence, being a licence –

    (a) whose terms as to payment for including the recordings in the broadcast ... would be acceptable to him or comply with an order of the Copyright Tribunal under section 135D relating to such a licence or any scheme under which it would be granted, and

    (b) allowing unlimited needletime or such needletime as he has demanded.

(3) Where he holds a licence to include the recordings in the broadcast ..., the condition is that the terms of the licence limit needletime and the licensing body refuses to substitute or procure the substitution of terms allowing unlimited needletime or such needletime as he has demanded, or refuses to do so on terms that fall within subsection (2)(a).

(4) The references in subsection (2) to refusing to grant, or procure the grant of, a licence, and in subsection (3) to refusing to substitute or procure the substitution of terms, include failing to do so within a reasonable time of being asked.

(5) In the group of sections from this section to section 135G –

['broadcast' does not include any broadcast which is a transmission of the kind specified in section 6(1A)(b) or (c);]

'needletime' means the time in any period (whether determined as a number of hours in the period or a proportion of the period, or otherwise) in which any proceedings may be included in a broadcast ... ;

'sound recording' does not include a film sound track when accompanying a film.

(6) In sections 135B to 135G, 'terms of payment' means terms as to payment for including sound recordings in a broadcast ... .

Amendments: Words omitted repealed: SI 2003/2498, reg 2(2), Sch 2. Definition inserted: SI 2003/ 2498, reg 2(1), Sch 1, Pt 1, paras 1, 15(1).

144A   Collective exercise of certain rights in relation to cable re-transmission

(1) This section applies to the right of the owner of copyright in a literary, dramatic, musical or artistic work, sound recording or film to grant or refuse authorisation for cable re-transmission of a [wireless] broadcast from another EEA member state in which the work is included.

That right is referred to below as 'cable re-transmission right'.

(2) Cable re-transmission right may be exercised against a cable operator only through a licensing body.

(3) Where a copyright owner has not transferred management of his cable re-transmission right to a licensing body, the licensing body which manages rights of the same category shall be deemed to be mandated to manage his right.

Where more than one licensing body manages rights of that category, he may choose which of them is deemed to be mandated to manage his right.

(4) A copyright owner to whom subsection (3) applies has the same rights and obligations resulting from any relevant agreement between the cable operator and the licensing body as have copyright owners who have transferred management of their cable re-transmission right to that licensing body.

(5) Any rights to which a copyright owner may be entitled by virtue of subsection (4) must be claimed within the period of three years beginning with the date of the cable re-transmission concerned.

(6) This section does not affect any rights exercisable by the maker of the broadcast, whether in relation to the broadcast or a work included in it.

[(7) In this section –

'cable operator' means a person responsible for cable re-transmission of a wireless broadcast; and

'cable re-transmission' means the reception and immediate re-transmission by cable, including the transmission of microwave energy between terrestrial fixed points, of a wireless broadcast.]

Amendments: Word in square brackets inserted: SI 2003/2498, regs 3, 5(6). Subsection (7) substituted: SI 2003/2498, reg 2(1), Sch 1, Pt 1, paras 1, 15(2).

Jurisdiction and procedure

149   Jurisdiction of the Tribunal

The function of the Copyright Tribunal has jurisdiction under this Part to hear and determine proceedings under –

(za) section 73 (determination of royalty or other remuneration to be paid with respect to re-transmission of broadcast including work);

(zb) section 93C (application to determine amount of equitable remuneration under section 93B);

(a) section 118, 119 or 120 (reference of licensing scheme);

(b) section 121 or 122 (application with respect to entitlement to licence under licensing scheme);

(c) section 125, 126 or 127 (reference or application with respect to licensing by licensing body);

[(ca) section 128B (reference by the Secretary of State under section 128A);]

(cc) section 135D or 135E (application or reference with respect to use as of right of sound recordings in broadcasts . . .);

(d) section 139 (appeal against order as to coverage of licensing scheme of licence);

(e) section 142 (application to settle royalty or other sum payable for lending of certain works);

(f) section 144(4) (application to settle terms of copyright licence available as of right).

Amendments: Paragraph inserted: SI 2003/2498, regs 3, 21(6). Words omitted repealed: SI 2003/2498, reg 2(2), Sch 2.

151A   Award of interest

(1) Any of the following, namely –

(a) a direction under section 123(3) so far as relating to a licence for [communicating a work to the public];

(b) a direction under section 128(3) so far as so relating;

(c) an order under section 135D(1); and

(d) an order under section 135F confirming or varying an order under section 135D(1),

may award simple interest at such rate and for such period, beginning not earlier than the relevant date and ending not later than the date of the order, as the Copyright Tribunal thinks reasonable in the circumstances.

(2) In this section 'the relevant date' means –

(a) in relation to a direction under section 123(3), the date on which the reference was made;

(b) in relation to a direction under section 128(3), the date on which the reference or application was made;

(c) in relation to an order under section 135D(1), the date on which the first payment under section 135C(2) became due; and

(d) in relation to an order under section 135F, the date on which the application was made.

Amendment: Words in square brackets substituted: SI 2003/2498, reg 2(1), Sch 1, Pt 1, paras 1, 7.

Chapter X

Miscellaneous and General

Crown and Parliamentary copyright

163 Crown copyright

(1) Where a work is made by Her Majesty or by an officer or servant of the Crown in the course of his duties –

(a) the work qualifies for copyright protection notwithstanding section 153(1) (ordinary requirement as to qualification for copyright protection), and

(b) Her Majesty is the first owner of any copyright in the work.

(1A) For the purposes of this section, works made by Her Majesty include any sound recording, film [or live broadcast] of the proceedings of the National Assembly for Wales (including proceedings of a committee of the Assembly or of a sub-committee of such a committee) which is made by or under the direction or control of the Assembly; but a work shall not be regarded as made by or under the direction or control of the Assembly by reason only of its being commissioned by or on behalf of the Assembly.

(2) Copyright in such a work is referred to in this Part as 'Crown copyright', notwithstanding that it may be, or have been, assigned to another person.

(3) Crown copyright in a literary, dramatic, musical or artistic work continues to subsist –

(a) until the end of the period of 125 years from the end of the calendar year in which the work was made, or

(b) if the work is published commercially before the end of the period of 75 years from the end of the calendar year in which it was made, until the end of the period of 50 years from the end of the calendar year in which it was first so published.

(4) In the case of a work of joint authorship where one or more but not all of the authors are persons falling within subsection (1), this section applies only in relation to those authors and the copyright subsisting by virtue of their contribution to the work.

(5) Except as mentioned above, and subject to any express exclusion elsewhere in this Part, the provisions of this Part apply in relation to Crown copyright as to other copyright.

(6) This section does not apply to work if, or to the extent that, Parliamentary copyright subsists in the work (see sections 165 to 166B).

Amendment: Words in square brackets substituted by SI 2003/2498, reg 2(1), Sch 1, Pt 1, paras 1, 11(a).

165 Parliamentary copyright

(1) Where a work is made by or under the direction or control of the House of Commons or the House of Lords –

(a) the work qualifies for copyright protection notwithstanding section 153(1) (ordinary requirement as to qualification for copyright protection), and

(b) the House by whom, or under whose direction or control, the work is made is the first owner of any copyright in the work, and if the work is made by or under the direction or control of both Houses, the two Houses are joint first owners of copyright.

(2) Copyright in such a work is referred to in this Part as 'Parliamentary copyright', notwithstanding that it may be, or have been, assigned to another person.

(3) Parliamentary copyright in a literary, dramatic, musical or artistic work continues to subsist until the end of the period of 50 years from the end of the calendar year in which the work was made.

(4) For the purposes of this section, works made by or under the direction or control of the House of Commons or the House of Lords include –

(a)　any work made by an officer or employee of that House in the course of his duties, and
(b)　any sound recording, film [or live broadcast] of the proceedings of that House;

but a work shall not be regarded as made by or under the direction or control of either House by reason only of its being commissioned by or on behalf of that House.

(5) In the case of a work of joint authorship where one or more but not all of the authors are acting on behalf of, or under the direction or control of, the House of Commons or the House of Lords, this section applies only in relation to those authors and the copyright subsisting by virtue of their contribution to the work.

(6) Except as mentioned above, and subject to any express exclusion elsewhere in this Part, the provisions of this Part apply in relation to Parliamentary copyright as to other copyright.

(7) The provisions of this section also apply, subject to any exceptions or modifications specified by Order in Council, to works made by or under the direction or control of any other legislative body of a country to which this Part extends; and references in this Part to 'Parliamentary copyright' shall be construed accordingly.

(8) A statutory instrument containing an Order in Council under subsection (7) shall be subject to annulment in pursuance of a resolution of either House of Parliament.

Amendment: Words in square brackets substituted: SI 2003/2498, reg 2(1), Sch 1, Pt 1, paras 1, 11(b).

175　Meaning of publication and commercial publication

(1) In this Part 'publication', in relation to a work –

(a)　means the issue of copies to the public, and
(b)　includes, in the case of a literary, dramatic, musical or artistic work, making it available to the public by means of an electronic retrieval system;

and related expressions shall be construed accordingly.

(2) In this Part 'commercial publication', in relation to a literary, dramatic, musical or artistic work means –

(a)　issuing copies of the work to the public at a time when copies made in advance of the receipt of orders are generally available to the public, or
(b)　making the work available to the public by means of an electronic retrieval system;

and related expressions shall be construed accordingly.

(3) In the case of a work of architecture in the form of a building, or an artistic work incorporated in a building, construction of the building shall be treated as equivalent to publication of the work.

(4) The following do not constitute publication for the purposes of this Part and references to commercial publication shall be construed accordingly –

(a)　in the case of a literary, dramatic or musical work –

(i)   the performance of the work, or

(ii)   the [communication to the public of the work] (otherwise than for the purposes of an electronic retrieval system);

(b) in the case of an artistic work –

(i)   the exhibition of the work,

(ii)   the issue to the public of copies of a graphic work representing, or of photographs of, a work of architecture in the form of a building or a model for a building, a sculpture or a work of artistic craftsmanship,

(iii)   the issue to the public of copies of a film including the work, or

(iv)   the [communication to the public of the work] (otherwise than for the purposes of an electronic retrieval system);

(c) in the case of a sound recording or film –

(i)   the work being played or shown in public, or

(ii)   the [communication to the public of the work].

(5) References in this Part to publication or commercial publication do not include publication which is merely colourable and not intended to satisfy the reasonable requirements of the public.

(6) No account shall be taken for the purposes of this section of any unauthorised act.

Amendment: Words substituted: SI 2003/2498, reg 2(1), Sch 1, Pt 1, paras 1, 6(1).

178   Minor definitions

In this Part –

'article', in the context of an article in a periodical, includes an item of any description;

'business' includes a trade or profession;

'collective work' means –

(a) a work of joint authorship, or

(b) a work in which there are distinct contributions by different authors or in which works or parts of works of different authors are incorporated;

'computer-generated', in relation to a work, means that the work is generated by computer in circumstances such that there is no human author of the work;

'country' includes any territory;

'the Crown' includes the Crown in right of the Scottish Administration or of Her Majesty's Government in Northern Ireland or in any country outside the United Kingdom to which this Part extends;

'electronic' means actuated by electric, magnetic, electro-magnetic, electro-chemical or electro-mechanical energy, and 'in electronic form' means in a form usable only by electronic means;

'employed', 'employee', 'employer' and 'employment' refer to employment under a contract of service or of apprenticeship;

'facsimile copy' includes a copy which is reduced or enlarged in scale;

'international organisation' means an organisation the members of which include one or more states;

'judicial proceedings' includes proceedings before any court, tribunal or person having authority to decide any matter affecting a person's legal rights or liabilities;

'parliamentary proceedings' includes proceedings of the Northern Ireland Assembly of the Scottish Parliament or of the European Parliament;

['private study' does not include any study which is directly or indirectly for a commercial purpose;]

'producer', in relation to a sound recording or a film, means the person by whom the arrangements necessary for the making of the sound recording or film are undertaken;

'public library' means a library administered by or on behalf of –

(a) in England and Wales, a library authority within the meaning of the Public Libraries and Museums Act 1964;
(b) in Scotland, a statutory library authority within the meaning of the Public Libraries (Scotland) Act 1955;
(c) in Northern Ireland, an Education or Library Board within the meaning of the Education and Libraries (Northern Ireland) Order 1986;

'rental right' means the right of a copyright owner to authorise or prohibit the rental of copies of the work (see section 18A);

'reprographic copy' and 'reprographic copying' refer to copying by means of a reprographic process;

'reprographic process' means a process –

(a) for making facsimile copies, or
(b) involving the use of an appliance for making multiple copies,

and includes, in relation to a work held in electronic form, any copying by electronic means, but does not include the making of a film or sound recording;

'sufficient acknowledgement' means an acknowledgement identifying the work in question by its title or other description, and identifying the author unless –

(a) in the case of a published work, it is published anonymously;
(b) in the case of an unpublished work, it is not possible for a person to ascertain the identity of the author by reasonable inquiry;

'sufficient disclaimer', in relation to an act capable of infringing the right conferred by section 80 (right to object to derogatory treatment of work), means a clear and reasonably prominent indication –

(a) given at the time of the act, and
(b) if the author or director is then identified, appearing along with the identification,

that the work has been subjected to treatment to which the author or director has not consented;

'telecommunications system' means a system for conveying visual images, sounds or other information by electronic means;

'typeface' includes an ornamental motif used in printing;

'unauthorised', as regards anything done in relation to a work, means done otherwise than –

(a)   by or with the licence of the copyright owner, or

(b)   if copyright does not subsist in the work, by or with the licence of the author or, in a case where section 11(2) would have applied, the author's employer or, in either case, persons lawfully claiming under him, or

(c)   in pursuance of section 48 (copying, etc of certain material by the Crown);

['wireless broadcast' means a broadcast by means of wireless telegraphy;]

'wireless telegraphy' means the sending of electro-magnetic energy over paths not provided by a material substance constructed or arranged for that purpose, but does not include the transmission of microwave energy between terrestrial fixed points;

'writing' includes any form of notation or code, whether by hand or otherwise and regardless of the method by which, or medium in or on which, it is recorded, and 'written' shall be construed accordingly.

Amendment: Definitions 'private study' and 'wireless broadcast' inserted by SI 2003/2498, reg 2(1), Sch 1, Pt 1, paras 1, 15(3).

179   Index of defined expressions

The following Table shows provisions defining or otherwise explaining expressions used in this Part (other than provisions defining or explaining an expression used only in the same section) –

accessible copy	section 31F(3)
account of profits and accounts (in Scotland)	section 177
acts restricted by copyright	section 16(1)
adaptation	section 21(3)
approved body	section 31B(12)
archivist (in sections 37 to 43)	section 37(6)
article (in a periodical)	section 178
artistic work	section 4(1)
assignment (in Scotland)	section 177
author	sections 9 and 10(3)
broadcast (and related expressions)	section 6
building	section 4(2)
business	section 178
. . .	. . .
collective work	section 178
commencement (in Schedule 1)	paragraph 1(2) of that Schedule
commercial publication	section 175
[communication to the public	section 20]
computer-generated	section 178
copy and copying	section 17
copyright (generally)	section 1
copyright (in Schedule 1)	paragraph 2(2) of that Schedule
copyright owner	sections 101(2) and 173
Copyright Tribunal	section 145
copyright work	section 1(2)
costs (in Scotland)	section 177
country	section 178
country of origin	section 15A
the Crown	section 178

Crown copyright	sections 163(2) and 164(3)
database	section 3A(1)
defendant (in Scotland)	section 177
delivery up (in Scotland)	section 177
dramatic work	section 3(1)
educational establishment	section 174(1) to (4)
EEA, EEA national and EEA state	section 172A
electronic and electronic form	section 178
employed, employee, employer and employment	section 178
[excepted sound recording	section 72(1A)]
exclusive licence	section 92(1)
existing works (in Schedule 1)	paragraph 1(3) of that Schedule
facsimile copy	section 178
film	section 5B
future copyright	section 91(2)
general licence (in sections 140 and 141)	section 140(7)
graphic work	section 4(2)
infringing copy	section 27
injunction (in Scotland)	section 177
interlocutory relief (in Scotland)	section 177
international organisation	section 178
issue of copies to the public	section 18
joint authorship (work of)	sections 10(1) and (2)
judicial proceedings	section 178
lawful user (in sections 50A to 50C)	section 50A(2)
lending	section 18A(2) to (6)
librarian (in sections 37 to 43)	section 37(6)
licence (in sections 125 to 128)	section 124
licence of copyright owner	sections 90(4), 91(3) and 173
licensing body (in Chapter VII)	section 116(2)
licensing scheme (generally)	section 116(1)
licensing scheme (in sections 118 to 121)	section 117
literary work	section 3(1)
made (in relation to a literary, dramatic or musical work)	section 3(2)
musical work	section 3(1)
needletime	section 135A
the new copyright provisions (in Schedule 1)	paragraph 1(1) of that Schedule
the 1911 Act (in Schedule 1)	paragraph 1(1) of that Schedule
the 1956 Act (in Schedule 1)	paragraph 1(1) of that Schedule
on behalf of (in relation to an educational establishment)	section 174(5)
original (in relation to a database)	section 3A(2)
Parliamentary copyright	sections 165(2) and (7), 166A(3) and 166B(3)
parliamentary proceedings	section 178
performance	section 19(2)
photograph	section 4(2)
plaintiff (in Scotland)	section 177

prescribed conditions (in sections 38 to 43)	section 37(1)(b)
prescribed library or archive (in sections 38 to 43)	section 37(1)(a)
[private study	section 178]
producer (in relation to a sound recording or film)	section 178
programme (in the context of broadcasting)	section 6(3)
prospective owner (of copyright)	section 91(2)
publication and related expressions	section 175
public library	section 178
published edition (in the context of copyright in the typographical arrangement)	section 8
pupil	section 174(5)
rental	section 18A(2) to (6)
rental right	section 178
reprographic copies and reprographic copying	section 178
reprographic process	section 178
sculpture	section 4(2)
signed	section 176
sound recording	sections 5A and 135A
sufficient acknowledgement	section 178
sufficient disclaimer	section 178
teacher	section 174(5)
telecommunications system	section 178
terms of payment	section 135A
typeface	section 178
unauthorised (as regards things done in relation to a work)	section 178
unknown (in relation to the author of a work)	section 9(5)
unknown authorship (work of)	section 9(4)
visually impaired person	section 31F(9)
[wireless broadcast	secion 178]
wireless telegraphy	section 178
work (in Schedule 1)	paragraph 2(1) of that Schedule
work of more than one author (in Chapter VII)	section 116(4)
writing and written	section 178

Amendments: Entry 'cable programme, cable programme service (and related expressions)' omitted repealed: SI 2003/2498, reg 2(2), Sch 2. Entries 'communication to the public', 'excepted sound recording', 'private study' and 'wireless broadcast' inserted: SI 2003/2498, reg 2(1), Sch 1, Pt 1, paras 1, 15(4).

182A   Consent required for copying of recording

(1) A performer's rights are infringed by a person who, without his consent, makes. . . a copy of a recording of the whole or any substantial part of a qualifying performance.

[(1A) In subsection (1), making a copy of a recording includes making a copy which is transient or is incidental to some other use of the original recording.]

(2) It is immaterial whether the copy is made directly or indirectly.

(3) The right of a performer under this section to authorise or prohibit the making of such copies is referred to in this Part as 'reproduction right'.

Amendments: Subsection (1A) inserted: SI 2003/2498, regs 3, 8(3). Words omitted repealed: SI 2003/2498, reg 2(2), Sch 2.

182C   Consent required for rental or lending of copies to public

(1) A performer's rights are infringed by a person who, without his consent, rents or lends to the public copies of a recording of the whole or any substantial part of a qualifying performance.

(2) In this Part, subject to the following provisions of this section –

(a) 'rental' means making a copy of a recording available for use, on terms that it will or may be returned, for direct or indirect economic or commercial advantage, and

(b) 'lending' means making a copy of a recording available for use, on terms that it will or may be returned, otherwise than for direct or indirect economic or commercial advantage, through an establishment which is accessible to the public.

(3) The expressions 'rental' and 'lending' do not include –

(a) making available for the purpose of public performance, playing or showing in public [or communication to the public];

(b) making available for the purpose of exhibition in public; or

(c) making available for on-the-spot reference use.

(4) The expression 'lending' does not include making available between establishments which are accessible to the public.

(5) Where lending by an establishment accessible to the public gives rise to a payment the amount of which does not go beyond what is necessary to cover the operating costs of the establishment, there is no direct or indirect economic or commercial advantage for the purposes of this section.

(6) References in this Part to the rental or lending of copies of a recording of a performance include the rental or lending of the original recording of the live performance.

(7) In this Part –

'rental right' means the right of a performer under this section to authorise or prohibit the rental of copies to the public, and

'lending right' means the right of a performer under this section to authorise or prohibit the lending of copies to the public.

Amendment: Words in square brackets substituted: SI 2003/2498, reg 2(1), Sch 1, Pt 1, paras 1, 6(2)(c).

[182CA   Consent required for making available to the public]

[(1) A performer's rights are infringed by a person who, without his consent, makes available to the public a recording of the whole or any substantial part of a qualifying performance by electronic transmission in such a way that members of the public may access the recording from a place and at a time individually chosen by them.

(2) The right of a performer under this section to authorise or prohibit the making available to the public of a recording is referred to in this Part as 'making available right.]

Amendment: Section inserted: SI 2003/2498, regs 3, 7(1).

182D   Right to equitable remuneration for exploitation of sound recording

(1) Where a commercially published sound recording of the whole or any substantial part of a qualifying performance –

(a)   is played in public, or

[(b) is communicated to the public otherwise than by its being made available to the public in the way mentioned in section 182CA(1),]

the performer is entitled to equitable remuneration from the owner of the copyright in the sound recording.

(2) The right to equitable remuneration under this section may not be assigned by the performer except to a collecting society for the purpose of enabling it to enforce the right on his behalf.

The right is, however, transmissible by testamentary disposition or by operation of law as personal or moveable property; and it may be assigned or further transmitted by any person into whose hands it passes.

(3) The amount payable by way of equitable remuneration is as agreed by or on behalf of the persons by and to whom it is payable, subject to the following provisions.

(4) In default of agreement as to the amount payable by way of equitable remuneration, the person by or to whom it is payable may apply to the Copyright Tribunal to determine the amount payable.

(5) A person to or by whom equitable remuneration is payable may also apply to the Copyright Tribunal –

(a)   to vary any agreement as to the amount payable, or

(b)   to vary any previous determination of the Tribunal as to that matter;

but except with the special leave of the Tribunal no such application may be made within twelve months from the date of a previous determination.

An order made on an application under this subsection has effect from the date on which it is made or such later date as may be specified by the Tribunal.

(6) On an application under this section the Tribunal shall consider the matter and make such order as to the method of calculating and paying equitable remuneration as it may determine to be reasonable in the circumstances, taking into account the importance of the contribution of the performer to the sound recording.

(7) An agreement is of no effect in so far as it purports –

(a)   to exclude or restrict the right to equitable remuneration under this section, or

(b)   to prevent a person questioning the amount of equitable remuneration or to restrict the powers of the Copyright Tribunal under this section.

Amendment: Paragraph substituted: SI 2003/2498, regs 3, 7(2).

183   Infringement of performer's rights by use of recording made without consent

A performer's rights are infringed by a person who, without his consent –

(a)   shows or plays in public the whole or any substantial part of a qualifying performance, or

(b) [communicates to the public] the whole or any substantial part of a qualifying performance,

by means of a recording which was, and which that person knows or has reason to believe was, made without the performer's consent.

Amendment: Words in square brackets substituted: SI 2003/2498, reg 2(1), Sch 1, Pt 1, paras 1, 13(1)(a).

187   Infringement of recording rights by use of recording made without consent

(1) A person infringes the rights of a person having recording rights in relation to a performance who, without his consent or, in the case of a qualifying performance, that of the performer –

(a) shows or plays in public the whole or any substantial part of the performance, or
(b) [communicates to the public] the whole or any substantial part of the performance,

by means of a recording which was, and which that person knows or has reason to believe was, made without the appropriate consent.

(2) The reference in subsection (1) to 'the appropriate consent' is to the consent of –

(a) the performer, or
(b) the person who at the time the consent was given had recording rights in relation to the performance (or, if there was more than one such person, of all of them).

Amendment: Words in square brackets substituted: SI 2003/2498, reg 2(1), Sch 1, Pt 1, paras 1, 13(1)(b).

191   Duration of rights

(1) The following provisions have effect with respect to the duration of the rights conferred by this Part.

(2) The rights conferred by this Part in relation to a performance expire –

(a) at the end of the period of 50 years from the end of the calendar year in which the performance takes place, or
(b) if during that period a recording of the performance is released, 50 years from the end of the calendar year in which it is released,

subject as follows.

(3) For the purposes of subsection (2) a recording is 'released' when it is first published, played or shown in public [or communicated to the public]; but in determining whether a recording has been released no account shall be taken of any unauthorised act.

(4) Where a performer is not a national of an EEA state, the duration of the rights conferred by this Part in relation to his performance is that to which the performance is entitled in the country of which he is a national, provided that does not exceed the period which would apply under subsections (2) and (3).

(5) If or to the extent that the application of subsection (4) would be at variance with an international obligation to which the United Kingdom became subject prior to 29th October 1993, the duration of the rights conferred by this Part shall be as specified in subsections (2) and (3).

Amendment: Words in square brackets substituted: SI 2003/2498, reg 2(1), Sch 1, Pt 1, paras 1, 8(1)(d).

Performers' property rights

191A   Performers' property rights

(1) The following rights conferred by this Part on a performer –

> reproduction right (section 182A),
> distribution right (section 182B),
> rental right and lending right (section 182C),
> [making available right (section 182CA),]

are property rights ('a performer's property rights').

(2) References in this Part to the consent of the performer shall be construed in relation to a performer's property rights as references to the consent of the rights owner.

(3) Where different persons are (whether in consequence of a partial assignment or otherwise) entitled to different aspects of a performer's property rights in relation to a performance, the rights owner for any purpose of this Part is the person who is entitled to the aspect of those rights relevant for that purpose.

(4) Where a performer's property rights (or any aspect of them) is owned by more than one person jointly, references in this Part to the rights owner are to all the owners, so that, in particular, any requirement of the licence of the rights owner requires the licence of all of them.

Amendment: Subsection (1): entry relating to 'making available right' inserted: SI 2003/2498, regs 3, 7(3).

[191JA   Injunctions against service providers]

[(1) The High Court (in Scotland, the Court of Session) shall have power to grant an injunction against a service provider, where that service provider has actual knowledge of another person using their service to infringe a performer's property right.

(2) In determining whether a service provider has actual knowledge for the purpose of this section, a court shall take into account all matters which appear to it in the particular circumstances to be relevant and, amongst other things, shall have regard to –

(a)   whether a service provider has received a notice through a means of contact made available in accordance with regulation 6(1)(c) of the Electronic Commerce (EC Directive) Regulations 2002 (SI 2002/2013); and
(b)   the extent to which any notice includes –
　　　(i)   the full name and address of the sender of the notice;
　　　(ii)   details of the infringement in question.

(3) In this section 'service provider' has the meaning given to it by regulation 2 of the Electronic Commerce (EC Directive) Regulations 2002.

(4) Section 177 applies in respect of this section as it applies in respect of Part 1.]

Amendment: Section inserted: SI 2003/2498, regs 3, 27(2).

197   Meaning of 'illicit recording'

(1) In this Part 'illicit recording', in relation to a performance, shall be construed in accordance with this section.

(2) For the purposes of a performer's rights, a recording of the whole or any substantial part of a performance of his is an illicit recording if it is made, otherwise than for private purposes, without his consent.

(3) For the purposes of the rights of a person having recording rights, a recording of the whole or any substantial part of a performance subject to the exclusive recording contract is an illicit recording if it is made, otherwise than for private purposes, without his consent or that of the performer.

(4) For the purposes of sections 198 and 199 (offences and orders for delivery up in criminal proceedings), a recording is an illicit recording if it is an illicit recording for the purposes mentioned in subsection (2) or subsection (3).

(5) In this Part 'illicit recording' includes a recording falling to be treated as an illicit recording by virtue of any of the following provisions of Schedule 2 –

paragraph 4(3) (recordings made for purposes of instruction or examination),

paragraph 6(2) (recordings made by educational establishments for educational purposes),

paragraph 12(2) (recordings of performance in electronic form retained on transfer of principal recording), ...

paragraph 16(3) (recordings made for purposes of broadcast ... ,

[paragraph 17A(2) (recording for the purposes of time-shifting), or

paragraph 17B(2) (photographs of broadcasts),]

but otherwise does not include a recording made in accordance with any of the provisions of that Schedule.

(6) It is immaterial for the purposes of this section where the recording was made.

Amendments: Entries relating to 'paragraph 17A(2)' and 'paragraph 17B(2)' inserted and words omitted repealed: SI 2003/2498, regs 3, 20(4).

Offences

198   Criminal liability for making, dealing with or using illicit recordings

(1) A person commits an offence who without sufficient consent –

(a)   makes for sale or hire, or
(b)   imports into the United Kingdom otherwise than for his private and domestic use, or
(c)   possesses in the course of a business with a view to committing any act infringing the rights conferred by this Part, or
(d)   in the course of a business –
  (i)   sells or lets for hire, or
  (ii)   offers or exposes for sale or hire, or
  (iii)   distributes,
  a recording which is, and which he knows or has reason to believe is, an illicit recording.

[(1A) A person who infringes a performer's making available right –

(a)   in the course of a business, or
(b)   otherwise than in the course of a business to such an extent as to affect prejudicially the owner of the making available right,

commits an offence if he knows or has reason to believe that, by doing so, he is infringing the making available right in the recording.]

(2) A person commits an offence who causes a recording of a performance made without sufficient consent to be –

    (a) shown or played in public, or
    [(b) communicated to the public,]

thereby infringing any of the rights conferred by this Part, if he knows or has reason to believe that those rights are thereby infringed.

(3) In subsections (1) and (2) 'sufficient consent' means –

    (a) in the case of a qualifying performance, the consent of the performer, and
    (b) in the case of a non-qualifying performance subject to an exclusive recording contract –
        (i)   for the purposes of subsection (1)(a) (making of recording), the consent of the performer or the person having recording rights, and
        (ii)   for the purposes of subsection (1)(b), (c) and (d) and subsection (2) (dealing with or using recording), the consent of the person having recording rights.

The references in this subsection to the person having recording rights are to the person having those rights at the time the consent is given or, if there is more than one such person, to all of them.

(4) No offence is committed under subsection (1) or (2) by the commission of an act which by virtue of any provision of Schedule 2 may be done without infringing the rights conferred by this Part.

(5) A person guilty of an offence under subsection (1)(a), (b) or (d)(iii) is liable –

    (a) on summary conviction to imprisonment for a term not exceeding six months or a fine not exceeding the statutory maximum, or both;
    (b) on conviction on indictment to a fine or imprisonment for a term not exceeding ten years, or both.

[(5A) A person guilty of an offence under subsection (1A) is liable –

    (a) on summary conviction to imprisonment for a term not exceeding three months or a fine not exceeding the statutory maximum, or both;
    (b) on conviction on indictment to a fine or imprisonment for a term not exceeding two years, or both.]

(6) A person guilty of any other offence under this section is liable on summary conviction to a fine not exceeding level 5 on the standard scale or imprisonment for a term not exceeding six months, or both.

Amendments: Subsections (1A) and (5A) inserted: SI 2003/2498, regs 3, 26(3). Paragraph (2)(b) inserted: SI 2003/2498, reg 2, Sch 1.

200   Search warrants

(1) Where a justice of the peace (in Scotland, a sheriff or justice of the peace) is satisfied by information on oath given by a constable (in Scotland, by evidence on oath) that there are reasonable grounds for believing –

(a) that an offence under [section 198(1) or (1A)] (offences of making, importing, possessing, selling etc or distributing illicit recordings) has been or is about to be committed in any premises, and

(b) that evidence that such an offence has been or is about to be committed is in those premises,

he may issue a warrant authorising a constable to enter and search the premises, using such reasonable force as is necessary.

(2) The power conferred by subsection (1) does not, in England and Wales, extend to authorising a search for material of the kinds mentioned in section 9(2) of the Police and Criminal Evidence Act 1984 (certain classes of personal or confidential material).

(3) A warrant under subsection (1) –

(a) may authorise persons to accompany any constable executing the warrant, and

(b) remains in force for 28 days from the date of its issue.

(3A) In executing a warrant issued under subsection (1) a constable may seize an article if he reasonably believes that it is evidence that any offence under [section 198(1) or (1A)] has been or is about to be committed.

(4) In this section 'premises' includes land, buildings, fixed or moveable structures, vehicles, vessels, aircraft and hovercraft.

Amendment: Words in square brackets substituted: SI 2003/2498, regs 3, 26(4).

204A   Forfeiture of illicit recordings: England and Wales or Northern Ireland

(1) In England and Wales or Northern Ireland where illicit recordings of a performance have come into the possession of any person in connection with the investigation or prosecution of a relevant offence, that person may apply under this section for an order for the forfeiture of the illicit recordings.

(2) For the purposes of this section 'relevant offence' means –

(a) an offence under [section 198(1) or (1A)] (criminal liability for making or dealing with illicit recordings),

(b) an offence under the Trade Descriptions Act 1968 (c 29), or

(c) an offence involving dishonesty or deception.

(3) An application under this section may be made –

(a) where proceedings have been brought in any court for a relevant offence relating to some or all of the illicit recordings, to that court, or

(b) where no application for the forfeiture of the illicit recordings has been made under paragraph (a), by way of complaint to a magistrates' court.

(4) On an application under this section, the court shall make an order for the forfeiture of any illicit recordings only if it is satisfied that a relevant offence has been committed in relation to the illicit recordings.

(5) A court may infer for the purposes of this section that such an offence has been committed in relation to any illicit recordings if it is satisfied that such an offence has been committed in relation to illicit recordings which are representative of the illicit recordings in question (whether by reason of being part of the same consignment or batch or otherwise).

(6) Any person aggrieved by an order made under this section by a magistrates' court, or by a decision of such a court not to make such an order, may appeal against that order or decision –

    (a) in England and Wales, to the Crown Court, or
    (b) in Northern Ireland, to the county court.

(7) An order under this section may contain such provision as appears to the court to be appropriate for delaying the coming into force of the order pending the making and determination of any appeal (including any application under section 111 of the Magistrates' Courts Act 1980 (c 43) or Article 146 of the Magistrates' Courts (Northern Ireland) Order 1981 (SI 1987/1675 (NI 26)) (statement of case)).

(8) Subject to subsection (9), where any illicit recordings are forfeited under this section they shall be destroyed in accordance with such directions as the court may give.

(9) On making an order under this section the court may direct that the illicit recordings to which the order relates shall (instead of being destroyed) be forfeited to the person having the performers' rights or recording rights in question or dealt with in such other way as the court considers appropriate.

Amendment: Words in square brackets substituted: SI 2003/2498, regs 3, 26(4).

204B Forfeiture: Scotland

(1) In Scotland the court may make an order under this section for the forfeiture of any illicit recordings.

(2) An order under this section may be made –

    (a) on an application by the procurator-fiscal made in the manner specified in section 134 of the Criminal Procedure (Scotland) Act 1995 (c 46), or
    (b) where a person is convicted of a relevant offence, in addition to any other penalty which the court may impose.

(3) On an application under subsection (2)(a), the court shall make an order for the forfeiture of any illicit recordings only if it is satisfied that a relevant offence has been committed in relation to the illicit recordings.

(4) The court may infer for the purposes of this section that such an offence has been committed in relation to any illicit recordings if it is satisfied that such an offence has been committed in relation to illicit recordings which are representative of the illicit recordings in question (whether by reason of being part of the same consignment or batch or otherwise).

(5) The procurator-fiscal making the application under subsection (2)(a) shall serve on any person appearing to him to be the owner of, or otherwise to have an interest in, the illicit recordings to which the application relates a copy of the application, together with a notice giving him the opportunity to appear at the hearing of the application to show cause why the illicit recordings should not be forfeited.

(6) Service under subsection (5) shall be carried out, and such service may be proved, in the manner specified for citation of an accused in summary proceedings under the Criminal Procedure (Scotland) Act 1995.

(7) Any person upon whom notice is served under subsection (5) and any other person claiming to be the owner of, or otherwise to have an interest in, illicit recordings to which an application under this section relates shall be entitled to appear at the hearing of the application to show cause why the illicit recordings should not be forfeited.

(8) The court shall not make an order following an application under subsection (2)(a) –

    (a)   if any person on whom notice is served under subsection (5) does not appear, unless service of the notice on that person is proved, or

    (b)   if no notice under subsection (5) has been served, unless the court is satisfied that in the circumstances it was reasonable not to serve such notice.

(9) Where an order for the forfeiture of any illicit recordings is made following an application under subsection (2)(a), any person who appeared, or was entitled to appear, to show cause why the illicit recordings should not be forfeited may, within 21 days of the making of the order, appeal to the High Court by Bill of Suspension.

(10) Section 182(5)(a) to (e) of the Criminal Procedure (Scotland) Act 1995 shall apply to an appeal under subsection (9) as it applies to a stated case under Part 2 of that Act.

(11) An order following an application under subsection (2)(a) shall not take effect –

    (a)   until the end of the period of 21 days beginning with the day after the day on which the order is made, or

    (b)   if an appeal is made under subsection (9) above within that period, until the appeal is determined or abandoned.

(12) An order under subsection (2)(b) shall not take effect –

    (a)   until the end of the period within which an appeal against the order could be brought under the Criminal Procedure (Scotland) Act 1995 (c 46), or

    (b)   if an appeal is made within that period, until the appeal is determined or abandoned.

(13) Subject to subsection (14), illicit recordings forfeited under this section shall be destroyed in accordance with such directions as the court may give.

(14) On making an order under this section the court may direct that the illicit recordings to which the order relates shall (instead of being destroyed) be forfeited to the person having the performers' rights or recording rights in question or dealt with in such other way as the court considers appropriate.

(15) For the purposes of this section –

    'relevant offence' means an offence under [section 198(1) or (1A)] (criminal liability for making or dealing with illicit recordings), or under the Trade Descriptions Act 1968 (c 29) or any offence involving dishonesty or deception;

    'the court' means –

    (a)   in relation to an order made on an application under subsection (2)(a), the sheriff, and

    (b)   in relation to an order made under subsection (2)(b), the court which imposed the penalty.

Amendment: Words in square brackets substituted: SI 2003/2498, regs 3, 26(4).

Interpretation

211   Expressions having same meaning as in copyright provisions

(1) The following expressions have the same meaning in this Part as in Part I (copyright) –

    broadcast,

business,

...

[communication to the public,]
country,
defendant (in Scotland),
delivery up (in Scotland),
EEA national,
film,
[injunction (in Scotland),]
literary work,
published, ...
[sound recording, and]
[wireless broadcast].

(2) The provisions of section [6(3) to (5A) and section 19(4)] (supplementary provisions relating to broadcasting ...) apply for the purposes of this Part, and in relation to an infringement of the rights conferred by this Part, as they apply for the purposes of Part I and in relation to an infringement of copyright.

Amendments: Entries 'cable programme' and 'cable programme service' and word omitted repealed: SI 2003/2498, reg 2(2), Sch 2. Entries 'communication to the public', 'injunction (in Scotland)'and 'wireless broadcast' inserted and entry 'sound recording' and words in square brackets substituted: SI 2003/2498, reg 2(1), Sch 1, Pt 1, paras 1, 15(5).

212   Index of defined expressions

The following Table shows provisions defining or otherwise explaining expressions used in this Part (other than provisions defining or explaining an expression used only in the same section) –

broadcast (and related expressions)	section 211 (and section 6)
business	section 211(1) (and section 178)
...	...
[communication to the public	section 211(1) (and section 20)]
consent of performer (in relation to performer's property rights)	section 191A(2)
country	section 211(1) (and section 178)
defendant (in Scotland)	section 211(1) (and section 177)
delivery up (in Scotland)	section 211(1) (and section 177)
distribution right	section 182B(5)
EEA national	section 211(1) (and section 172A)
exclusive recording contract	section 185(1)
film	section 211(1) (and [section 5B])
illicit recording	section 197
[injunction (in Scotland)	section 211(1) (and section 177)]
lending right	section 182C(7)
literary work	section 211(1) (and section 3(1))
[making available right	section 182CA]
performance	section 180(2)
performer's non-property rights	section 192A(1)
performer's property rights	section 191A(1)
published	section 211(1) (and section 175)
qualifying country	section 206(1)
qualifying individual	section 206(1) and (2)

qualifying performance	section 181
qualifying person	section 206(1) and (3)
recording (of a performance)	section 180(2)
recording rights (person having)	section 185(2) and (3)
rental right	section 182C(7)
reproduction right	section 182A(3)
rights owner (in relation to performer's property rights)	section 191A(3) and (4)
sound recording	section 211(1) (and section 5A)

Amendments: Entry 'cable programme, cable programme service (and related expressions)' (omitted) repealed: SI 2003/2498, reg 2(2), Sch 2. Entries 'communication to the public', 'injunction (in Scotland)' and 'making available right' inserted: SI 2003/2498, reg 2(1), Sch 1, Pt 1, paras 1, 15(6).

PART VII

MISCELLANEOUS AND GENERAL

[Circumvention of protection measures]

Amendment: Heading substituted: SI 2003/2498, regs 3, 24(1).

[296   Circumvention of technical devices applied to computer programs]

[(1) This section applies where –

(a)   a technical device has been applied to a computer program; and

(b)   a person (A) knowing or having reason to believe that it will be used to make infringing copies –

  (i)   manufactures for sale or hire, imports, distributes, sells or lets for hire, offers or exposes for sale or hire, advertises for sale or hire or has in his possession for commercial purposes any means the sole intended purpose of which is to facilitate the unauthorised removal or circumvention of the technical device; or

  (ii)   publishes information intended to enable or assist persons to remove or circumvent the technical device.

(2) The following persons have the same rights against A as a copyright owner has in respect of an infringement of copyright –

(a)   a person –

  (i)   issuing to the public copies of, or

  (ii)   communicating to the public,

  the computer program to which the technical device has been applied;

(b)   the copyright owner or his exclusive licensee, if he is not the person specified in paragraph (a);

(c)   the owner or exclusive licensee of any intellectual property right in the technical device applied to the computer program.

(3) The rights conferred by subsection (2) are concurrent, and sections 101(3) and 102(1) to (4) apply, in proceedings under this section, in relation to persons with concurrent rights as they apply, in proceedings mentioned in those provisions, in relation to a copyright owner and exclusive licensee with concurrent rights.

(4) Further, the persons in subsection (2) have the same rights under section 99 or 100 (delivery up or seizure of certain articles) in relation to any such means as is referred to in subsection (1) which a person has in his possession, custody or control with the intention that it should be used

to facilitate the unauthorised removal or circumvention of any technical device which has been applied to a computer program, as a copyright owner has in relation to an infringing copy.

(5) The rights conferred by subsection (4) are concurrent, and section 102(5) shall apply, as respects anything done under section 99 or 100 by virtue of subsection (4), in relation to persons with concurrent rights as it applies, as respects anything done under section 99 or 100, in relation to a copyright owner and exclusive licensee with concurrent rights.

(6) In this section references to a technical device in relation to a computer program are to any device intended to prevent or restrict acts that are not authorised by the copyright owner of that computer program and are restricted by copyright.

(7) The following provisions apply in relation to proceedings under this section as in relation to proceedings under Part 1 (copyright) –

(a) sections 104 to 106 of this Act (presumptions as to certain matters relating to copyright); and

(b) section 72 of the Supreme Court Act 1981, section 15 of the Law Reform (Miscellaneous Provisions) (Scotland) Act 1985 and section 94A of the Judicature (Northern Ireland) Act 1978 (withdrawal of privilege against self-incrimination in certain proceedings relating to intellectual property);

and section 114 of this Act applies, with the necessary modifications, in relation to the disposal of anything delivered up or seized by virtue of subsection (4).

(8) Expressions used in this section which are defined for the purposes of Part 1 of this Act (copyright) have the same meaning as in that Part.]

Amendment: Section substituted, together with ss 296ZA–296ZF, for this section as originally enacted: SI 2003/2498, regs 3, 24(1).

[296ZA   Circumvention of technological measures]

[(1) This section applies where –

(a) effective technological measures have been applied to a copyright work other than a computer program; and

(b) a person (B) does anything which circumvents those measures knowing, or with reasonable grounds to know, that he is pursuing that objective.

(2) This section does not apply where a person, for the purposes of research into cryptography, does anything which circumvents effective technological measures unless in so doing, or in issuing information derived from that research, he affects prejudicially the rights of the copyright owner.

(3) The following persons have the same rights against B as a copyright owner has in respect of an infringement of copyright –

(a) a person –
(i)   issuing to the public copies of, or
(ii) communicating to the public,
the work to which effective technological measures have been applied; and

(b) the copyright owner or his exclusive licensee, if he is not the person specified in paragraph (a).

(4) The rights conferred by subsection (3) are concurrent, and sections 101(3) and 102(1) to (4) apply, in proceedings under this section, in relation to persons with concurrent rights as they

apply, in proceedings mentioned in those provisions, in relation to a copyright owner and exclusive licensee with concurrent rights.

(5) The following provisions apply in relation to proceedings under this section as in relation to proceedings under Part 1 (copyright) –

   (a) sections 104 to 106 of this Act (presumptions as to certain matters relating to copyright); and
   (b) section 72 of the Supreme Court Act 1981, section 15 of the Law Reform (Miscellaneous Provisions) (Scotland) Act 1985 and section 94A of the Judicature (Northern Ireland) Act 1978 (withdrawal of privilege against self-incrimination in certain proceedings relating to intellectual property).

(6) Subsections (1) to (4) and (5)(b) and any other provision of this Act as it has effect for the purposes of those subsections apply, with any necessary adaptations, to rights in performances, publication right and database right.

(7) The provisions of regulation 22 (presumptions relevant to database right) of the Copyright and Rights in Databases Regulations 1997 (SI 1997/3032) apply in proceedings brought by virtue of this section in relation to database right.]

Amendment: Section substituted, together with ss 296, 296ZB–296ZF, for s 296 as originally enacted: SI 2003/2498, regs 3, 24(1).

[296ZB   Devices and services designed to circumvent technological measures]

[(1) A person commits an offence if he –

   (a) manufactures for sale or hire, or
   (b) imports otherwise than for his private and domestic use, or
   (c) in the course of a business –
       (i)   sells or lets for hire, or
       (ii)   offers or exposes for sale or hire, or
       (iii) advertises for sale or hire, or
       (iv)   possesses, or
       (v)   distributes, or
   (d) distributes otherwise than in the course of a business to such an extent as to affect prejudicially the copyright owner,

any device, product or component which is primarily designed, produced, or adapted for the purpose of enabling or facilitating the circumvention of effective technological measures.

(2) A person commits an offence if he provides, promotes, advertises or markets –

   (a) in the course of a business, or
   (b) otherwise than in the course of a business to such an extent as to affect prejudicially the copyright owner,

a service the purpose of which is to enable or facilitate the circumvention of effective technological measures.

(3) Subsections (1) and (2) do not make unlawful anything done by, or on behalf of, law enforcement agencies or any of the intelligence services –

   (a) in the interests of national security; or
   (b) for the purpose of the prevention or detection of crime, the investigation of an offence, or the conduct of a prosecution,

and in this subsection 'intelligence services' has the meaning given in section 81 of the Regulation of Investigatory Powers Act 2000.

(4) A person guilty of an offence under subsection (1) or (2) is liable –

    (a) on summary conviction, to imprisonment for a term not exceeding three months, or to a fine not exceeding the statutory maximum, or both;

    (b) on conviction on indictment to a fine or imprisonment for a term not exceeding two years, or both.

(5) It is a defence to any prosecution for an offence under this section for the defendant to prove that he did not know, and had no reasonable ground for believing, that –

    (a) the device, product or component; or

    (b) the service,

enabled or facilitated the circumvention of effective technological measures.]

Amendment: Section substituted, together with ss 296, 296ZA, 296ZC–296ZF, for s 296 as originally enacted: SI 2003/2498, regs 3, 24(1).

[296ZC   Devices and services designed to circumvent technological measures: search warrants and forfeiture]

[(1) The provisions of sections 297B (search warrants), 297C (forfeiture of unauthorised decoders: England and Wales or Northern Ireland) and 297D (forfeiture of unauthorised decoders: Scotland) apply to offences under section 296ZB with the following modifications.

(2) In section 297B the reference to an offence under section 297A(1) shall be construed as a reference to an offence under section 296ZB(1) or (2).

(3) In sections 297C(2)(a) and 297D(15) the references to an offence under section 297A(1) shall be construed as a reference to an offence under section 296ZB(1).

(4) In sections 297C and 297D references to unauthorised decoders shall be construed as references to devices, products or components for the purpose of circumventing effective technological measures.]

Amendment: Section substituted, together with ss 296, 296ZA, 296ZB, 296ZD–296ZF, for s 296 as originally enacted: SI 2003/2498, regs 3, 24(1).

[296ZD   Rights and remedies in respect of devices and services designed to circumvent technological measures]

[(1) This section applies where –

    (a) effective technological measures have been applied to a copyright work other than a computer program; and

    (b) a person (C) manufactures, imports, distributes, sells or lets for hire, offers or exposes for sale or hire, advertises for sale or hire, or has in his possession for commercial purposes any device, product or component, or provides services which –

        (i)   are promoted, advertised or marketed for the purpose of the circumvention of, or

        (ii) have only a limited commercially significant purpose or use other than to circumvent, or

        (iii) are primarily designed, produced, adapted or performed for the purpose of enabling or facilitating the circumvention of,

        those measures.

(2) The following persons have the same rights against C as a copyright owner has in respect of an infringement of copyright –

   (a) a person –
      (i)   issuing to the public copies of, or
      (ii) communicating to the public,
     the work to which effective technological measures have been applied;
   (b) the copyright owner or his exclusive licensee, if he is not the person specified in paragraph (a); and
   (c) the owner or exclusive licensee of any intellectual property right in the effective technological measures applied to the work.

(3) The rights conferred by subsection (2) are concurrent, and sections 101(3) and 102(1) to (4) apply, in proceedings under this section, in relation to persons with concurrent rights as they apply, in proceedings mentioned in those provisions, in relation to a copyright owner and exclusive licensee with concurrent rights.

(4) Further, the persons in subsection (2) have the same rights under section 99 or 100 (delivery up or seizure of certain articles) in relation to any such device, product or component which a person has in his possession, custody or control with the intention that it should be used to circumvent effective technological measures, as a copyright owner has in relation to any infringing copy.

(5) The rights conferred by subsection (4) are concurrent, and section 102(5) shall apply, as respects anything done under section 99 or 100 by virtue of subsection (4), in relation to persons with concurrent rights as it applies, as respects anything done under section 99 or 100, in relation to a copyright owner and exclusive licensee with concurrent rights.

(6) The following provisions apply in relation to proceedings under this section as in relation to proceedings under Part 1 (copyright) –

   (a) sections 104 to 106 of this Act (presumptions as to certain matters relating to copyright); and
   (b) section 72 of the Supreme Court Act 1981, section 15 of the Law Reform (Miscellaneous Provisions) (Scotland) Act 1985 and section 94A of the Judicature (Northern Ireland) Act 1978 (withdrawal of privilege against self-incrimination in certain proceedings relating to intellectual property);

and section 114 of this Act applies, with the necessary modifications, in relation to the disposal of anything delivered up or seized by virtue of subsection (4).

(7) In section 97(1) (innocent infringement of copyright) as it applies to proceedings for infringement of the rights conferred by this section, the reference to the defendant not knowing or having reason to believe that copyright subsisted in the work shall be construed as a reference to his not knowing or having reason to believe that his acts enabled or facilitated an infringement of copyright.

(8) Subsections (1) to (5), (6)(b) and (7) and any other provision of this Act as it has effect for the purposes of those subsections apply, with any necessary adaptations, to rights in performances, publication right and database right.

(9) The provisions of regulation 22 (presumptions relevant to database right) of the Copyright and Rights in Databases Regulations 1997 (SI 1997/3032) apply in proceedings brought by virtue of this section in relation to database right.]

Amendment: Section substituted, together with ss 296, 296ZA–296ZC, 296ZE, 296ZF, for s 296 as originally enacted: SI 2003/2498, regs 3, 24(1).

[296ZE   Remedy where effective technological measures prevent permitted acts]

[(1) In this section –

'permitted act' means an act which may be done in relation to copyright works, notwithstanding the subsistence of copyright, by virtue of a provision of this Act listed in Part 1 of Schedule 5A;

'voluntary measure or agreement' means –

(a)   any measure taken voluntarily by a copyright owner, his exclusive licensee or a person issuing copies of, or communicating to the public, a work other than a computer program, or

(b)   any agreement between a copyright owner, his exclusive licensee or a person issuing copies of, or communicating to the public, a work other than a computer program and another party,

the effect of which is to enable a person to carry out a permitted act.

(2) Where the application of any effective technological measure to a copyright work other than a computer program prevents a person from carrying out a permitted act in relation to that work then that person or a person being a representative of a class of persons prevented from carrying out a permitted act may issue a notice of complaint to the Secretary of State.

(3) Following receipt of a notice of complaint, the Secretary of State may give to the owner of that copyright work or an exclusive licensee such directions as appear to the Secretary of State to be requisite or expedient for the purpose of –

(a)   establishing whether any voluntary measure or agreement relevant to the copyright work the subject of the complaint subsists; or

(b)   (where it is established there is no subsisting voluntary measure or agreement) ensuring that the owner or exclusive licensee of that copyright work makes available to the complainant the means of carrying out the permitted act the subject of the complaint to the extent necessary to so benefit from that permitted act.

(4) The Secretary of State may also give directions –

(a)   as to the form and manner in which a notice of complaint in subsection (2) may be delivered to him;

(b)   as to the form and manner in which evidence of any voluntary measure or agreement may be delivered to him; and

(c)   generally as to the procedure to be followed in relation to a complaint made under this section;

and shall publish directions given under this subsection in such manner as in his opinion will secure adequate publicity for them.

(5) It shall be the duty of any person to whom a direction is given under subsection (3)(a) or (b) to give effect to that direction.

(6) The obligation to comply with a direction given under subsection (3)(b) is a duty owed to the complainant or, where the complaint is made by a representative of a class of persons, to that representative and to each person in the class represented; and a breach of the duty is actionable accordingly (subject to the defences and other incidents applying to actions for breach of statutory duty).

(7) Any direction under this section may be varied or revoked by a subsequent direction under this section.

(8) Any direction given under this section shall be in writing.

(9) This section does not apply to copyright works made available to the public on agreed contractual terms in such a way that members of the public may access them from a place and at a time individually chosen by them.

(10) This section applies only where a complainant has lawful access to the protected copyright work, or where the complainant is a representative of a class of persons, where the class of persons have lawful access to the work.

(11) Subsections (1) to (10) apply with any necessary adaptations to –

(a) rights in performances, and in this context the expression 'permitted act' refers to an act that may be done by virtue of a provision of this Act listed in Part 2 of Schedule 5A;

(b) database right, and in this context the expression 'permitted act' refers to an act that may be done by virtue of a provision of this Act listed in Part 3 of Schedule 5A; and

(c) publication right.]

Amendment: Section substituted, together with ss 296, 296ZA–296ZD, 296ZF, for s 296 as originally enacted: SI 2003/2498, regs 3, 24(1).

[296ZF   Interpretation of sections 296ZA to 296ZE]

[(1) In sections 296ZA to 296ZE, 'technological measures' are any technology, device or component which is designed, in the normal course of its operation, to protect a copyright work other than a computer program.

(2) Such measures are 'effective' if the use of the work is controlled by the copyright owner through –

(a) an access control or protection process such as encryption, scrambling or other transformation of the work, or

(b) a copy control mechanism,

which achieves the intended protection.

(3) In this section, the reference to –

(a) protection of a work is to the prevention or restriction of acts that are not authorised by the copyright owner of that work and are restricted by copyright; and

(b) use of a work does not extend to any use of the work that is outside the scope of the acts restricted by copyright.

(4) Expressions used in sections 296ZA to 296ZE which are defined for the purposes of Part 1 of this Act (copyright) have the same meaning as in that Part.]

Amendment: Section substituted, together with ss 296, 296ZA–296ZE, for s 296 as originally enacted: SI 2003/2498, regs 3, 24(1).

[Rights management information]

Amendment: Heading inserted: SI 2003/2498, regs 3, 25.

[296ZG   Electronic rights management information]

[(1) This section applies where a person (D), knowingly and without authority, removes or alters electronic rights management information which –

(a) is associated with a copy of a copyright work, or

(b) appears in connection with the communication to the public of a copyright work, and

where D knows, or has reason to believe, that by so doing he is inducing, enabling, facilitating or concealing an infringement of copyright.

(2) This section also applies where a person (E), knowingly and without authority, distributes, imports for distribution or communicates to the public copies of a copyright work from which electronic rights management information –

(a) associated with the copies, or

(b) appearing in connection with the communication to the public of the work,

has been removed or altered without authority and where E knows, or has reason to believe, that by so doing he is inducing, enabling, facilitating or concealing an infringement of copyright.

(3) A person issuing to the public copies of, or communicating, the work to the public, has the same rights against D and E as a copyright owner has in respect of an infringement of copyright.

(4) The copyright owner or his exclusive licensee, if he is not the person issuing to the public copies of, or communicating, the work to the public, also has the same rights against D and E as he has in respect of an infringement of copyright.

(5) The rights conferred by subsections (3) and (4) are concurrent, and sections 101(3) and 102(1) to (4) apply, in proceedings under this section, in relation to persons with concurrent rights as they apply, in proceedings mentioned in those provisions, in relation to a copyright owner and exclusive licensee with concurrent rights.

(6) The following provisions apply in relation to proceedings under this section as in relation to proceedings under Part 1 (copyright) –

(a) sections 104 to 106 of this Act (presumptions as to certain matters relating to copyright); and

(b) section 72 of the Supreme Court Act 1981, section 15 of the Law Reform (Miscellaneous Provisions) (Scotland) Act 1985 and section 94A of the Judicature (Northern Ireland) Act 1978 (withdrawal of privilege against self-incrimination in certain proceedings relating to intellectual property).

(7) In this section –

(a) expressions which are defined for the purposes of Part 1 of this Act (copyright) have the same meaning as in that Part; and

(b) 'rights management information' means any information provided by the copyright owner or the holder of any right under copyright which identifies the work, the author, the copyright owner or the holder of any intellectual property rights, or information about the terms and conditions of use of the work, and any numbers or codes that represent such information.

(8) Subsections (1) to (5) and (6)(b), and any other provision of this Act as it has effect for the purposes of those subsections, apply, with any necessary adaptations, to rights in performances, publication right and database right.

(9) The provisions of regulation 22 (presumptions relevant to database right) of the Copyright and Rights in Databases Regulations 1997 (SI 1997/3032) apply in proceedings brought by virtue of this section in relation to database right.]

Amendment: Section inserted: SI 2003/2498, regs 3, 25.

Computer programs

296A   Avoidance of certain terms

(1) Where a person has the use of a computer program under an agreement, any term or condition in the agreement shall be void in so far as it purports to prohibit or restrict –

  (a)   the making of any back up copy of the program which it is necessary for him to have for the purposes of the agreed use;
  (b)   where the conditions in section 50B(2) are met, the decompiling of the program; or
  [(c)   the observing, studying or testing of the functioning of the program in accordance with section 50BA].

(2) In this section, decompile, in relation to a computer program, has the same meaning as in section 50B.

Amendment: Paragraph (c) substituted: SI 2003/2498, regs 3, 15(4).

Databases

299   Supplementary provisions as to fraudulent reception

(1) Her Majesty may by Order in Council –

  (a)   provide that section 297 applies in relation to programmes included in services provided from a country or territory outside the United Kingdom, and
  (b)   provide that section 298 applies in relation to such programmes and to encrypted transmissions sent from such a country or territory.

(2) ...

(3) A statutory instrument containing an Order in Council under subsection (1) shall be subject to annulment in pursuance of a resolution of either House of Parliament.

(4) Where sections 297 and 298 apply in relation to a broadcasting service . . . , they also apply to any service run for the person providing that service, or a person providing programmes for that service, which consists wholly or mainly in the sending by means of a telecommunications system of sounds or visual images, or both.

(5) In sections 297, 297A and 298, and this section, 'programme' [and 'broadcasting'], and related expressions, have the same meaning as in Part I (copyright).

Amendments: Words omitted repealed: SI 2003/2498, reg 2(2), Sch 2. Words in square brackets substituted: SI 2003/2498, reg 2(1), Sch 1, Pt 1, paras 1, 3(3).

301   Provisions for the benefit of the Hospital for Sick Children

The provisions of Schedule 6 have effect for conferring on trustees for the benefit of the Hospital for Sick Children, Great Ormond Street, London, a right to a royalty in respect of the public performance, commercial publication [or communication to the public] of the play 'Peter Pan' by Sir James Matthew Barrie, or of any adaptation of that work, notwithstanding that copyright in the work expired on 31st December 1987.

Amendment: Words in square brackets substituted: SI 2003/2498, reg 2(1), Sch 1, Pt 1, paras 1, 6(2)(d).

SCHEDULES

SCHEDULE 1

COPYRIGHT: TRANSITIONAL PROVISIONS AND SAVINGS

Section 170

Introductory

[9 No copyright subsists in –

    (a) a wireless broadcast made before 1st June 1957, or
    (b) a broadcast by cable made before 1st January 1985;

and any such broadcast shall be disregarded for the purposes of section 14(5) (duration of copyright in repeats).]

12(1) The following provisions have effect with respect to the duration of copyright in existing works.

The question which provision applies to a work shall be determined by reference to the facts immediately before commencement; and expressions used in this paragraph which were defined for the purposes of the 1956 Act have the same meaning as in that Act.

(2) Copyright in the following descriptions of work continues to subsist until the date on which it would have expired under the 1956 Act –

    (a) literary, dramatic or musical works in relation to which the period of 50 years mentioned in the proviso to section 2(3) of the 1956 Act (duration of copyright in works made available to the public after the death of the author) has begun to run;
    (b) engravings in relation to which the period of 50 years mentioned in the proviso to section 3(4) of the 1956 Act (duration of copyright in works published after the death of the author) has begun to run;
    (c) published photographs and photographs taken before 1st June 1957;
    (d) published sound recordings and sound recordings made before 1st June 1957;
    (e) published films and films falling within section 13(3)(a) of the 1956 Act (films registered under former enactments relating to registration of films).

(3) Copyright in anonymous or pseudonymous literary, dramatic, musical or artistic works (other than photographs) continues to subsist –

    (a) if the work is published, until the date on which it would have expired in accordance with the 1956 Act, and
    (b) if the work is unpublished, until the end of the period of 50 years from the end of the calendar year in which the new copyright provisions come into force or, if during that period the work is first made available to the public within the meaning of [section 12(3)] (duration of copyright in works of unknown authorship), the date on which copyright expires in accordance with that provision;

unless, in any case, the identity of the author becomes known before that date, in which case [section 12(2)] applies (general rule: life of the author [plus 70] years).

(4) Copyright in the following descriptions of work continues to subsist until the end of the period of 50 years from the end of the calendar year in which the new copyright provisions come into force –

(a) literary, dramatic and musical works of which the author has died and in relation to which none of the acts mentioned in paragraphs (a) to (e) of the proviso to section 2(3) of the 1956 Act has been done;

(b) unpublished engravings of which the author has died;

(c) unpublished photographs taken on or after 1st June 1957.

(5) Copyright in the following descriptions of work continues to subsist until the end of the period of 50 years from the end of the calendar year in which the new copyright provisions come into force –

(a) unpublished sound recordings made on or after 1st June 1957;

(b) films not falling within sub-paragraph (2)(e) above,

unless the recording or film is published before the end of that period in which case copyright in it shall continue until the end of the period of 50 years from the end of the calendar year in which the recording or film is published.

(6) Copyright in any other description of existing work continues to subsist until the date on which copyright in that description of work expires in accordance with sections 12 to 15 of this Act.

(7) The above provisions do not apply to works subject to Crown or Parliamentary copyright (see paragraphs 41 to 43 below).

15(1) Section 57 (anonymous or pseudonymous works: acts permitted on assumptions as to expiry of copyright or death of author) has effect in relation to existing works subject to the following provisions.

(2) Subsection (1)(b)(i) (assumption as to expiry of copyright) does not apply in relation to –

(a) photographs, or

(b) the rights mentioned in paragraph 13 above (rights conferred by the Copyright Act 1775).

(3) . . .

17 Where in the case of a dramatic or musical work made before 1st July 1912, the right conferred by the 1911 Act did not include the sole right to perform the work in public, the acts restricted by the copyright shall be treated as not including –

(a) performing the work in public,

[(b) communicating the work to the public, or]

(c) doing any of the above in relation to an adaptation of the work;

and where the right conferred by the 1911 Act consisted only of the sole right to perform the work in public, the acts restricted by the copyright shall be treated as consisting only of those acts.

Amendments: Paragraph 9 substituted: SI 2003/2498, reg 2(1), Sch 1, Pt 1, paras 1, 16(a). Words in square brackets in para 12(3) substituted: SI 2003/2498, reg 2(1), Sch 1, Pt 1, paras 1, 18(3). Paragraph 15(3) repealed: SI 2003/2498, reg 2, Sch 1, Pt 1, paras 1, 16(b), Sch 2. Paragraph 17(b) substituted by SI 2003/2498, reg 2(1), Sch 1, Pt 1, paras 1, 4(6).

SCHEDULE 2

RIGHTS IN PERFORMANCES: PERMITTED ACTS

Section 189

[Making of temporary copies

1A The rights conferred by Part 2 are not infringed by the making of a temporary copy of a recording of a performance which is transient or incidental, which is an integral and essential part of a technological process and the sole purpose of which is to enable –

   (a)   a transmission of the recording in a network between third parties by an intermediary; or
   (b)   a lawful use of the recording;

and which has no independent economic significance.]

Criticism, reviews and news reporting

2 [(1) Fair dealing with a performance or recording for the purpose of criticism or review, of that or another performance or recording, or of a work, does not infringe any of the rights conferred by Part 2 provided that the performance or recording has been made available to the public.

(1A) Fair dealing with a performance or recording for the purpose of reporting current events does not infringe any of the rights conferred by Part 2.]

(2) Expressions used in this paragraph have the same meaning as in section 30.

Incidental inclusion of performance or recording

3(1) The rights conferred by Part II are not infringed by the incidental inclusion of a performance or recording in a sound recording, film [or broadcast].

(2) Nor are those rights infringed by anything done in relation to copies of, or the playing, showing [or communication to the public] of, anything whose making was, by virtue of sub-paragraph (1), not an infringement of those rights.

(3) A performance or recording so far as it consists of music, or words spoken or sung with music, shall not be regarded as incidentally included in a sound recording [or broadcast] if it is deliberately included.

(4) Expressions used in this paragraph have the same meaning as in section 31.

Things done for purposes of instruction or examination

4(1) The rights conferred by Part II are not infringed by the copying of a recording of a performance in the course of instruction, or of preparation for instruction, in the making of films or film sound-tracks, provided the copying is done by a person giving or receiving instruction [and the instruction is for a non-commercial purpose].

(2) The rights conferred by Part II are not infringed –

   (a)   by the copying of a recording of a performance for the purposes of setting or answering the questions in an examination, or

(b) by anything done for the purposes of an examination by way of communicating the questions to the candidates.

(3) Where a recording which would otherwise be an illicit recording is made in accordance with this paragraph but is subsequently dealt with, it shall be treated as an illicit recording for the purposes of that dealing, and if that dealing infringes any right conferred by Part II for all subsequent purposes.

[For this purpose 'dealt with' means –

(a) sold or let for hire, offered or exposed for sale or hire; or
(b) communicated to the public, unless that communication, by virtue of sub-paragraph (2)(b), is not an infringement of the rights conferred by Part 2.]

(4) Expressions used in this paragraph have the same meaning as in section 32.

Playing or showing sound recording, film [or broadcast] at educational establishment

5(1) The playing or showing of a sound recording, film [or broadcast] at an educational establishment for the purposes of instruction before an audience consisting of teachers and pupils at the establishment and other persons directly connected with the activities of the establishment is not a playing or showing of a performance in public for the purposes of infringement of the rights conferred by Part II.

(2) A person is not for this purpose directly connected with the activities of the educational establishment simply because he is the parent of a pupil at the establishment.

(3) Expressions used in this paragraph have the same meaning as in section 34 and any provision made under section 174(2) with respect to the application of that section also applies for the purposes of this paragraph.

Recording of broadcasts ... by educational establishments

6(1) A recording of a broadcast ... , or a copy of such a recording, may be made by or on behalf of an educational establishment for the educational purposes of that establishment without thereby infringing any of the rights conferred by Part II in relation to any performance or recording included in it[, provided that the educational purposes are non-commercial].

[(1A) The rights conferred by Part 2 are not infringed where a recording of a broadcast or a copy of such a recording, whose making was by virtue of sub-paragraph (1) not an infringement of such rights, is communicated to the public by a person situated within the premises of an educational establishment provided that the communication cannot be received by any person situated outside the premises of that establishment.

(1B) This paragraph does not apply if or to the extent that there is a licensing scheme certified for the purposes of this paragraph under paragraph 16 of Schedule 2A providing for the grant of licences.]

(2) Where a recording which would otherwise be an illicit recording is made in accordance with this paragraph but is subsequently dealt with, it shall be treated as an illicit recording for the purposes of that dealing, and if that dealing infringes any right conferred by Part II for all subsequent purposes.

For this purpose 'dealt with' means sold or let for hire[, offered or exposed for sale or hire, or communicated from within the premises of an educational establishment to any person situated outside those premises].

(3) Expressions used in this paragraph have the same meaning as in section 35 and any provision made under section 174(2) with respect to the application of that section also applies for the purposes of this paragraph.

Use of recordings of spoken works in certain cases

13(1) Where a recording of the reading or recitation of a literary work is made for the purpose –

    (a) of reporting current events, or
    (b) of [communicating to the public] the whole or part of the reading or recitation,

it is not an infringement of the rights conferred by Part II to use the recording (or to copy the recording and use the copy) for that purpose, provided the following conditions are met.

(2) The conditions are that –

    (a) the recording is a direct recording of the reading or recitation and is not taken from a previous recording or from a broadcast . . .;
    (b) the making of the recording was not prohibited by or on behalf of the person giving the reading or recitation;
    (c) the use made of the recording is not of a kind prohibited by or on behalf of that person before the recording was made; and
    (d) the use is by or with the authority of a person who is lawfully in possession of the recording.

(3) Expressions used in this paragraph have the same meaning as in section 58.

15(1) It is not an infringement of any right conferred by Part II to play a sound recording as part of the activities of, or for the benefit of, a club, society or other organisation if the following conditions are met.

(2) The conditions are –

    (a) that the organisation is not established or conducted for profit and its main objects are charitable or are otherwise concerned with the advancement of religion, education or social welfare,
    [(b) that the sound recording is played by a person who is acting primarily and directly for the benefit of the organisation and who is not acting with a view to gain,
    (c) that the proceeds of any charge for admission to the place where the recording is to be heard are applied solely for the purposes of the organisation, and
    (d) that the proceeds from any goods or services sold by, or on behalf of, the organisation –
        (i)   in the place where the sound recording is heard, and
        (ii)   on the occasion when the sound recording is played,
        are applied solely for the purposes of the organisation].

(3) Expressions used in this paragraph have the same meaning as in section 67.

Incidental recording for purposes of broadcast . . .

16(1) A person who proposes to broadcast a recording of a performance. . . in circumstances not infringing the rights conferred by Part II shall be treated as having consent for the purposes of that Part for the making of a further recording for the purposes of the broadcast . . ..

(2) That consent is subject to the condition that the further recording –

    (a) shall not be used for any other purpose, and

(b) shall be destroyed within 28 days of being first used for broadcasting the performance

. . ..

(3) A recording made in accordance with this paragraph shall be treated as an illicit recording –

(a) for the purposes of any use in breach of the condition mentioned in sub-paragraph (2)(a), and
(b) for all purposes after that condition or the condition mentioned in sub-paragraph (2)(b) is broken.

(4) Expressions used in this paragraph have the same meaning as in section 68.

Recordings for purposes of supervision and control of broadcasts and [other services]

17(1) The rights conferred by Part II are not infringed by the making or use by the British Broadcasting Corporation, for the purpose of maintaining supervision and control over programmes broadcast by them, of recordings of those programmes.

[(2) The rights conferred by Part II are not infringed by anything done in pursuance of –

(a) section 11(1), 95(1) or 167(1) of the Broadcasting Act 1990 or section 115(4) or (6), 116(5) or 117 of the Broadcasting Act 1996;
(b) a condition which, by virtue of section 11(2) or 95(2) of the Broadcasting Act 1990, is included in a licence granted under Part I or III of that Act or Part I or II of the Broadcasting Act 1996; or
(c) a direction given under section 109(2) of the Broadcasting Act 1990 (power of Radio Authority to require production of recordings etc).

(3) The rights conferred by Part II are not infringed by –

(a) the use by the Independent Television Commission or the Radio Authority, in connection with the performance of any of their functions under the Broadcasting Act 1990 or the Broadcasting Act 1996, of any recording, script or transcript which is provided to them under or by virtue of any provision of those Acts; or
(b) the use by the Broadcasting Standards Commission, in connection with any complaint made to them under the Broadcasting Act 1996, of any recording or transcript requested or required to be provided to them, and so provided, under section 115(4) or (6) or 116(5) of that Act.

(3) The rights conferred by Part 2 are not infringed by the use by OFCOM in connection with the performance of any of their functions under the Broadcasting Act 1990, the Broadcasting Act 1996 or the Communications Act 2003 of –

(a) any recording, script or transcript which is provided to them under or by virtue of any provision of those Acts; or
(b) any existing material which is transferred to them by a scheme made under section 30 of the Communications Act 2003.

(4) In subsection (3), 'existing material' means –

(a) any recording, script or transcript which was provided to the Independent Television Commission or the Radio Authority under or by virtue of any provision of the Broadcasting Act 1990 or the Broadcasting Act 1996; and
(b) any recording or transcript which was provided to the Broadcasting Standards Commission under section 115(4) or (6) or 116(5) of the Broadcasting Act 1996.

[Recording for the purposes of time-shifting

17A(1) The making in domestic premises for private and domestic use of a recording of a broadcast solely for the purpose of enabling it to be viewed or listened to at a more convenient time does not infringe any right conferred by Part 2 in relation to a performance or recording included in the broadcast.

(2) Where a recording which would otherwise be an illicit recording is made in accordance with this paragraph but is subsequently dealt with –

(a)   it shall be treated as an illicit recording for the purposes of that dealing; and
(b)   if that dealing infringes any right conferred by Part 2, it shall be treated as an illicit recording for all subsequent purposes.

(3) In sub-paragraph (2), 'dealt with' means sold or let for hire, offered or exposed for sale or hire or communicated to the public.

(4) Expressions used in this paragraph have the same meaning as in section 70.]

[Photographs of broadcasts

17B(1) The making in domestic premises for private and domestic use of a photograph of the whole or any part of an image forming part of a broadcast, or a copy of such a photograph, does not infringe any right conferred by Part 2 in relation to a performance or recording included in the broadcast.

(2) Where a recording which would otherwise be an illicit recording is made in accordance with this paragraph but is subsequently dealt with –

(a)   it shall be treated as an illicit recording for the purposes of that dealing; and
(b)   if that dealing infringes any right conferred by Part 2, it shall be treated as an illicit recording for all subsequent purposes.

(3) In sub-paragraph (2), 'dealt with' means sold or let for hire, offered or exposed for sale or hire or communicated to the public.

(4) Expressions used in this paragraph have the same meaning as in section 71.]

Free public showing or playing of broadcast …

18(1) The showing or playing in public of a broadcast … to an audience who have not paid for admission to the place where the broadcast … is to be seen or heard does not infringe any right conferred by Part II in relation to a performance or recording included in –

(a)   the broadcast … , or
(b)   any sound recording [(except so far as it is an excepted sound recording)] or film which is played or shown in public by reception of the broadcast ….

[(1A) The showing or playing in public of a broadcast to an audience who have not paid for admission to the place where the broadcast is to be seen or heard does not infringe any right conferred by Part 2 in relation to a performance or recording included in any excepted sound recording which is played in public by reception of the broadcast, if the playing or showing of that broadcast in public –

(a)   forms part of the activities of an organisation that is not established or conducted for profit; or
(b)   is necessary for the purposes of –

(i)   repairing equipment for the reception of broadcasts;

(ii)   demonstrating that a repair to such equipment has been carried out; or

(iii)   demonstrating such equipment which is being sold or let for hire or offered or exposed for sale or hire.]

(2) The audience shall be treated as having paid for admission to a place –

(a)   if they have paid for admission to a place of which that place forms part; or

(b)   if goods or services are supplied at that place (or a place of which it forms part) –

    (i)   at prices which are substantially attributable to the facilities afforded for seeing or hearing the broadcast ... , or

    (ii)   at prices exceeding those usually charged there and which are partly attributable to those facilities.

(3) The following shall not be regarded as having paid for admission to a place –

(a)   persons admitted as residents or inmates of the place;

(b)   persons admitted as members of a club or society where the payment is only for membership of the club or society and the provision of facilities for seeing or hearing broadcasts ... is only incidental to the main purposes of the club or society.

(4) Where the making of the broadcast ... was an infringement of the rights conferred by Part II in relation to a performance or recording, the fact that it was heard or seen in public by the reception of the broadcast ... shall be taken into account in assessing the damages for that infringement.

(5) Expressions used in this paragraph have the same meaning as in section 72.

Reception and re-transmission of [wireless broadcast by cable]

19(1) This paragraph applies where a [wireless] broadcast made from a place in the United Kingdom is [received and immediately re-transmitted by cable].

(2) The rights conferred by Part II in relation to a performance or recording included in the broadcast are not infringed if and to the extent that the broadcast is made for reception in the area in which [it is re-transmitted by cable]; but where the making of the broadcast was an infringement of those rights, the fact that the broadcast was re-transmitted [by cable] shall be taken into account in assessing the damages for that infringement.

(3) Where –

(a)   the [re-transmission by cable] is in pursuance of a relevant requirement, but

(b)   to any extent, the area in which the [re-transmission by cable takes place] ('the cable area') falls outside the area for reception in which the broadcast is made ('the broadcast area'),

the [re-transmission by cable] (to the extent that it is provided for so much of the cable area as falls outside the broadcast area) of any performance or recording included in the broadcast shall, subject to sub-paragraph (4), be treated as licensed by the owner of the rights conferred by Part II in relation to the performance or recording, subject only to the payment to him by the person making the broadcast of such reasonable royalty or other payment in respect of the [re-transmission by cable of the broadcast] as may be agreed or determined in default of agreement by the Copyright Tribunal.

(4) Sub-paragraph (3) does not apply if, or to the extent that, the [re-transmission of the performance or recording by cable] is (apart from that sub-paragraph) licensed by the owner of the rights conferred by Part II in relation to the performance or recording.

(5) The Secretary of State may by order –

    (a) provide that in specified cases sub-paragraph (2) is to apply in relation to broadcasts of a specified description which are not made as mentioned in that sub-paragraph, or

    (b) exclude the application of that sub-paragraph in relation to broadcasts of a specified description made as mentioned in that sub-paragraph.

(6) Where the Secretary of State exercises the power conferred by sub-paragraph (5)(b) in relation to broadcasts of any description, the order may also provide for sub-paragraph (3) to apply, subject to such modifications as may be specified in the order, in relation to broadcasts of that description.

(7) An order under this paragraph may contain such transitional provision as appears to the Secretary of State to be appropriate.

(8) An order under this paragraph shall be made by statutory instrument which shall be subject to annulment in pursuance of a resolution of either House of Parliament.

(9) Expressions used in this paragraph have the same meaning as in section 73.

Provision of sub-titled copies of broadcast . . .

20(1) A designated body may, for the purpose of providing people who are deaf or hard of hearing, or physically or mentally handicapped in other ways, with copies which are sub-titled or otherwise modified for their special needs, make recordings of [broadcasts and copies of such recordings, and issue or lend copies to the public,] without infringing any right conferred by Part II in relation to a performance or recording included in the broadcast . . .

[(1A) This paragraph does not apply if, or to the extent that, there is a licensing scheme certified for the purposes of this paragraph under paragraph 16 of Schedule 2A providing for the grant of licences.]

(2) In this paragraph 'designated body' means a body designated for the purposes of section 74 and other expressions used in this paragraph have the same meaning as in that section.

Recording of broadcast . . . for archival purposes

21(1) A recording of a broadcast . . . of a designated class, or a copy of such a recording, may be made for the purpose of being placed in an archive maintained by a designated body without thereby infringing any right conferred by Part II in relation to a performance or recording included in the broadcast . . . .

(2) In this paragraph 'designated class' and 'designated body' means a class or body designated for the purposes of section 75 and other expressions used in this paragraph have the same meaning as in that section.

Amendment: Paragraph 1A inserted: SI 2003/2498, regs 3, 8(2). Paragraph 2(1), (1A) substituted for sub-para (1) as originally enacted: SI 2003/2498, regs 3, 10(2). Paragraph 6(1A), (1B) inserted: SI 2003/2498, regs 3, 12(2)(b). Paragraph 15(2)(b)–(d) substituted, for sub-para (2)(b) and word 'and' immediately preceding it as originally enacted: SI 2003/2498, regs 3, 18(2). Paragraph 17A inserted: SI 2003/2498, regs 3, 19(3). Paragraph 17B inserted: SI 2003/2498, regs 3, 20(2). Paragraph 18(1A) inserted: SI 2003/2498, regs 3, 21(2)(b). Paragraph 20(1A) inserted: SI 2003/2498, regs 3, 23(2)(b). Words in square brackets substituted or inserted: SI 2003/2498, reg 2(1), Sch 1, Pt 1, paras 1, 2(1),(2), 3(1), 6(2)(e), 11(2), 12, 21(2)(a), 22(3)(b), (c), (d), (e), 23(2). Words omitted repealed: SI 2003/2498, reg 2(2), Sch 2.

[SCHEDULE 5A

PERMITTED ACTS TO WHICH SECTION 296ZE APPLIES]

Amendment: Heading inserted: SI 2003/2498, regs 3, 24(2), Sch 3.

[Section 296ZE]

Amendment: Heading inserted: SI 2003/2498, regs 3, 24(2), Sch 3.

[PART 1

COPYRIGHT EXCEPTIONS]

Amendment: Heading inserted: SI 2003/2498, regs 3, 24(2), Sch 3.

[section 29 (research and private study)

section 31A (making a single accessible copy for personal use)

section 31B (multiple copies for visually impaired persons)

section 31C (intermediate copies and records)]

section 32(1), (2) and (3) (things done for purposes of instruction or examination)

section 35 (recording by educational establishments of broadcasts)

section 36 (reprographic copying by educational establishments of passages from published works)

section 38 (copying by librarians: articles in periodicals)

section 39 (copying by librarians: parts of published works)

section 41 (copying by librarians: supply of copies to other libraries)

section 42 (copying by librarians or archivists: replacement copies of works)

section 43 (copying by librarians or archivists: certain unpublished works)

section 44 (copy of work required to be made as condition of export)

section 45 (Parliamentary and judicial proceedings)

section 46 (Royal Commissions and statutory inquiries)

section 47 (material open to public inspection or on official register)

section 48 (material communicated to the Crown in the course of public business)

section 49 (public records)

section 50 (acts done under statutory authority)

section 61 (recordings of folksongs)

section 68 (incidental recording for purposes of broadcast)

section 69 (recording for purposes of supervision and control of broadcasts)

section 70 (recording for purposes of time-shifting)

section 71 (photographs of broadcasts)

section 74 (provision of sub-titled copies of broadcast)

section 75 (recording for archival purposes)]

Amendment: Part inserted: SI 2003/2498, regs 3, 24(2), Sch 3.

[PART 2

RIGHTS IN PERFORMANCES EXCEPTIONS]

Amendment: Heading inserted: SI 2003/2498, regs 3, 24(2), Sch 3.

[paragraph 4 of Schedule 2 (things done for purposes of instruction or examination)

paragraph 6 of Schedule 2 (recording of broadcasts by educational establishments)

paragraph 7 of Schedule 2 (copy of work required to be made as condition of export)

paragraph 8 of Schedule 2 (Parliamentary and judicial proceedings)

paragraph 9 of Schedule 2 (Royal Commissions and statutory inquiries)

paragraph 10 of Schedule 2 (public records)

paragraph 11 of Schedule 2 (acts done under statutory authority)

paragraph 14 of Schedule 2 (recordings of folksongs)

paragraph 16 of Schedule 2 (incidental recording for purposes of broadcast)

paragraph 17 of Schedule 2 (recordings for purposes of supervision and control of broadcasts)

paragraph 17A of Schedule 2 (recording for the purposes of time-shifting)

paragraph 17B of Schedule 2 (photographs of broadcasts)

paragraph 20 of Schedule 2 (provision of sub-titled copies of broadcast)

paragraph 21 of Schedule 2 (recording of broadcast for archival purposes)]

Amendment: Part inserted: SI 2003/2498, regs 3, 24(2), Sch 3.

[PART 3

DATABASE RIGHT EXCEPTIONS]

Amendment: Heading inserted: SI 2003/2498, regs 3, 24(2), Sch 3.

[regulation 20 of and Schedule 1 to the Copyright and Rights in Databases Regulations 1997 (SI 1997/3032)]

Amendment: Part inserted: SI 2003/2498, regs 3, 24(2), Sch 3.

SCHEDULE 6

PROVISIONS FOR THE BENEFIT OF THE HOSPITAL FOR SICK CHILDREN

Section 301

Interpretation

1(1) In this Schedule –

'the Hospital' means The Hospital for Sick Children, Great Ormond Street, London,

'the trustees' means the special trustees appointed for the Hospital under the National Health Service Act 1977; and

'the work' means the play 'Peter Pan' by Sir James Matthew Barrie.

(2) Expressions used in this Schedule which are defined for the purposes of Part I of this Act (copyright) have the same meaning as in that Part.

Entitlement to royalty

2(1) The trustees are entitled, subject to the following provisions of this Schedule, to a royalty in respect of any public performance, commercial publication [or communication to the public] of the whole or any substantial part of the work or an adaptation of it.

(2) Where the trustees are or would be entitled to a royalty, another form of remuneration may be agreed.

Exceptions

3 No royalty is payable in respect of –

    (a) anything which immediately before copyright in the work expired on 31st December 1987 could lawfully have been done without the licence, or further licence, of the trustees as copyright owners; or

    (b) anything which if copyright still subsisted in the work could, by virtue of any provision of Chapter III of Part I of this Act (acts permitted notwithstanding copyright), be done without infringing copyright.

Saving

4 No royalty is payable in respect of anything done in pursuance of arrangements made before the passing of this Act.

Procedure for determining amount payable

5(1) In default of agreement application may be made to the Copyright Tribunal which shall consider the matter and make such order regarding the royalty or other remuneration to be paid as it may determine to be reasonable in the circumstances.

(2) Application may subsequently be made to the Tribunal to vary its order, and the Tribunal shall consider the matter and make such order confirming or varying the original order as it may determine to be reasonable in the circumstances.

(3) An application for variation shall not, except with the special leave of the Tribunal, be made within twelve months from the date of the original order or of the order on a previous application for variation.

(4) A variation order has effect from the date on which it is made or such later date as may be specified by the Tribunal.

(5) The provisions of Chapter VIII of Part I (general provisions relating to the Copyright Tribunal) apply in relation to the Tribunal when exercising any jurisdiction under this paragraph.

Sums received to be held on trust

6 The sums received by the trustees by virtue of this Schedule, after deduction of any relevant expenses, shall be held by them on trust for the purposes of the Hospital.

Right only for the benefit of the Hospital

7(1) The right of the trustees under this Schedule may not be assigned and shall cease if the trustees purport to assign or charge it.

(2) The right may not be the subject of an order under section 92 of the National Health Service Act 1977 (transfers of trust property by order of the Secretary of State) and shall cease if the Hospital ceases to have a separate identity or ceases to have purposes which include the care of sick children.

(3) Any power of Her Majesty, the court (within the meaning of the Charities Act 1993) or any other person to alter the trusts of a charity is not exercisable in relation to the trust created by this Schedule.

Amendment: Words in square brackets substituted: SI 2003/2498, reg 2(1), Sch 1, Pt 1, paras 1, 6(2)(f).

Appendix 3

COPYRIGHT AND RELATED RIGHTS REGULATIONS 2003, PART 3

SI 2003/2498

[Parts 1 and 2 of these Regulations amend the Copyright, Designs and Patents Act 1988. The effect of these amendments is shown in Appendix 2.]

30 Introductory

(1) In this Part –

'commencement' means the date upon which these regulations come into force;

'extended copyright' means any copyright in sound recordings which subsists by virtue of section 13A of the 1988 Act (as amended by regulation 29) after the date on which it would have expired under the 1988 provisions;

'prospective owner' includes a person who is prospectively entitled to extended copyright in a sound recording by virtue of such an agreement as is mentioned in regulation 37(1);

'the 1988 Act' means the Copyright, Designs and Patents Act 1988; and

'the 1988 provisions' means the provisions of the 1988 Act as they stood immediately before commencement (including the provisions of Schedule 1 to that Act continuing the effect of earlier enactments).

(2) Expressions used in this Part which are defined for the purposes of Part 1 or 2 of the 1988 Act have the same meaning as in that Part.

31 General rules

(1) Subject to regulation 32, these Regulations apply to –

(a) copyright works made,
(b) performances given,
(c) databases, in which database right vests, made, and
(d) works, in which publication right vests, first published,

before or after commencement.

(2) No act done before commencement shall be regarded as an infringement of any new or extended right arising by virtue of these Regulations.

32 Savings for certain existing agreements

(1) Nothing in these Regulations affects any agreement made before 22nd December 2002.

(2) No act done after commencement, in pursuance of an agreement made before 22nd December 2002, shall be regarded as an infringement of any new or extended right arising by virtue of these Regulations.

Special provisions

33 Permitted acts

The provisions of Chapter 3 of Part 1 (acts permitted in relation to copyright works) and Schedule 2 (rights in performances: permitted acts) in the 1988 provisions shall continue to apply to anything done after commencement in completion of an act begun before commencement which was permitted by those provisions.

34 Performers' rights: making available to the public

(1) Those parts of section 182D in the 1988 provisions which confer a right to equitable remuneration in relation to the making available to the public in the way mentioned in section 182CA(1) (regulation 7) of a commercially published sound recording shall cease to apply on commencement.

(2) Any assignment made before commencement under the provisions of section 182D(2) shall, on commencement, cease to apply insofar as it relates to the new making available to the public right conferred by section 182CA (regulation 7).

35 Exercise of rights in relation to performances

(1) The new right conferred by section 182CA (consent required for making available to the public) (in regulation 7) is exercisable as from commencement by the performer or (if he has died) by the person who immediately before commencement was entitled by virtue of section 192A(2) to exercise the rights conferred on the performer by Part 2 in relation to that performance.

(2) Any damages received by a person's personal representatives by virtue of the right conferred by paragraph (1) shall devolve as part of that person's estate as if the right had subsisted and been vested in him immediately before his death.

36 Ownership of extended copyright in sound recordings

The person who is the owner of the copyright in a sound recording immediately before commencement is as from commencement the owner of any extended copyright in that sound recording.

37 Prospective ownership of extended copyright in sound recordings

(1) Where by an agreement made before commencement in relation to extended copyright in a sound recording, and signed by or on behalf of the prospective owner of the copyright, the prospective owner purports to assign the extended copyright (wholly or partially) to another person, then, if on commencement the assignee or another person claiming under him would be entitled as against all other persons to require the copyright to be vested in him, the copyright shall vest in the assignee or his successor in title by virtue of this paragraph.

(2) A licence granted by a prospective owner of extended copyright in a sound recording is binding on every successor in title to his interest (or prospective interest) in the right, except a purchaser in good faith for valuable consideration and without notice (actual or constructive) of the licence or a person deriving title from such a purchaser; and references in Part 1 of the 1988 Act to doing anything with, or without, the licence of the copyright owner shall be construed accordingly.

38   Extended copyright in sound recordings: existing licences, agreements, etc

(1) Any copyright licence or any term or condition of an agreement relating to the exploitation of a sound recording which –

   (a)   subsists immediately before commencement in relation to an existing sound recording, and
   (b)   is not to expire before the end of the copyright period under the 1988 provisions,

shall continue to have effect during the period of any extended copyright in that sound recording, subject to any agreement to the contrary.

(2) Any copyright licence, or term or condition relating to the exploitation of a sound recording, imposed by order of the Copyright Tribunal which –

   (a)   subsists immediately before commencement in relation to an existing sound recording, and
   (b)   is not to expire before the end of the copyright period under the 1988 provisions,

shall continue to have effect during the period of any extended copyright, subject to any further order of the Tribunal.

39   Duration of copyright in sound recordings: general saving

Copyright in an existing sound recording shall continue to subsist until the date it would have expired under regulation 15 of the Duration of Copyright and Rights in Performances Regulations 1995 (SI 1995/3297) if that date is later than the date on which copyright would expire under the provisions of section 13A of the 1988 Act as amended by regulation 29.

40   Sanctions and remedies

(1) Section 296 in the 1988 provisions (devices designed to circumvent copy-protection) shall continue to apply to acts done in relation to computer programs or other works prior to commencement.

(2) Section 296 as substituted by regulation 24(1) (circumvention of technical devices applied to computer programs), and sections 296ZA (circumvention of technological measures) and 296ZD (rights and remedies in respect of devices designed to circumvent technological measures), introduced by regulation 24(1), shall apply to acts done in relation to computer programs or other works on or after commencement.

(3) Sections 107(2A), 198(1A) and 296ZB(1) and (2) (offences) do not have effect in relation to any act committed before commencement.

Appendix 4

BERNE CONVENTION FOR THE PROTECTION OF LITERARY AND ARTISTIC WORKS, Arts 1–20

Paris Act
of July 24, 1971, as amended on September 28, 1979

The countries of the Union, being equally animated by the desire to protect, in as effective and uniform a manner as possible, the rights of authors in their literary and artistic works,

Recognizing the importance of the work of the Revision Conference held at Stockholm in 1967,

Have resolved to revise the Act adopted by the Stockholm Conference, while maintaining without change Articles 1 to 20 and 22 to 26 of that Act.

Consequently, the undersigned Plenipotentiaries, having presented their full powers, recognized as in good and due form, have agreed as follows:

Article 1
[Establishment of a Union][1]

The countries to which this Convention applies constitute a Union for the protection of the rights of authors in their literary and artistic works.

Article 2
[Protected Works: 1. 'Literary and artistic works'; 2. Possible requirement of fixation; 3. Derivative works; 4. Official texts; 5. Collections; 6. Obligation to protect; beneficiaries of protection; 7. Works of applied art and industrial designs; 8. News]

(1)   The expression 'literary and artistic works' shall include every production in the literary, scientific and artistic domain, whatever may be the mode or form of its expression, such as books, pamphlets and other writings; lectures, addresses, sermons and other works of the same nature; dramatic or dramatico-musical works; choreographic works and entertainments in dumb show; musical compositions with or without words; cinematographic works to which are assimilated works expressed by a process analogous to cinematography; works of drawing, painting, architecture, sculpture, engraving and lithography; photographic works to which are assimilated works expressed by a process analogous to photography; works of applied art; illustrations, maps, plans, sketches and three-dimensional works relative to geography, topography, architecture or science.

(2)   It shall, however, be a matter for legislation in the countries of the Union to prescribe that works in general or any specified categories of works shall not be protected unless they have been fixed in some material form.

---

1   Each Article and the Appendix have been given titles to facilitate their identification. There are no titles in the signed (English) text.

(3)   Translations, adaptations, arrangements of music and other alterations of a literary or artistic work shall be protected as original works without prejudice to the copyright in the original work.

(4)   It shall be a matter for legislation in the countries of the Union to determine the protection to be granted to official texts of a legislative, administrative and legal nature, and to official translations of such texts.

(5)   Collections of literary or artistic works such as encyclopaedias and anthologies which, by reason of the selection and arrangement of their contents, constitute intellectual creations shall be protected as such, without prejudice to the copyright in each of the works forming part of such collections.

(6)   The works mentioned in this Article shall enjoy protection in all countries of the Union. This protection shall operate for the benefit of the author and his successors in title.

(7)   Subject to the provisions of Article 7(4) of this Convention, it shall be a matter for legislation in the countries of the Union to determine the extent of the application of their laws to works of applied art and industrial designs and models, as well as the conditions under which such works, designs and models shall be protected. Works protected in the country of origin solely as designs and models shall be entitled in another country of the Union only to such special protection as is granted in that country to designs and models; however, if no such special protection is granted in that country, such works shall be protected as artistic works.

(8)   The protection of this Convention shall not apply to news of the day or to miscellaneous facts having the character of mere items of press information.

Article 2bis
[Possible Limitation of Protection of Certain Works: **1. Certain speeches; 2. Certain uses of lectures and addresses; 3. Right to make collections of such works]**

(1)   It shall be a matter for legislation in the countries of the Union to exclude, wholly or in part, from the protection provided by the preceding Article political speeches and speeches delivered in the course of legal proceedings.

(2)   It shall also be a matter for legislation in the countries of the Union to determine the conditions under which lectures, addresses and other works of the same nature which are delivered in public may be reproduced by the press, broadcast, communicated to the public by wire and made the subject of public communication as envisaged in Article 11bis(1) of this Convention, when such use is justified by the informatory purpose.

(3)   Nevertheless, the author shall enjoy the exclusive right of making a collection of his works mentioned in the preceding paragraphs.

Article 3
[Criteria of Eligibility for Protection: **1. Nationality of author; place of publication of work; 2. Residence of author; 3: 'Published' works; 4. 'Simultaneously published' works]**

(1)   The protection of this Convention shall apply to:

  (a)   authors who are nationals of one of the countries of the Union, for their works, whether published or not;
  (b)   authors who are not nationals of one of the countries of the Union, for their works first published in one of those countries, or simultaneously in a country outside the Union and in a country of the Union.

(2)   Authors who are not nationals of one of the countries of the Union but who have their habitual residence in one of them shall, for the purposes of this Convention, be assimilated to nationals of that country.

(3)   The expression 'published works' means works published with the consent of their authors, whatever may be the means of manufacture of the copies, provided that the availability of such copies has been such as to satisfy the reasonable requirements of the public, having regard to the nature of the work. The performance of a dramatic, dramatico-musical, cinematographic or musical work, the public recitation of a literary work, the communication by wire or the broadcasting of literary or artistic works, the exhibition of a work of art and the construction of a work of architecture shall not constitute publication.

(4)   A work shall be considered as having been published simultaneously in several countries if it has been published in two or more countries within thirty days of its first publication.

Article 4
[*Criteria of Eligibility for Protection of Cinematographic Works, Works of Architecture and Certain Artistic Works*]

The protection of this Convention shall apply, even if the conditions of Article 3 are not fulfilled, to:

  (a)   authors of cinematographic works the maker of which has his headquarters or habitual residence in one of the countries of the Union;
  (b)   authors of works of architecture erected in a country of the Union or of other artistic works incorporated in a building or other structure located in a country of the Union.

Article 5
[*Rights Guaranteed:* 1. and 2. Outside the country of origin; 3. In the country of origin; 4. 'Country of origin']

(1)   Authors shall enjoy, in respect of works for which they are protected under this Convention, in countries of the Union other than the country of origin, the rights which their respective laws do now or may hereafter grant to their nationals, as well as the rights specially granted by this Convention.

(2)   The enjoyment and the exercise of these rights shall not be subject to any formality; such enjoyment and such exercise shall be independent of the existence of protection in the country of origin of the work. Consequently, apart from the provisions of this Convention, the extent of protection, as well as the means of redress afforded to the author to protect his rights, shall be governed exclusively by the laws of the country where protection is claimed.

(3)   Protection in the country of origin is governed by domestic law. However, when the author is not a national of the country of origin of the work for which he is protected under this Convention, he shall enjoy in that country the same rights as national authors.

(4)   The country of origin shall be considered to be:

  (a)   in the case of works first published in a country of the Union, that country; in the case of works published simultaneously in several countries of the Union which grant different terms of protection, the country whose legislation grants the shortest term of protection;
  (b)   in the case of works published simultaneously in a country outside the Union and in a country of the Union, the latter country;
  (c)   in the case of unpublished works or of works first published in a country outside the Union, without simultaneous publication in a country of the Union, the country of the Union of which the author is a national, provided that:

(i)   when these are cinematographic works the maker of which has his headquarters or his habitual residence in a country of the Union, the country of origin shall be that country, and

(ii)   when these are works of architecture erected in a country of the Union or other artistic works incorporated in a building or other structure located in a country of the Union, the country of origin shall be that country.

Article 6
[Possible Restriction of Protection in Respect of Certain Works of Nationals of Certain Countries Outside the Union: **1. In the country of the first publication and in other countries; 2. No retroactivity; 3. Notice]**

(1)   Where any country outside the Union fails to protect in an adequate manner the works of authors who are nationals of one of the countries of the Union, the latter country may restrict the protection given to the works of authors who are, at the date of the first publication thereof, nationals of the other country and are not habitually resident in one of the countries of the Union. If the country of first publication avails itself of this right, the other countries of the Union shall not be required to grant to works thus subjected to special treatment a wider protection than that granted to them in the country of first publication.

(2)   No restrictions introduced by virtue of the preceding paragraph shall affect the rights which an author may have acquired in respect of a work published in a country of the Union before such restrictions were put into force.

(3)   The countries of the Union which restrict the grant of copyright in accordance with this Article shall give notice thereof to the Director General of the World Intellectual Property Organization (hereinafter designated as 'the Director General') by a written declaration specifying the countries in regard to which protection is restricted, and the restrictions to which rights of authors who are nationals of those countries are subjected. The Director General shall immediately communicate this declaration to all the countries of the Union.

Article 6bis
[Moral Rights: **1. To claim authorship; to object to certain modifications and other derogatory actions; 2. After the author's death; 3. Means of redress]**

(1)   Independently of the author's economic rights, and even after the transfer of the said rights, the author shall have the right to claim authorship of the work and to object to any distortion, mutilation or other modification of, or other derogatory action in relation to, the said work, which would be prejudicial to his honor or reputation.

(2)   The rights granted to the author in accordance with the preceding paragraph shall, after his death, be maintained, at least until the expiry of the economic rights, and shall be exercisable by the persons or institutions authorized by the legislation of the country where protection is claimed. However, those countries whose legislation, at the moment of their ratification of or accession to this Act, does not provide for the protection after the death of the author of all the rights set out in the preceding paragraph may provide that some of these rights may, after his death, cease to be maintained.

(3)   The means of redress for safeguarding the rights granted by this Article shall be governed by the legislation of the country where protection is claimed.

Article 7
[*Term of Protection:* 1. Generally; 2. For cinematographic works; 3. For anonymous and pseudonymous works; 4. For photographic works and works of applied art; 5. Starting date of computation; 6. Longer terms; 7. Shorter terms; 8. Applicable law; 'comparison' of terms]

(1)   The term of protection granted by this Convention shall be the life of the author and fifty years after his death.

(2)   However, in the case of cinematographic works, the countries of the Union may provide that the term of protection shall expire fifty years after the work has been made available to the public with the consent of the author, or, failing such an event within fifty years from the making of such a work, fifty years after the making.

(3)   In the case of anonymous or pseudonymous works, the term of protection granted by this Convention shall expire fifty years after the work has been lawfully made available to the public. However, when the pseudonym adopted by the author leaves no doubt as to his identity, the term of protection shall be that provided in paragraph (1). If the author of an anonymous or pseudonymous work discloses his identity during the above-mentioned period, the term of protection applicable shall be that provided in paragraph (1). The countries of the Union shall not be required to protect anonymous or pseudonymous works in respect of which it is reasonable to presume that their author has been dead for fifty years.

(4)   It shall be a matter for legislation in the countries of the Union to determine the term of protection of photographic works and that of works of applied art in so far as they are protected as artistic works; however, this term shall last at least until the end of a period of twenty-five years from the making of such a work.

(5)   The term of protection subsequent to the death of the author and the terms provided by paragraphs (2), (3) and (4) shall run from the date of death or of the event referred to in those paragraphs, but such terms shall always be deemed to begin on the first of January of the year following the death or such event.

(6)   The countries of the Union may grant a term of protection in excess of those provided by the preceding paragraphs.

(7)   Those countries of the Union bound by the Rome Act of this Convention which grant, in their national legislation in force at the time of signature of the present Act, shorter terms of protection than those provided for in the preceding paragraphs shall have the right to maintain such terms when ratifying or acceding to the present Act.

(8)   In any case, the term shall be governed by the legislation of the country where protection is claimed; however, unless the legislation of that country otherwise provides, the term shall not exceed the term fixed in the country of origin of the work.

Article 7bis
[*Term of Protection for Works of Joint Authorship*]

The provisions of the preceding Article shall also apply in the case of a work of joint authorship, provided that the terms measured from the death of the author shall be calculated from the death of the last surviving author.

Article 8
[*Right of Translation*]

Authors of literary and artistic works protected by this Convention shall enjoy the exclusive right of making and of authorizing the translation of their works throughout the term of protection of their rights in the original works.

Article 9
[*Right of Reproduction:* 1. Generally; 2. Possible exceptions; 3. Sound and visual recordings]

(1)   Authors of literary and artistic works protected by this Convention shall have the exclusive right of authorizing the reproduction of these works, in any manner or form.

(2)   It shall be a matter for legislation in the countries of the Union to permit the reproduction of such works in certain special cases, provided that such reproduction does not conflict with a normal exploitation of the work and does not unreasonably prejudice the legitimate interests of the author.

(3)   Any sound or visual recording shall be considered as a reproduction for the purposes of this Convention.

Article 10
[*Certain Free Uses of Works:* 1. Quotations; 2. Illustrations for teaching; 3. Indication of source and author]

(1)   It shall be permissible to make quotations from a work which has already been lawfully made available to the public, provided that their making is compatible with fair practice, and their extent does not exceed that justified by the purpose, including quotations from newspaper articles and periodicals in the form of press summaries.

(2)   It shall be a matter for legislation in the countries of the Union, and for special agreements existing or to be concluded between them, to permit the utilization, to the extent justified by the purpose, of literary or artistic works by way of illustration in publications, broadcasts or sound or visual recordings for teaching, provided such utilization is compatible with fair practice.

(3)   Where use is made of works in accordance with the preceding paragraphs of this Article, mention shall be made of the source, and of the name of the author if it appears thereon.

Article 10bis
[*Further Possible Free Uses of Works:* 1. Of certain articles and broadcast works; 2. Of works seen or heard in connection with current events]

(1)   It shall be a matter for legislation in the countries of the Union to permit the reproduction by the press, the broadcasting or the communication to the public by wire of articles published in newspapers or periodicals on current economic, political or religious topics, and of broadcast works of the same character, in cases in which the reproduction, broadcasting or such communication thereof is not expressly reserved. Nevertheless, the source must always be clearly indicated; the legal consequences of a breach of this obligation shall be determined by the legislation of the country where protection is claimed.

(2)   It shall also be a matter for legislation in the countries of the Union to determine the conditions under which, for the purpose of reporting current events by means of photography, cinematography, broadcasting or communication to the public by wire, literary or artistic works seen or heard in the course of the event may, to the extent justified by the informatory purpose, be reproduced and made available to the public.

Article 11
[*Certain Rights in Dramatic and Musical Works:* 1. Right of public performance and of communication to the public of a performance; 2. In respect of translations]

(1)　Authors of dramatic, dramatico-musical and musical works shall enjoy the exclusive right of authorizing:

(i)　the public performance of their works, including such public performance by any means or process;

(ii)　any communication to the public of the performance of their works.

(2)　Authors of dramatic or dramatico-musical works shall enjoy, during the full term of their rights in the original works, the same rights with respect to translations thereof.

Article 11bis
[*Broadcasting and Related Rights:* 1. Broadcasting and other wireless communications, public communication of broadcast by wire or rebroadcast, public communication of broadcast by loudspeaker or analogous instruments; 2. Compulsory licenses; 3. Recording; ephemeral recordings]

(1)　Authors of literary and artistic works shall enjoy the exclusive right of authorizing:

(i)　the broadcasting of their works or the communication thereof to the public by any other means of wireless diffusion of signs, sounds or images;

(ii)　any communication to the public by wire or by rebroadcasting of the broadcast of the work, when this communication is made by an organization other than the original one;

(iii)　the public communication by loudspeaker or any other analogous instrument transmitting, by signs, sounds or images, the broadcast of the work.

(2)　It shall be a matter for legislation in the countries of the Union to determine the conditions under which the rights mentioned in the preceding paragraph may be exercised, but these conditions shall apply only in the countries where they have been prescribed. They shall not in any circumstances be prejudicial to the moral rights of the author, nor to his right to obtain equitable remuneration which, in the absence of agreement, shall be fixed by competent authority.

(3)　In the absence of any contrary stipulation, permission granted in accordance with paragraph (1) of this Article shall not imply permission to record, by means of instruments recording sounds or images, the work broadcast. It shall, however, be a matter for legislation in the countries of the Union to determine the regulations for ephemeral recordings made by a broadcasting organization by means of its own facilities and used for its own broadcasts. The preservation of these recordings in official archives may, on the ground of their exceptional documentary character, be authorized by such legislation.

Article 11ter
[*Certain Rights in Literary Works:* 1. Right of public recitation and of communication to the public of a recitation; 2. In respect of translations]

(1)　Authors of literary works shall enjoy the exclusive right of authorizing:

(i)　the public recitation of their works, including such public recitation by any means or process;

(ii)　any communication to the public of the recitation of their works.

(2)　Authors of literary works shall enjoy, during the full term of their rights in the original works, the same rights with respect to translations thereof.

Article 12
[*Right of Adaptation, Arrangement and Other Alteration*]

Authors of literary or artistic works shall enjoy the exclusive right of authorizing adaptations, arrangements and other alterations of their works.

Article 13
[*Possible Limitation of the Right of Recording of Musical Works and Any Words Pertaining Thereto:* 1. Compulsory licenses; 2. Transitory measures; 3. Seizure on importation of copies made without the author's permission]

(1)   Each country of the Union may impose for itself reservations and conditions on the exclusive right granted to the author of a musical work and to the author of any words, the recording of which together with the musical work has already been authorized by the latter, to authorize the sound recording of that musical work, together with such words, if any; but all such reservations and conditions shall apply only in the countries which have imposed them and shall not, in any circumstances, be prejudicial to the rights of these authors to obtain equitable remuneration which, in the absence of agreement, shall be fixed by competent authority.

(2)   Recordings of musical works made in a country of the Union in accordance with Article 13(3) of the Conventions signed at Rome on June 2, 1928, and at Brussels on June 26, 1948, may be reproduced in that country without the permission of the author of the musical work until a date two years after that country becomes bound by this Act.

(3)   Recordings made in accordance with paragraphs (1) and (2) of this Article and imported without permission from the parties concerned into a country where they are treated as infringing recordings shall be liable to seizure.

Article 14
[*Cinematographic and Related Rights:* 1. Cinematographic adaptation and reproduction; distribution; public performance and public communication by wire of works thus adapted or reproduced; 2. Adaptation of cinematographic productions; 3. No compulsory licenses]

(1)   Authors of literary or artistic works shall have the exclusive right of authorizing:

   (i)   the cinematographic adaptation and reproduction of these works, and the distribution of the works thus adapted or reproduced;
   (ii) the public performance and communication to the public by wire of the works thus adapted or reproduced.

(2)   The adaptation into any other artistic form of a cinematographic production derived from literary or artistic works shall, without prejudice to the authorization of the author of the cinematographic production, remain subject to the authorization of the authors of the original works.

(3)   The provisions of Article 13(1) shall not apply.

Article 14bis
[*Special Provisions Concerning Cinematographic Works:* 1. Assimilation to 'original' works; 2. Ownership; limitation of certain rights of certain contributors; 3. Certain other contributors]

(1)   Without prejudice to the copyright in any work which may have been adapted or reproduced, a cinematographic work shall be protected as an original work. The owner of

copyright in a cinematographic work shall enjoy the same rights as the author of an original work, including the rights referred to in the preceding Article.

(2)

(a) Ownership of copyright in a cinematographic work shall be a matter for legislation in the country where protection is claimed.

(b) However, in the countries of the Union which, by legislation, include among the owners of copyright in a cinematographic work authors who have brought contributions to the making of the work, such authors, if they have undertaken to bring such contributions, may not, in the absence of any contrary or special stipulation, object to the reproduction, distribution, public performance, communication to the public by wire, broadcasting or any other communication to the public, or to the subtitling or dubbing of texts, of the work.

(c) The question whether or not the form of the undertaking referred to above should, for the application of the preceding subparagraph (b), be in a written agreement or a written act of the same effect shall be a matter for the legislation of the country where the maker of the cinematographic work has his headquarters or habitual residence. However, it shall be a matter for the legislation of the country of the Union where protection is claimed to provide that the said undertaking shall be in a written agreement or a written act of the same effect. The countries whose legislation so provides shall notify the Director General by means of a written declaration, which will be immediately communicated by him to all the other countries of the Union.

(d) By 'contrary or special stipulation' is meant any restrictive condition which is relevant to the aforesaid undertaking.

(3) Unless the national legislation provides to the contrary, the provisions of paragraph (2)(b) above shall not be applicable to authors of scenarios, dialogues and musical works created for the making of the cinematographic work, or to the principal director thereof. However, those countries of the Union whose legislation does not contain rules providing for the application of the said paragraph (2)(b) to such director shall notify the Director General by means of a written declaration, which will be immediately communicated by him to all the other countries of the Union.

Article 14ter
[*'Droit de suite' in Works of Art and Manuscripts:* 1. Right to an interest in resales;
2. Applicable law; 3. Procedure]

(1) The author, or after his death the persons or institutions authorized by national legislation, shall, with respect to original works of art and original manuscripts of writers and composers, enjoy the inalienable right to an interest in any sale of the work subsequent to the first transfer by the author of the work.

(2) The protection provided by the preceding paragraph may be claimed in a country of the Union only if legislation in the country to which the author belongs so permits, and to the extent permitted by the country where this protection is claimed.

(3) The procedure for collection and the amounts shall be matters for determination by national legislation.

Article 15
[Right to Enforce Protected Rights: **1. Where author's name is indicated or where pseudonym leaves no doubt as to author's identity; 2. In the case of cinematographic works; 3. In the case of anonymous and pseudonymous works; 4. In the case of certain unpublished works of unknown authorship]**

(1)   In order that the author of a literary or artistic work protected by this Convention shall, in the absence of proof to the contrary, be regarded as such, and consequently be entitled to institute infringement proceedings in the countries of the Union, it shall be sufficient for his name to appear on the work in the usual manner. This paragraph shall be applicable even if this name is a pseudonym, where the pseudonym adopted by the author leaves no doubt as to his identity.

(2)   The person or body corporate whose name appears on a cinematographic work in the usual manner shall, in the absence of proof to the contrary, be presumed to be the maker of the said work.

(3)   In the case of anonymous and pseudonymous works, other than those referred to in paragraph (1) above, the publisher whose name appears on the work shall, in the absence of proof to the contrary, be deemed to represent the author, and in this capacity he shall be entitled to protect and enforce the author's rights. The provisions of this paragraph shall cease to apply when the author reveals his identity and establishes his claim to authorship of the work.

(4)

    (a)   In the case of unpublished works where the identity of the author is unknown, but where there is every ground to presume that he is a national of a country of the Union, it shall be a matter for legislation in that country to designate the competent authority which shall represent the author and shall be entitled to protect and enforce his rights in the countries of the Union.

    (b)   Countries of the Union which make such designation under the terms of this provision shall notify the Director General by means of a written declaration giving full information concerning the authority thus designated. The Director General shall at once communicate this declaration to all other countries of the Union.

Article 16
[Infringing Copies: **1. Seizure; 2. Seizure on importation; 3. Applicable law]**

(1)   Infringing copies of a work shall be liable to seizure in any country of the Union where the work enjoys legal protection.

(2)   The provisions of the preceding paragraph shall also apply to reproductions coming from a country where the work is not protected, or has ceased to be protected.

(3)   The seizure shall take place in accordance with the legislation of each country.

Article 17
[Possibility of Control of Circulation, Presentation and Exhibition of Works]

The provisions of this Convention cannot in any way affect the right of the Government of each country of the Union to permit, to control, or to prohibit, by legislation or regulation, the circulation, presentation, or exhibition of any work or production in regard to which the competent authority may find it necessary to exercise that right.

Article 18
[*Works Existing on Convention's Entry Into Force:* 1. Protectable where protection not yet expired in country of origin; 2. Non-protectable where protection already expired in country where it is claimed; 3. Application of these principles; 4. Special cases]

(1)   This Convention shall apply to all works which, at the moment of its coming into force, have not yet fallen into the public domain in the country of origin through the expiry of the term of protection.

(2)   If, however, through the expiry of the term of protection which was previously granted, a work has fallen into the public domain of the country where protection is claimed, that work shall not be protected anew.

(3)   The application of this principle shall be subject to any provisions contained in special conventions to that effect existing or to be concluded between countries of the Union. In the absence of such provisions, the respective countries shall determine, each in so far as it is concerned, the conditions of application of this principle.

(4)   The preceding provisions shall also apply in the case of new accessions to the Union and to cases in which protection is extended by the application of Article 7 or by the abandonment of reservations.

Article 19
[*Protection Greater than Resulting from Convention*]

The provisions of this Convention shall not preclude the making of a claim to the benefit of any greater protection which may be granted by legislation in a country of the Union.

Article 20
[*Special Agreements Among Countries of the Union*]

The Governments of the countries of the Union reserve the right to enter into special agreements among themselves, in so far as such agreements grant to authors more extensive rights than those granted by the Convention, or contain other provisions not contrary to this Convention. The provisions of existing agreements which satisfy these conditions shall remain applicable.

Appendix 5

AGREEMENT ON TRADE-RELATED ASPECTS OF INTELLECTUAL PROPERTY RIGHTS ('the TRIPs Agreement'), Arts 1–21, 39, 40–50

Article 1
Nature and Scope of Obligations

1.   Members shall give effect to the provisions of this Agreement. Members may, but shall not be obliged to, implement in their law more extensive protection than is required by this Agreement, provided that such protection does not contravene the provisions of this Agreement. Members shall be free to determine the appropriate method of implementing the provisions of this Agreement within their own legal system and practice.

2.   For the purposes of this Agreement, the term 'intellectual property' refers to all categories of intellectual property that are the subject of Sections 1 through 7 of Part II.

3.   Members shall accord the treatment provided for in this Agreement to the nationals of other Members.[1] In respect of the relevant intellectual property right, the nationals of other Members shall be understood as those natural or legal persons that would meet the criteria for eligibility for protection provided for in the Paris Convention (1967), the Berne Convention (1971), the Rome Convention and the Treaty on Intellectual Property in Respect of Integrated Circuits, were all Members of the WTO members of those conventions.[2] Any Member availing itself of the possibilities provided in paragraph 3 of Article 5 or paragraph 2 of Article 6 of the Rome Convention shall make a notification as foreseen in those provisions to the Council for Trade-Related Aspects of Intellectual Property Rights (the 'Council for TRIPS').

---

1   When 'nationals' are referred to in this Agreement, they shall be deemed, in the case of a separate customs territory Member of the WTO, to mean persons, natural or legal, who are domiciled or who have a real and effective industrial or commercial establishment in that customs territory.

2   In this Agreement, 'Paris Convention' refers to the Paris Convention for the Protection of Industrial Property; 'Paris Convention (1967)' refers to the Stockholm Act of this Convention of 14 July 1967. 'Berne Convention' refers to the Berne Convention for the Protection of Literary and Artistic Works; 'Berne Convention (1971)' refers to the Paris Act of this Convention of 24 July 1971. 'Rome Convention' refers to the International Convention for the Protection of Performers, Producers of Phonograms and Broadcasting Organizations, adopted at Rome on 26 October 1961. 'Treaty on Intellectual Property in Respect of Integrated Circuits' (IPIC Treaty) refers to the Treaty on Intellectual Property in Respect of Integrated Circuits, adopted at Washington on 26 May 1989. 'WTO Agreement' refers to the Agreement Establishing the WTO.

Article 2
Intellectual Property Conventions

1.   In respect of Parts II, III and IV of this Agreement, Members shall comply with Articles 1 through 12, and Article 19, of the Paris Convention (1967).

2.   Nothing in Parts I to IV of this Agreement shall derogate from existing obligations that Members may have to each other under the Paris Convention, the Berne Convention, the Rome Convention and the Treaty on Intellectual Property in Respect of Integrated Circuits.

Article 3
National Treatment

1.   Each Member shall accord to the nationals of other Members treatment no less favourable than that it accords to its own nationals with regard to the protection[3] of intellectual property, subject to the exceptions already provided in, respectively, the Paris Convention (1967), the Berne Convention (1971), the Rome Convention or the Treaty on Intellectual Property in Respect of Integrated Circuits. In respect of performers, producers of phonograms and broadcasting organizations, this obligation only applies in respect of the rights provided under this Agreement. Any Member availing itself of the possibilities provided in Article 6 of the Berne Convention (1971) or paragraph 1(b) of Article 16 of the Rome Convention shall make a notification as foreseen in those provisions to the Council for TRIPS.

2.   Members may avail themselves of the exceptions permitted under paragraph 1 in relation to judicial and administrative procedures, including the designation of an address for service or the appointment of an agent within the jurisdiction of a Member, only where such exceptions are necessary to secure compliance with laws and regulations which are not inconsistent with the provisions of this Agreement and where such practices are not applied in a manner which would constitute a disguised restriction on trade.

Article 4
Most-Favoured-Nation Treatment

With regard to the protection of intellectual property, any advantage, favour, privilege or immunity granted by a Member to the nationals of any other country shall be accorded immediately and unconditionally to the nationals of all other Members. Exempted from this obligation are any advantage, favour, privilege or immunity accorded by a Member:

   (a)   deriving from international agreements on judicial assistance or law enforcement of a general nature and not particularly confined to the protection of intellectual property;

   (b)   granted in accordance with the provisions of the Berne Convention (1971) or the Rome Convention authorizing that the treatment accorded be a function not of national treatment but of the treatment accorded in another country;

   (c)   in respect of the rights of performers, producers of phonograms and broadcasting organizations not provided under this Agreement;

   (d)   deriving from international agreements related to the protection of intellectual property which entered into force prior to the entry into force of the WTO Agreement, provided that such agreements are notified to the Council for TRIPS and do not constitute an arbitrary or unjustifiable discrimination against nationals of other Members.

---

3   For the purposes of Articles 3 and 4, 'protection' shall include matters affecting the availability, acquisition, scope, maintenance and enforcement of intellectual property rights as well as those matters affecting the use of intellectual property rights specifically addressed in this Agreement.

Article 5
Multilateral Agreements on Acquisition or Maintenance of Protection

The obligations under Articles 3 and 4 do not apply to procedures provided in multilateral agreements concluded under the auspices of WIPO relating to the acquisition or maintenance of intellectual property rights.

Article 6
Exhaustion

For the purposes of dispute settlement under this Agreement, subject to the provisions of Articles 3 and 4 nothing in this Agreement shall be used to address the issue of the exhaustion of intellectual property rights.

Article 7
Objectives

The protection and enforcement of intellectual property rights should contribute to the promotion of technological innovation and to the transfer and dissemination of technology, to the mutual advantage of producers and users of technological knowledge and in a manner conducive to social and economic welfare, and to a balance of rights and obligations.

Article 8
Principles

1.   Members may, in formulating or amending their laws and regulations, adopt measures necessary to protect public health and nutrition, and to promote the public interest in sectors of vital importance to their socio-economic and technological development, provided that such measures are consistent with the provisions of this Agreement.

2.   Appropriate measures, provided that they are consistent with the provisions of this Agreement, may be needed to prevent the abuse of intellectual property rights by right holders or the resort to practices which unreasonably restrain trade or adversely affect the international transfer of technology.

PART II
STANDARDS CONCERNING THE AVAILABILITY, SCOPE AND USE OF INTELLECTUAL PROPERTY RIGHTS

SECTION 1: COPYRIGHT AND RELATED RIGHTS

Article 9
Relation to the Berne Convention

1.   Members shall comply with Articles 1 through 21 of the Berne Convention (1971) and the Appendix thereto. However, Members shall not have rights or obligations under this Agreement in respect of the rights conferred under Article 6*bis* of that Convention or of the rights derived therefrom.

2.   Copyright protection shall extend to expressions and not to ideas, procedures, methods of operation or mathematical concepts as such.

Article 10
Computer Programs and Compilations of Data

1. Computer programs, whether in source or object code, shall be protected as literary works under the Berne Convention (1971).

2. Compilations of data or other material, whether in machine readable or other form, which by reason of the selection or arrangement of their contents constitute intellectual creations shall be protected as such. Such protection, which shall not extend to the data or material itself, shall be without prejudice to any copyright subsisting in the data or material itself.

Article 11
Rental Rights

In respect of at least computer programs and cinematographic works, a Member shall provide authors and their successors in title the right to authorize or to prohibit the commercial rental to the public of originals or copies of their copyright works. A Member shall be excepted from this obligation in respect of cinematographic works unless such rental has led to widespread copying of such works which is materially impairing the exclusive right of reproduction conferred in that Member on authors and their successors in title. In respect of computer programs, this obligation does not apply to rentals where the program itself is not the essential object of the rental.

Article 12
Term of Protection

Whenever the term of protection of a work, other than a photographic work or a work of applied art, is calculated on a basis other than the life of a natural person, such term shall be no less than 50 years from the end of the calendar year of authorized publication, or, failing such authorized publication within 50 years from the making of the work, 50 years from the end of the calendar year of making.

Article 13
Limitations and Exceptions

Members shall confine limitations or exceptions to exclusive rights to certain special cases which do not conflict with a normal exploitation of the work and do not unreasonably prejudice the legitimate interests of the right holder.

Article 14
Protection of Performers, Producers of Phonograms
(Sound Recordings) and Broadcasting Organizations

1. In respect of a fixation of their performance on a phonogram, performers shall have the possibility of preventing the following acts when undertaken without their authorization: the fixation of their unfixed performance and the reproduction of such fixation. Performers shall also have the possibility of preventing the following acts when undertaken without their authorization: the broadcasting by wireless means and the communication to the public of their live performance.

2. Producers of phonograms shall enjoy the right to authorize or prohibit the direct or indirect reproduction of their phonograms.

3. Broadcasting organizations shall have the right to prohibit the following acts when undertaken without their authorization: the fixation, the reproduction of fixations, and the

rebroadcasting by wireless means of broadcasts, as well as the communication to the public of television broadcasts of the same. Where Members do not grant such rights to broadcasting organizations, they shall provide owners of copyright in the subject matter of broadcasts with the possibility of preventing the above acts, subject to the provisions of the Berne Convention (1971).

4.   The provisions of Article 11 in respect of computer programs shall apply *mutatis mutandis* to producers of phonograms and any other right holders in phonograms as determined in a Member's law. If on 15 April 1994 a Member has in force a system of equitable remuneration of right holders in respect of the rental of phonograms, it may maintain such system provided that the commercial rental of phonograms is not giving rise to the material impairment of the exclusive rights of reproduction of right holders.

5.   The term of the protection available under this Agreement to performers and producers of phonograms shall last at least until the end of a period of 50 years computed from the end of the calendar year in which the fixation was made or the performance took place. The term of protection granted pursuant to paragraph 3 shall last for at least 20 years from the end of the calendar year in which the broadcast took place.

6.   Any Member may, in relation to the rights conferred under paragraphs 1, 2 and 3, provide for conditions, limitations, exceptions and reservations to the extent permitted by the Rome Convention. However, the provisions of Article 18 of the Berne Convention (1971) shall also apply, *mutatis mutandis*, to the rights of performers and producers of phonograms in phonograms.

SECTION 2: TRADEMARKS

Article 15
Protectable Subject Matter

1.   Any sign, or any combination of signs, capable of distinguishing the goods or services of one undertaking from those of other undertakings, shall be capable of constituting a trademark. Such signs, in particular words including personal names, letters, numerals, figurative elements and combinations of colours as well as any combination of such signs, shall be eligible for registration as trademarks. Where signs are not inherently capable of distinguishing the relevant goods or services, Members may make registrability depend on distinctiveness acquired through use. Members may require, as a condition of registration, that signs be visually perceptible.

2.   Paragraph 1 shall not be understood to prevent a Member from denying registration of a trademark on other grounds, provided that they do not derogate from the provisions of the Paris Convention (1967).

3.   Members may make registrability depend on use. However, actual use of a trademark shall not be a condition for filing an application for registration. An application shall not be refused solely on the ground that intended use has not taken place before the expiry of a period of three years from the date of application.

4.   The nature of the goods or services to which a trademark is to be applied shall in no case form an obstacle to registration of the trademark.

5.   Members shall publish each trademark either before it is registered or promptly after it is registered and shall afford a reasonable opportunity for petitions to cancel the registration. In addition, Members may afford an opportunity for the registration of a trademark to be opposed.

Article 16
Rights Conferred

1.   The owner of a registered trademark shall have the exclusive right to prevent all third parties not having the owner's consent from using in the course of trade identical or similar signs for goods or services which are identical or similar to those in respect of which the trademark is registered where such use would result in a likelihood of confusion. In case of the use of an identical sign for identical goods or services, a likelihood of confusion shall be presumed. The rights described above shall not prejudice any existing prior rights, nor shall they affect the possibility of Members making rights available on the basis of use.

2.   Article 6*bis* of the Paris Convention (1967) shall apply, *mutatis mutandis*, to services. In determining whether a trademark is well-known, Members shall take account of the knowledge of the trademark in the relevant sector of the public, including knowledge in the Member concerned which has been obtained as a result of the promotion of the trademark.

3.   Article 6*bis* of the Paris Convention (1967) shall apply, *mutatis mutandis*, to goods or services which are not similar to those in respect of which a trademark is registered, provided that use of that trademark in relation to those goods or services would indicate a connection between those goods or services and the owner of the registered trademark and provided that the interests of the owner of the registered trademark are likely to be damaged by such use.

Article 17
Exceptions

Members may provide limited exceptions to the rights conferred by a trademark, such as fair use of descriptive terms, provided that such exceptions take account of the legitimate interests of the owner of the trademark and of third parties.

Article 18
Term of Protection

Initial registration, and each renewal of registration, of a trademark shall be for a term of no less than seven years. The registration of a trademark shall be renewable indefinitely.

Article 19
Requirement of Use

1.   If use is required to maintain a registration, the registration may be cancelled only after an uninterrupted period of at least three years of non-use, unless valid reasons based on the existence of obstacles to such use are shown by the trademark owner. Circumstances arising independently of the will of the owner of the trademark which constitute an obstacle to the use of the trademark, such as import restrictions on or other government requirements for goods or services protected by the trademark, shall be recognized as valid reasons for non-use.

2.   When subject to the control of its owner, use of a trademark by another person shall be recognized as use of the trademark for the purpose of maintaining the registration.

Article 20
Other Requirements

The use of a trademark in the course of trade shall not be unjustifiably encumbered by special requirements, such as use with another trademark, use in a special form or use in a manner detrimental to its capability to distinguish the goods or services of one undertaking from those of other undertakings. This will not preclude a requirement prescribing the use of the trademark identifying the undertaking producing the goods or services along with, but without linking it to, the trademark distinguishing the specific goods or services in question of that undertaking.

Article 21
Licensing and Assignment

Members may determine conditions on the licensing and assignment of trademarks, it being understood that the compulsory licensing of trademarks shall not be permitted and that the owner of a registered trademark shall have the right to assign the trademark with or without the transfer of the business to which the trademark belongs.

SECTION 7: PROTECTION OF UNDISCLOSED INFORMATION

Article 39

1.   In the course of ensuring effective protection against unfair competition as provided in Article 10*bis* of the Paris Convention (1967), Members shall protect undisclosed information in accordance with paragraph 2 and data submitted to governments or governmental agencies in accordance with paragraph 3.

2.   Natural and legal persons shall have the possibility of preventing information lawfully within their control from being disclosed to, acquired by, or used by others without their consent in a manner contrary to honest commercial practices[4] so long as such information:

   (a)   is secret in the sense that it is not, as a body or in the precise configuration and assembly of its components, generally known among or readily accessible to persons within the circles that normally deal with the kind of information in question;
   (b)   has commercial value because it is secret; and
   (c)   has been subject to reasonable steps under the circumstances, by the person lawfully in control of the information, to keep it secret.

3.   Members, when requiring, as a condition of approving the marketing of pharmaceutical or of agricultural chemical products which utilize new chemical entities, the submission of undisclosed test or other data, the origination of which involves a considerable effort, shall protect such data against unfair commercial use. In addition, Members shall protect such data against disclosure, except where necessary to protect the public, or unless steps are taken to ensure that the data are protected against unfair commercial use.

SECTION 8: CONTROL OF ANTI-COMPETITIVE PRACTICES IN CONTRACTUAL LICENCES

Article 40

1.   Members agree that some licensing practices or conditions pertaining to intellectual property rights which restrain competition may have adverse effects on trade and may impede the transfer and dissemination of technology.

2.   Nothing in this Agreement shall prevent Members from specifying in their legislation licensing practices or conditions that may in particular cases constitute an abuse of intellectual property rights having an adverse effect on competition in the relevant market. As provided

---

4   For the purpose of this provision, 'a manner contrary to honest commercial practices' shall mean at least practices such as breach of contract, breach of confidence and inducement to breach, and includes the acquisition of undisclosed information by third parties who knew, or were grossly negligent in failing to know, that such practices were involved in the acquisition.

above, a Member may adopt, consistently with the other provisions of this Agreement, appropriate measures to prevent or control such practices, which may include for example exclusive grantback conditions, conditions preventing challenges to validity and coercive package licensing, in the light of the relevant laws and regulations of that Member.

3.   Each Member shall enter, upon request, into consultations with any other Member which has cause to believe that an intellectual property right owner that is a national or domiciliary of the Member to which the request for consultations has been addressed is undertaking practices in violation of the requesting Member's laws and regulations on the subject matter of this Section, and which wishes to secure compliance with such legislation, without prejudice to any action under the law and to the full freedom of an ultimate decision of either Member. The Member addressed shall accord full and sympathetic consideration to, and shall afford adequate opportunity for, consultations with the requesting Member, and shall cooperate through supply of publicly available non-confidential information of relevance to the matter in question and of other information available to the Member, subject to domestic law and to the conclusion of mutually satisfactory agreements concerning the safeguarding of its confidentiality by the requesting Member.

4.   A Member whose nationals or domiciliaries are subject to proceedings in another Member concerning alleged violation of that other Member's laws and regulations on the subject matter of this Section shall, upon request, be granted an opportunity for consultations by the other Member under the same conditions as those foreseen in paragraph 3.

PART III
ENFORCEMENT OF INTELLECTUAL PROPERTY RIGHTS

SECTION 1: GENERAL OBLIGATIONS

Article 41

1.   Members shall ensure that enforcement procedures as specified in this Part are available under their law so as to permit effective action against any act of infringement of intellectual property rights covered by this Agreement, including expeditious remedies to prevent infringements and remedies which constitute a deterrent to further infringements. These procedures shall be applied in such a manner as to avoid the creation of barriers to legitimate trade and to provide for safeguards against their abuse.

2.   Procedures concerning the enforcement of intellectual property rights shall be fair and equitable. They shall not be unnecessarily complicated or costly, or entail unreasonable time-limits or unwarranted delays.

3.   Decisions on the merits of a case shall preferably be in writing and reasoned. They shall be made available at least to the parties to the proceeding without undue delay. Decisions on the merits of a case shall be based only on evidence in respect of which parties were offered the opportunity to be heard.

4.   Parties to a proceeding shall have an opportunity for review by a judicial authority of final administrative decisions and, subject to jurisdictional provisions in a Member's law concerning the importance of a case, of at least the legal aspects of initial judicial decisions on the merits of a case. However, there shall be no obligation to provide an opportunity for review of acquittals in criminal cases.

5.   It is understood that this Part does not create any obligation to put in place a judicial system for the enforcement of intellectual property rights distinct from that for the enforcement of law

in general, nor does it affect the capacity of Members to enforce their law in general. Nothing in this Part creates any obligation with respect to the distribution of resources as between enforcement of intellectual property rights and the enforcement of law in general.

SECTION 2: CIVIL AND ADMINISTRATIVE PROCEDURES AND REMEDIES

Article 42
Fair and Equitable Procedures

Members shall make available to right holders[5] civil judicial procedures concerning the enforcement of any intellectual property right covered by this Agreement. Defendants shall have the right to written notice which is timely and contains sufficient detail, including the basis of the claims. Parties shall be allowed to be represented by independent legal counsel, and procedures shall not impose overly burdensome requirements concerning mandatory personal appearances. All parties to such procedures shall be duly entitled to substantiate their claims and to present all relevant evidence. The procedure shall provide a means to identify and protect confidential information, unless this would be contrary to existing constitutional requirements.

Article 43
Evidence

1.   The judicial authorities shall have the authority, where a party has presented reasonably available evidence sufficient to support its claims and has specified evidence relevant to substantiation of its claims which lies in the control of the opposing party, to order that this evidence be produced by the opposing party, subject in appropriate cases to conditions which ensure the protection of confidential information.

2.   In cases in which a party to a proceeding voluntarily and without good reason refuses access to, or otherwise does not provide necessary information within a reasonable period, or significantly impedes a procedure relating to an enforcement action, a Member may accord judicial authorities the authority to make preliminary and final determinations, affirmative or negative, on the basis of the information presented to them, including the complaint or the allegation presented by the party adversely affected by the denial of access to information, subject to providing the parties an opportunity to be heard on the allegations or evidence.

Article 44
Injunctions

1.   The judicial authorities shall have the authority to order a party to desist from an infringement, *inter alia* to prevent the entry into the channels of commerce in their jurisdiction of imported goods that involve the infringement of an intellectual property right, immediately after customs clearance of such goods. Members are not obliged to accord such authority in respect of protected subject matter acquired or ordered by a person prior to knowing or having reasonable grounds to know that dealing in such subject matter would entail the infringement of an intellectual property right.

2.   Notwithstanding the other provisions of this Part and provided that the provisions of Part II specifically addressing use by governments, or by third parties authorized by a government, without the authorization of the right holder are complied with, Members may limit the remedies available against such use to payment of remuneration in accordance with subparagraph (h) of Article 31. In other cases, the remedies under this Part shall apply or, where

---

5   For the purpose of this Part, the term 'right holder' includes federations and associations having legal standing to assert such rights.

these remedies are inconsistent with a Member's law, declaratory judgments and adequate compensation shall be available.

Article 45
Damages

1.   The judicial authorities shall have the authority to order the infringer to pay the right holder damages adequate to compensate for the injury the right holder has suffered because of an infringement of that person's intellectual property right by an infringer who knowingly, or with reasonable grounds to know, engaged in infringing activity.

2.   The judicial authorities shall also have the authority to order the infringer to pay the right holder expenses, which may include appropriate attorney's fees. In appropriate cases, Members may authorize the judicial authorities to order recovery of profits and/or payment of pre-established damages even where the infringer did not knowingly, or with reasonable grounds to know, engage in infringing activity.

Article 46
Other Remedies

In order to create an effective deterrent to infringement, the judicial authorities shall have the authority to order that goods that they have found to be infringing be, without compensation of any sort, disposed of outside the channels of commerce in such a manner as to avoid any harm caused to the right holder, or, unless this would be contrary to existing constitutional requirements, destroyed. The judicial authorities shall also have the authority to order that materials and implements the predominant use of which has been in the creation of the infringing goods be, without compensation of any sort, disposed of outside the channels of commerce in such a manner as to minimize the risks of further infringements. In considering such requests, the need for proportionality between the seriousness of the infringement and the remedies ordered as well as the interests of third parties shall be taken into account. In regard to counterfeit trademark goods, the simple removal of the trademark unlawfully affixed shall not be sufficient, other than in exceptional cases, to permit release of the goods into the channels of commerce.

Article 47
Right of Information

Members may provide that the judicial authorities shall have the authority, unless this would be out of proportion to the seriousness of the infringement, to order the infringer to inform the right holder of the identity of third persons involved in the production and distribution of the infringing goods or services and of their channels of distribution.

Article 48
Indemnification of the Defendant

1.   The judicial authorities shall have the authority to order a party at whose request measures were taken and who has abused enforcement procedures to provide to a party wrongfully enjoined or restrained adequate compensation for the injury suffered because of such abuse. The judicial authorities shall also have the authority to order the applicant to pay the defendant expenses, which may include appropriate attorney's fees.

2.   In respect of the administration of any law pertaining to the protection or enforcement of intellectual property rights, Members shall only exempt both public authorities and officials from liability to appropriate remedial measures where actions are taken or intended in good faith in the course of the administration of that law.

Article 49
Administrative Procedures

To the extent that any civil remedy can be ordered as a result of administrative procedures on the merits of a case, such procedures shall conform to principles equivalent in substance to those set forth in this Section.

SECTION 3: PROVISIONAL MEASURES

Article 50

1. The judicial authorities shall have the authority to order prompt and effective provisional measures:

    (a) to prevent an infringement of any intellectual property right from occurring, and in particular to prevent the entry into the channels of commerce in their jurisdiction of goods, including imported goods immediately after customs clearance;

    (b) to preserve relevant evidence in regard to the alleged infringement.

2. The judicial authorities shall have the authority to adopt provisional measures *inaudita altera parte* where appropriate, in particular where any delay is likely to cause irreparable harm to the right holder, or where there is a demonstrable risk of evidence being destroyed.

3. The judicial authorities shall have the authority to require the applicant to provide any reasonably available evidence in order to satisfy themselves with a sufficient degree of certainty that the applicant is the right holder and that the applicant's right is being infringed or that such infringement is imminent, and to order the applicant to provide a security or equivalent assurance sufficient to protect the defendant and to prevent abuse.

4. Where provisional measures have been adopted *inaudita altera parte*, the parties affected shall be given notice, without delay after the execution of the measures at the latest. A review, including a right to be heard, shall take place upon request of the defendant with a view to deciding, within a reasonable period after the notification of the measures, whether these measures shall be modified, revoked or confirmed.

5. The applicant may be required to supply other information necessary for the identification of the goods concerned by the authority that will execute the provisional measures.

6. Without prejudice to paragraph 4, provisional measures taken on the basis of paragraphs 1 and 2 shall, upon request by the defendant, be revoked or otherwise cease to have effect, if proceedings leading to a decision on the merits of the case are not initiated within a reasonable period, to be determined by the judicial authority ordering the measures where a Member's law so permits or, in the absence of such a determination, not to exceed 20 working days or 31 calendar days, whichever is the longer.

7. Where the provisional measures are revoked or where they lapse due to any act or omission by the applicant, or where it is subsequently found that there has been no infringement or threat of infringement of an intellectual property right, the judicial authorities shall have the authority to order the applicant, upon request of the defendant, to provide the defendant appropriate compensation for any injury caused by these measures.

8. To the extent that any provisional measure can be ordered as a result of administrative procedures, such procedures shall conform to principles equivalent in substance to those set forth in this Section.

Appendix 6

WIPO COPYRIGHT TREATY AND AGREED STATEMENTS

Article 1
Relation to the Berne Convention

(1)   This Treaty is a special agreement within the meaning of Article 20 of the Berne Convention for the Protection of Literary and Artistic Works, as regards Contracting Parties that are countries of the Union established by that Convention. This Treaty shall not have any connection with treaties other than the Berne Convention, nor shall it prejudice any rights and obligations under any other treaties.

(2)   Nothing in this Treaty shall derogate from existing obligations that Contracting Parties have to each other under the Berne Convention for the Protection of Literary and Artistic Works.

(3)   Hereinafter, 'Berne Convention' shall refer to the Paris Act of July 24, 1971 of the Berne Convention for the Protection of Literary and Artistic Works.

(4)   Contracting Parties shall comply with Articles 1 to 21 and the Appendix of the Berne Convention.[1]

Article 2
Scope of Copyright Protection

Copyright protection extends to expressions and not to ideas, procedures, methods of operation or mathematical concepts as such.

Article 3
Application of Articles 2 to 6 of the Berne Convention

Contracting Parties shall apply *mutatis mutandis* the provisions of Articles 2 to 6 of the Berne Convention in respect of the protection provided for in this Treaty.[2]

---

1   **Agreed statements concerning Article 1(4)**: The reproduction right, as set out in Article 9 of the Berne Convention, and the exceptions permitted thereunder, fully apply in the digital environment, in particular to the use of works in digital form. It is understood that the storage of a protected work in digital form in an electronic medium constitutes a reproduction within the meaning of Article 9 of the Berne Convention.

2   **Agreed statements concerning Article 3:** It is understood that in applying Article 3 of this Treaty, the expression 'country of the Union' in Articles 2 to 6 of the Berne Convention will be read as if it were a reference to a Contracting Party to this Treaty, in the application of those Berne Articles in respect of protection provided for in this Treaty. It is also understood that the expression 'country outside the Union' in those Articles in the Berne Convention will, in the same circumstances, be read as if it were a reference to a country that is not a Contracting Party to this Treaty, and that 'this Convention' in Articles 2(8), 2bis(2), 3, 4 and 5 of the Berne Convention will be read as if it were a reference to the Berne Convention and this Treaty. Finally, it is understood that a reference in Articles 3 to 6 of the Berne Convention to a 'national of one of the countries of

Article 4
Computer Programs

Computer programs are protected as literary works within the meaning of Article 2 of the Berne Convention. Such protection applies to computer programs, whatever may be the mode or form of their expression.[3]

Article 5
Compilations of Data (Databases)

Compilations of data or other material, in any form, which by reason of the selection or arrangement of their contents constitute intellectual creations, are protected as such. This protection does not extend to the data or the material itself and is without prejudice to any copyright subsisting in the data or material contained in the compilation.[4]

Article 6
Right of Distribution

(1)   Authors of literary and artistic works shall enjoy the exclusive right of authorizing the making available to the public of the original and copies of their works through sale or other transfer of ownership.

(2)   Nothing in this Treaty shall affect the freedom of Contracting Parties to determine the conditions, if any, under which the exhaustion of the right in paragraph (1) applies after the first sale or other transfer of ownership of the original or a copy of the work with the authorization of the author.[5]

Article 7
Right of Rental

(1)   Authors of

(i)   computer programs;
(ii)   cinematographic works; and
(iii)   works embodied in phonograms, as determined in the national law of Contracting Parties,

shall enjoy the exclusive right of authorizing commercial rental to the public of the originals or copies of their works.

(2)   Paragraph (1) shall not apply

---

the Union' will, when these Articles are applied to this Treaty, mean, in regard to an intergovernmental organization that is a Contracting Party to this Treaty, a national of one of the countries that is member of that organization.

3   **Agreed statements concerning Article 4:** The scope of protection for computer programs under Article 4 of this Treaty, read with Article 2, is consistent with Article 2 of the Berne Convention and on a par with the relevant provisions of the TRIPS Agreement.

4   **Agreed statements concerning Article 5:** The scope of protection for compilations of data (databases) under Article 5 of this Treaty, read with Article 2, is consistent with Article 2 of the Berne Convention and on a par with the relevant provisions of the TRIPS Agreement.

5   **Agreed statements concerning Articles 6 and 7:** As used in these Articles, the expressions 'copies' and 'original and copies,' being subject to the right of distribution and the right of rental under the said Articles, refer exclusively to fixed copies that can be put into circulation as tangible objects.

(i)   in the case of computer programs, where the program itself is not the essential object of the rental; and

(ii) in the case of cinematographic works, unless such commercial rental has led to widespread copying of such works materially impairing the exclusive right of reproduction.

(3) Notwithstanding the provisions of paragraph (1), a Contracting Party that, on April 15, 1994, had and continues to have in force a system of equitable remuneration of authors for the rental of copies of their works embodied in phonograms may maintain that system provided that the commercial rental of works embodied in phonograms is not giving rise to the material impairment of the exclusive right of reproduction of authors.[6, 7]

Article 8
Right of Communication to the Public

Without prejudice to the provisions of Articles 11(1)(ii), 11*bis*(1)(i) and (ii), 11*ter*(1)(ii), 14(1)(ii) and 14*bis*(1) of the Berne Convention, authors of literary and artistic works shall enjoy the exclusive right of authorizing any communication to the public of their works, by wire or wireless means, including the making available to the public of their works in such a way that members of the public may access these works from a place and at a time individually chosen by them.[8]

Article 9
Duration of the Protection of Photographic Works

In respect of photographic works, the Contracting Parties shall not apply the provisions of Article 7(4) of the Berne Convention.

Article 10
Limitations and Exceptions

(1) Contracting Parties may, in their national legislation, provide for limitations of or exceptions to the rights granted to authors of literary and artistic works under this Treaty in certain special cases that do not conflict with a normal exploitation of the work and do not unreasonably prejudice the legitimate interests of the author.

(2) Contracting Parties shall, when applying the Berne Convention, confine any limitations of or exceptions to rights provided for therein to certain special cases that do not conflict with a

---

6   **Agreed statements concerning Articles 6 and 7:** As used in these Articles, the expressions 'copies' and 'original and copies,' being subject to the right of distribution and the right of rental under the said Articles, refer exclusively to fixed copies that can be put into circulation as tangible objects.

7   **Agreed statements concerning Article 7:** It is understood that the obligation under Article 7(1) does not require a Contracting Party to provide an exclusive right of commercial rental to authors who, under that Contracting Party's law, are not granted rights in respect of phonograms. It is understood that this obligation is consistent with Article 14(4) of the TRIPs Agreement.

8   **Agreed statements concerning Article 8:** It is understood that the mere provision of physical facilities for enabling or making a communication does not in itself amount to communication within the meaning of this Treaty or the Berne Convention. It is further understood that nothing in Article 8 precludes a Contracting Party from applying Article 11*bis*(2).

normal exploitation of the work and do not unreasonably prejudice the legitimate interests of the author.[9]

Article 11
Obligations concerning Technological Measures

Contracting Parties shall provide adequate legal protection and effective legal remedies against the circumvention of effective technological measures that are used by authors in connection with the exercise of their rights under this Treaty or the Berne Convention and that restrict acts, in respect of their works, which are not authorized by the authors concerned or permitted by law.

Article 12
Obligations concerning Rights Management Information

(1)   Contracting Parties shall provide adequate and effective legal remedies against any person knowingly performing any of the following acts knowing, or with respect to civil remedies having reasonable grounds to know, that it will induce, enable, facilitate or conceal an infringement of any right covered by this Treaty or the Berne Convention:

  (i)   to remove or alter any electronic rights management information without authority;
  (ii) to distribute, import for distribution, broadcast or communicate to the public, without authority, works or copies of works knowing that electronic rights management information has been removed or altered without authority.

(2)   As used in this Article, 'rights management information' means information which identifies the work, the author of the work, the owner of any right in the work, or information about the terms and conditions of use of the work, and any numbers or codes that represent such information, when any of these items of information is attached to a copy of a work or appears in connection with the communication of a work to the public.[10]

Article 13
Application in Time

Contracting Parties shall apply the provisions of Article 18 of the Berne Convention to all protection provided for in this Treaty.

Article 14
Provisions on Enforcement of Rights

(1)   Contracting Parties undertake to adopt, in accordance with their legal systems, the measures necessary to ensure the application of this Treaty.

---

9   **Agreed statement concerning Article 10:** It is understood that the provisions of Article 10 permit Contracting Parties to carry forward and appropriately extend into the digital environment limitations and exceptions in their national laws which have been considered acceptable under the Berne Convention. Similarly, these provisions should be understood to permit Contracting Parties to devise new exceptions and limitations that are appropriate in the digital network environment.
   It is also understood that Article 10(2) neither reduces nor extends the scope of applicability of the limitations and exceptions permitted by the Berne Convention.

10 **Agreed statements concerning Article 12:** It is understood that the reference to 'infringement of any right covered by this Treaty or the Berne Convention' includes both exclusive rights and rights of remuneration.
   It is further understood that Contracting Parties will not rely on this Article to devise or implement rights management systems that would have the effect of imposing formalities which

(2) Contracting Parties shall ensure that enforcement procedures are available under their law so as to permit effective action against any act of infringement of rights covered by this Treaty, including expeditious remedies to prevent infringements and remedies which constitute a deterrent to further infringements.

Article 15
Assembly

(1)

   (a) The Contracting Parties shall have an Assembly.

   (b) Each Contracting Party shall be represented by one delegate who may be assisted by alternate delegates, advisors and experts.

   (c) The expenses of each delegation shall be borne by the Contracting Party that has appointed the delegation. The Assembly may ask the World Intellectual Property Organization (hereinafter referred to as 'WIPO') to grant financial assistance to facilitate the participation of delegations of Contracting Parties that are regarded as developing countries in conformity with the established practice of the General Assembly of the United Nations or that are countries in transition to a market economy.

(2)

   (a) The Assembly shall deal with matters concerning the maintenance and development of this Treaty and the application and operation of this Treaty.

   (b) The Assembly shall perform the function allocated to it under Article 17(2) in respect of the admission of certain intergovernmental organizations to become party to this Treaty.

   (c) The Assembly shall decide the convocation of any diplomatic conference for the revision of this Treaty and give the necessary instructions to the Director General of WIPO for the preparation of such diplomatic conference.

(3)

   (a) Each Contracting Party that is a State shall have one vote and shall vote only in its own name.

   (b) Any Contracting Party that is an intergovernmental organization may participate in the vote, in place of its Member States, with a number of votes equal to the number of its Member States which are party to this Treaty. No such intergovernmental organization shall participate in the vote if any one of its Member States exercises its right to vote and *vice versa*.

(4) The Assembly shall meet in ordinary session once every two years upon convocation by the Director General of WIPO.

(5) The Assembly shall establish its own rules of procedure, including the convocation of extraordinary sessions, the requirements of a quorum and, subject to the provisions of this Treaty, the required majority for various kinds of decisions.

Article 16
International Bureau

The International Bureau of WIPO shall perform the administrative tasks concerning the Treaty.

---

are not permitted under the Berne Convention or this Treaty, prohibiting the free movement of goods or impeding the enjoyment of rights under this Treaty.

Article 17
Eligibility for Becoming Party to the Treaty

(1)   Any Member State of WIPO may become party to this Treaty.

(2)   The Assembly may decide to admit any intergovernmental organization to become party to this Treaty which declares that it is competent in respect of, and has its own legislation binding on all its Member States on, matters covered by this Treaty and that it has been duly authorized, in accordance with its internal procedures, to become party to this Treaty.

(3)   The European Community, having made the declaration referred to in the preceding paragraph in the Diplomatic Conference that has adopted this Treaty, may become party to this Treaty.

Article 18
Rights and Obligations under the Treaty

Subject to any specific provisions to the contrary in this Treaty, each Contracting Party shall enjoy all of the rights and assume all of the obligations under this Treaty.

Article 19
Signature of the Treaty

This Treaty shall be open for signature until December 31, 1997, by any Member State of WIPO and by the European Community.

Article 20
Entry into Force of the Treaty

This Treaty shall enter into force three months after 30 instruments of ratification or accession by States have been deposited with the Director General of WIPO.

Article 21
Effective Date of Becoming Party to the Treaty

This Treaty shall bind

  (i)   the 30 States referred to in Article 20, from the date on which this Treaty has entered into force;
 (ii)   each other State from the expiration of three months from the date on which the State has deposited its instrument with the Director General of WIPO;
(iii)   the European Community, from the expiration of three months after the deposit of its instrument of ratification or accession if such instrument has been deposited after the entry into force of this Treaty according to Article 20, or, three months after the entry into force of this Treaty if such instrument has been deposited before the entry into force of this Treaty;
 (iv)   any other intergovernmental organization that is admitted to become party to this Treaty, from the expiration of three months after the deposit of its instrument of accession.

Article 22
No Reservations to the Treaty

No reservation to this Treaty shall be admitted.

Article 23
Denunciation of the Treaty

This Treaty may be denounced by any Contracting Party by notification addressed to the Director General of WIPO. Any denunciation shall take effect one year from the date on which the Director General of WIPO received the notification.

Article 24
Languages of the Treaty

(1)   This Treaty is signed in a single original in English, Arabic, Chinese, French, Russian and Spanish languages, the versions in all these languages being equally authentic.

(2)   An official text in any language other than those referred to in paragraph (1) shall be established by the Director General of WIPO on the request of an interested party, after consultation with all the interested parties. For the purposes of this paragraph, 'interested party' means any Member State of WIPO whose official language, or one of whose official languages, is involved and the European Community, and any other intergovernmental organization that may become party to this Treaty, if one of its official languages is involved.

Article 25
Depositary

The Director General of WIPO is the depositary of this Treaty.

Appendix 7

WIPO PERFORMANCES AND PHONOGRAMS TREATY AND AGREED STATEMENTS

CHAPTER I
GENERAL PROVISIONS

Article 1
Relation to Other Conventions

(1)   Nothing in this Treaty shall derogate from existing obligations that Contracting Parties have to each other under the International Convention for the Protection of Performers, Producers of Phonograms and Broadcasting Organizations done in Rome, October 26, 1961 (hereinafter the 'Rome Convention').

(2)   Protection granted under this Treaty shall leave intact and shall in no way affect the protection of copyright in literary and artistic works. Consequently, no provision of this Treaty may be interpreted as prejudicing such protection.[1]

(3)   This Treaty shall not have any connection with, nor shall it prejudice any rights and obligations under, any other treaties.

Article 2
Definitions

For the purposes of this Treaty:

(a)   'performers' are actors, singers, musicians, dancers, and other persons who act, sing, deliver, declaim, play in, interpret, or otherwise perform literary or artistic works or expressions of folklore;

---

1   **Agreed statement concerning Article 1(2):** It is understood that Article 1(2) clarifies the relationship between rights in phonograms under this Treaty and copyright in works embodied in the phonograms. In cases where authorization is needed from both the author of a work embodied in the phonogram and a performer or producer owning rights in the phonogram, the need for the authorization of the author does not cease to exist because the authorization of the performer or producer is also required, and vice versa.

It is further understood that nothing in Article 1(2) precludes a Contracting Party from providing exclusive rights to a performer or producer of phonograms beyond those required to be provided under this Treaty.

(b) 'phonogram' means the fixation of the sounds of a performance or of other sounds, or of a representation of sounds, other than in the form of a fixation incorporated in a cinematographic or other audiovisual work;[2]

(c) 'fixation' means the embodiment of sounds, or of the representations thereof, from which they can be perceived, reproduced or communicated through a device;

(d) 'producer of a phonogram' means the person, or the legal entity, who or which takes the initiative and has the responsibility for the first fixation of the sounds of a performance or other sounds, or the representations of sounds;

(e) 'publication' of a fixed performance or a phonogram means the offering of copies of the fixed performance or the phonogram to the public, with the consent of the rightholder, and provided that copies are offered to the public in reasonable quantity;[3]

(f) 'broadcasting' means the transmission by wireless means for public reception of sounds or of images and sounds or of the representations thereof; such transmission by satellite is also 'broadcasting'; transmission of encrypted signals is 'broadcasting' where the means for decrypting are provided to the public by the broadcasting organization or with its consent;

(g) 'communication to the public' of a performance or a phonogram means the transmission to the public by any medium, otherwise than by broadcasting, of sounds of a performance or the sounds or the representations of sounds fixed in a phonogram. For the purposes of Article 15, 'communication to the public' includes making the sounds or representations of sounds fixed in a phonogram audible to the public.

Article 3
Beneficiaries of Protection under this Treaty

(1) Contracting Parties shall accord the protection provided under this Treaty to the performers and producers of phonograms who are nationals of other Contracting Parties.

(2) The nationals of other Contracting Parties shall be understood to be those performers or producers of phonograms who would meet the criteria for eligibility for protection provided under the Rome Convention, were all the Contracting Parties to this Treaty Contracting States of that Convention. In respect of these criteria of eligibility, Contracting Parties shall apply the relevant definitions in Article 2 of this Treaty.[4]

(3) Any Contracting Party availing itself of the possibilities provided in Article 5(3) of the Rome Convention or, for the purposes of Article 5 of the same Convention, Article 17 thereof shall make a notification as foreseen in those provisions to the Director General of the World Intellectual Property Organization (WIPO).[5]

---

2   **Agreed statement concerning Article 2(b):** It is understood that the definition of phonogram provided in Article 2(b) does not suggest that rights in the phonogram are in any way affected through their incorporation into a cinematographic or other audiovisual work.

3   **Agreed statement concerning Articles 2(e), 8, 9, 12, and 13:** As used in these Articles, the expressions 'copies' and 'original and copies,' being subject to the right of distribution and the right of rental under the said Articles, refer exclusively to fixed copies that can be put into circulation as tangible objects.

4   **Agreed statement concerning Article 3(2):** For the application of Article 3(2), it is understood that fixation means the finalization of the master tape ('bande-mère').

5   **Agreed statement concerning Article 3:** It is understood that the reference in Articles 5(a) and 16(a)(iv) of the Rome Convention to 'national of another Contracting State' will, when applied to this Treaty, mean, in regard to an intergovernmental organization that is a Contracting Party to this Treaty, a national of one of the countries that is a member of that organization.

Article 4
National Treatment

(1) Each Contracting Party shall accord to nationals of other Contracting Parties, as defined in Article 3(2), the treatment it accords to its own nationals with regard to the exclusive rights specifically granted in this Treaty, and to the right to equitable remuneration provided for in Article 15 of this Treaty.

(2) The obligation provided for in paragraph (1) does not apply to the extent that another Contracting Party makes use of the reservations permitted by Article 15(3) of this Treaty.

CHAPTER II
RIGHTS OF PERFORMERS

Article 5
Moral Rights of Performers

(1) Independently of a performer's economic rights, and even after the transfer of those rights, the performer shall, as regards his live aural performances or performances fixed in phonograms, have the right to claim to be identified as the performer of his performances, except where omission is dictated by the manner of the use of the performance, and to object to any distortion, mutilation or other modification of his performances that would be prejudicial to his reputation.

(2) The rights granted to a performer in accordance with paragraph (1) shall, after his death, be maintained, at least until the expiry of the economic rights, and shall be exercisable by the persons or institutions authorized by the legislation of the Contracting Party where protection is claimed. However, those Contracting Parties whose legislation, at the moment of their ratification of or accession to this Treaty, does not provide for protection after the death of the performer of all rights set out in the preceding paragraph may provide that some of these rights will, after his death, cease to be maintained.

(3) The means of redress for safeguarding the rights granted under this Article shall be governed by the legislation of the Contracting Party where protection is claimed.

Article 6
Economic Rights of Performers in their Unfixed Performances

Performers shall enjoy the exclusive right of authorizing, as regards their performances:

(i)   the broadcasting and communication to the public of their unfixed performances except where the performance is already a broadcast performance; and

(ii) the fixation of their unfixed performances.

Article 7
Right of Reproduction

Performers shall enjoy the exclusive right of authorizing the direct or indirect reproduction of their performances fixed in phonograms, in any manner or form.[6]

Article 8
Right of Distribution

(1) Performers shall enjoy the exclusive right of authorizing the making available to the public of the original and copies of their performances fixed in phonograms through sale or other transfer of ownership.

(2) Nothing in this Treaty shall affect the freedom of Contracting Parties to determine the conditions, if any, under which the exhaustion of the right in paragraph (1) applies after the first sale or other transfer of ownership of the original or a copy of the fixed performance with the authorization of the performer.[7]

Article 9
Right of Rental

(1) Performers shall enjoy the exclusive right of authorizing the commercial rental to the public of the original and copies of their performances fixed in phonograms as determined in the national law of Contracting Parties, even after distribution of them by, or pursuant to, authorization by the performer.

(2) Notwithstanding the provisions of paragraph (1), a Contracting Party that, on April 15, 1994, had and continues to have in force a system of equitable remuneration of performers for the rental of copies of their performances fixed in phonograms, may maintain that system provided that the commercial rental of phonograms is not giving rise to the material impairment of the exclusive right of reproduction of performers.[8]

Article 10
Right of Making Available of Fixed Performances

Performers shall enjoy the exclusive right of authorizing the making available to the public of their performances fixed in phonograms, by wire or wireless means, in such a way that members of the public may access them from a place and at a time individually chosen by them.

---

6   **Agreed statement concerning Articles 7, 11 and 16:** The reproduction right, as set out in Articles 7 and 11, and the exceptions permitted thereunder through Article 16, fully apply in the digital environment, in particular to the use of performances and phonograms in digital form. It is understood that the storage of a protected performance or phonogram in digital form in an electronic medium constitutes a reproduction within the meaning of these Articles.

7   **Agreed statement concerning Articles 2(e), 8, 9, 12, and 13:** As used in these Articles, the expressions 'copies' and 'original and copies,' being subject to the right of distribution and the right of rental under the said Articles, refer exclusively to fixed copies that can be put into circulation as tangible objects.

8   **Agreed statement concerning Articles 2(e), 8, 9, 12, and 13:** As used in these Articles, the expressions 'copies' and 'original and copies,' being subject to the right of distribution and the

CHAPTER III
RIGHTS OF PRODUCERS OF PHONOGRAMS

Article 11
Right of Reproduction

Producers of phonograms shall enjoy the exclusive right of authorizing the direct or indirect reproduction of their phonograms, in any manner or form.[9]

Article 12
Right of Distribution

(1) Producers of phonograms shall enjoy the exclusive right of authorizing the making available to the public of the original and copies of their phonograms through sale or other transfer of ownership.

(2) Nothing in this Treaty shall affect the freedom of Contracting Parties to determine the conditions, if any, under which the exhaustion of the right in paragraph (1) applies after the first sale or other transfer of ownership of the original or a copy of the phonogram with the authorization of the producer of the phonogram.[10]

Article 13
Right of Rental

(1) Producers of phonograms shall enjoy the exclusive right of authorizing the commercial rental to the public of the original and copies of their phonograms, even after distribution of them by or pursuant to authorization by the producer.

(2) Notwithstanding the provisions of paragraph (1), a Contracting Party that, on April 15, 1994, had and continues to have in force a system of equitable remuneration of producers of phonograms for the rental of copies of their phonograms, may maintain that system provided that the commercial rental of phonograms is not giving rise to the material impairment of the exclusive right of reproduction of producers of phonograms.[11]

---

right of rental under the said Articles, refer exclusively to fixed copies that can be put into circulation as tangible objects.

9   **Agreed statement concerning Articles 7, 11 and 16:** The reproduction right, as set out in Articles 7 and 11, and the exceptions permitted thereunder through Article 16, fully apply in the digital environment, in particular to the use of performances and phonograms in digital form. It is understood that the storage of a protected performance or phonogram in digital form in an electronic medium constitutes a reproduction within the meaning of these Articles.

10   **Agreed statement concerning Articles 2(e), 8, 9, 12, and 13:** As used in these Articles, the expressions 'copies' and 'original and copies,' being subject to the right of distribution and the right of rental under the said Articles, refer exclusively to fixed copies that can be put into circulation as tangible objects.

11   **Agreed statement concerning Articles 2(e), 8, 9, 12, and 13:** As used in these Articles, the expressions 'copies' and 'original and copies,' being subject to the right of distribution and the right of rental under the said Articles, refer exclusively to fixed copies that can be put into circulation as tangible objects.

Article 14
Right of Making Available of Phonograms

Producers of phonograms shall enjoy the exclusive right of authorizing the making available to the public of their phonograms, by wire or wireless means, in such a way that members of the public may access them from a place and at a time individually chosen by them.

CHAPTER IV
COMMON PROVISIONS

Article 15
Right to Remuneration for Broadcasting and Communication to the Public

(1)   Performers and producers of phonograms shall enjoy the right to a single equitable remuneration for the direct or indirect use of phonograms published for commercial purposes for broadcasting or for any communication to the public.

(2)   Contracting Parties may establish in their national legislation that the single equitable remuneration shall be claimed from the user by the performer or by the producer of a phonogram or by both. Contracting Parties may enact national legislation that, in the absence of an agreement between the performer and the producer of a phonogram, sets the terms according to which performers and producers of phonograms shall share the single equitable remuneration.

(3)   Any Contracting Party may in a notification deposited with the Director General of WIPO, declare that it will apply the provisions of paragraph (1) only in respect of certain uses, or that it will limit their application in some other way, or that it will not apply these provisions at all.

(4)   For the purposes of this Article, phonograms made available to the public by wire or wireless means in such a way that members of the public may access them from a place and at a time individually chosen by them shall be considered as if they had been published for commercial purposes.[12, 13]

Article 16
Limitations and Exceptions

(1)   Contracting Parties may, in their national legislation, provide for the same kinds of limitations or exceptions with regard to the protection of performers and producers of phonograms as they provide for, in their national legislation, in connection with the protection of copyright in literary and artistic works.

---

12   **Agreed statement concerning Article 15:** It is understood that Article 15 does not represent a complete resolution of the level of rights of broadcasting and communication to the public that should be enjoyed by performers and phonogram producers in the digital age. Delegations were unable to achieve consensus on differing proposals for aspects of exclusivity to be provided in certain circumstances or for rights to be provided without the possibility of reservations, and have therefore left the issue to future resolution.

13   **Agreed statement concerning Article 15:** It is understood that Article 15 does not prevent the granting of the right conferred by this Article to performers of folklore and producers of phonograms recording folklore where such phonograms have not been published for commercial gain.

(2) Contracting Parties shall confine any limitations of or exceptions to rights provided for in this Treaty to certain special cases which do not conflict with a normal exploitation of the performance or phonogram and do not unreasonably prejudice the legitimate interests of the performer or of the producer of the phonogram.[14, 15]

Article 17
Term of Protection

(1) The term of protection to be granted to performers under this Treaty shall last, at least, until the end of a period of 50 years computed from the end of the year in which the performance was fixed in a phonogram.

(2) The term of protection to be granted to producers of phonograms under this Treaty shall last, at least, until the end of a period of 50 years computed from the end of the year in which the phonogram was published, or failing such publication within 50 years from fixation of the phonogram, 50 years from the end of the year in which the fixation was made.

Article 18
Obligations concerning Technological Measures

Contracting Parties shall provide adequate legal protection and effective legal remedies against the circumvention of effective technological measures that are used by performers or producers of phonograms in connection with the exercise of their rights under this Treaty and that restrict acts, in respect of their performances or phonograms, which are not authorized by the performers or the producers of phonograms concerned or permitted by law.

Article 19
Obligations concerning Rights Management Information

(1) Contracting Parties shall provide adequate and effective legal remedies against any person knowingly performing any of the following acts knowing, or with respect to civil remedies having reasonable grounds to know, that it will induce, enable, facilitate or conceal an infringement of any right covered by this Treaty:

---

14 **Agreed statement concerning Articles 7, 11 and 16:** The reproduction right, as set out in Articles 7 and 11, and the exceptions permitted thereunder through Article 16, fully apply in the digital environment, in particular to the use of performances and phonograms in digital form. It is understood that the storage of a protected performance or phonogram in digital form in an electronic medium constitutes a reproduction within the meaning of these Articles.

15 **Agreed statement concerning Article 16:** The agreed statement concerning Article 10 (on Limitations and Exceptions) of the WIPO Copyright Treaty is applicable *mutatis mutandis* also to Article 16 (on Limitations and Exceptions) of the WIPO Performances and Phonograms Treaty. [The text of the agreed statement concerning Article 10 of the WCT reads as follows: 'It is understood that the provisions of Article 10 permit Contracting Parties to carry forward and appropriately extend into the digital environment limitations and exceptions in their national laws which have been considered acceptable under the Berne Convention. Similarly, these provisions should be understood to permit Contracting Parties to devise new exceptions and limitations that are appropriate in the digital network environment.

'It is also understood that Article 10(2) neither reduces nor extends the scope of applicability of the limitations and exceptions permitted by the Berne Convention.']

(i)   to remove or alter any electronic rights management information without authority;

(ii) to distribute, import for distribution, broadcast, communicate or make available to the public, without authority, performances, copies of fixed performances or phonograms knowing that electronic rights management information has been removed or altered without authority.

(2)   As used in this Article, 'rights management information' means information which identifies the performer, the performance of the performer, the producer of the phonogram, the phonogram, the owner of any right in the performance or phonogram, or information about the terms and conditions of use of the performance or phonogram, and any numbers or codes that represent such information, when any of these items of information is attached to a copy of a fixed performance or a phonogram or appears in connection with the communication or making available of a fixed performance or a phonogram to the public.[16]

Article 20
Formalities

The enjoyment and exercise of the rights provided for in this Treaty shall not be subject to any formality.

Article 21
Reservations

Subject to the provisions of Article 15(3), no reservations to this Treaty shall be permitted.

Article 22
Application in Time

(1)   Contracting Parties shall apply the provisions of Article 18 of the Berne Convention, *mutatis mutandis*, to the rights of performers and producers of phonograms provided for in this Treaty.

(2)   Notwithstanding paragraph (1), a Contracting Party may limit the application of Article 5 of this Treaty to performances which occurred after the entry into force of this Treaty for that Party.

Article 23
Provisions on Enforcement of Rights

(1)   Contracting Parties undertake to adopt, in accordance with their legal systems, the measures necessary to ensure the application of this Treaty.

---

16 **Agreed statement concerning Article 19:** The agreed statement concerning Article 12 (on Obligations concerning Rights Management Information) of the WIPO Copyright Treaty is applicable *mutatis mutandis* also to Article 19 (on Obligations concerning Rights Management Information) of the WIPO Performances and Phonograms Treaty. [The text of the agreed statement concerning Article 12 of the WCT reads as follows: 'It is understood that the reference to 'infringement of any right covered by this Treaty or the Berne Convention' includes both exclusive rights and rights of remuneration.

(2)   Contracting Parties shall ensure that enforcement procedures are available under their law so as to permit effective action against any act of infringement of rights covered by this Treaty, including expeditious remedies to prevent infringements and remedies which constitute a deterrent to further infringements.

CHAPTER V
ADMINISTRATIVE AND FINAL CLAUSES

Article 24
Assembly

(1)

   (a)   The Contracting Parties shall have an Assembly.

   (b)   Each Contracting Party shall be represented by one delegate who may be assisted by alternate delegates, advisors and experts.

   (c)   The expenses of each delegation shall be borne by the Contracting Party that has appointed the delegation. The Assembly may ask WIPO to grant financial assistance to facilitate the participation of delegations of Contracting Parties that are regarded as developing countries in conformity with the established practice of the General Assembly of the United Nations or that are countries in transition to a market economy.

(2)

   (a)   The Assembly shall deal with matters concerning the maintenance and development of this Treaty and the application and operation of this Treaty.

   (b)   The Assembly shall perform the function allocated to it under Article 26(2) in respect of the admission of certain intergovernmental organizations to become party to this Treaty.

   (c)   The Assembly shall decide the convocation of any diplomatic conference for the revision of this Treaty and give the necessary instructions to the Director General of WIPO for the preparation of such diplomatic conference.

(3)

   (a)   Each Contracting Party that is a State shall have one vote and shall vote only in its own name.

   (b)   Any Contracting Party that is an intergovernmental organization may participate in the vote, in place of its Member States, with a number of votes equal to the number of its Member States which are party to this Treaty. No such intergovernmental organization shall participate in the vote if any one of its Member States exercises its right to vote and vice versa.

(4)   The Assembly shall meet in ordinary session once every two years upon convocation by the Director General of WIPO.

(5)   The Assembly shall establish its own rules of procedure, including the convocation of extraordinary sessions, the requirements of a quorum and, subject to the provisions of this Treaty, the required majority for various kinds of decisions.

'It is further understood that Contracting Parties will not rely on this Article to devise or implement rights management systems that would have the effect of imposing formalities which are not permitted under the Berne Convention or this Treaty, prohibiting the free movement of goods or impending the enjoyment of rights under this Treaty.']

Article 25
International Bureau

The International Bureau of WIPO shall perform the administrative tasks concerning the Treaty.

Article 26
Eligibility for Becoming Party to the Treaty

(1)   Any Member State of WIPO may become party to this Treaty.

(2)   The Assembly may decide to admit any intergovernmental organization to become party to this Treaty which declares that it is competent in respect of, and has its own legislation binding on all its Member States on, matters covered by this Treaty and that it has been duly authorized, in accordance with its internal procedures, to become party to this Treaty.

(3)   The European Community, having made the declaration referred to in the preceding paragraph in the Diplomatic Conference that has adopted this Treaty, may become party to this Treaty.

Article 27
Rights and Obligations under the Treaty

Subject to any specific provisions to the contrary in this Treaty, each Contracting Party shall enjoy all of the rights and assume all of the obligations under this Treaty.

Article 28
Signature of the Treaty

This Treaty shall be open for signature until December 31, 1997, by any Member State of WIPO and by the European Community.

Article 29
Entry into Force of the Treaty

This Treaty shall enter into force three months after 30 instruments of ratification or accession by States have been deposited with the Director General of WIPO.

Article 30
Effective Date of Becoming Party to the Treaty

This Treaty shall bind

   (i)   the 30 States referred to in Article 29, from the date on which this Treaty has entered into force;
   (ii) each other State from the expiration of three months from the date on which the State has deposited its instrument with the Director General of WIPO;

(iii) the European Community, from the expiration of three months after the deposit of its instrument of ratification or accession if such instrument has been deposited after the entry into force of this Treaty according to Article 29, or, three months after the entry into force of this Treaty if such instrument has been deposited before the entry into force of this Treaty;

(iv) any other intergovernmental organization that is admitted to become party to this Treaty, from the expiration of three months after the deposit of its instrument of accession.

Article 31
Denunciation of the Treaty

This Treaty may be denounced by any Contracting Party by notification addressed to the Director General of WIPO. Any denunciation shall take effect one year from the date on which the Director General of WIPO received the notification.

Article 32
Languages of the Treaty

(1)   This Treaty is signed in a single original in English, Arabic, Chinese, French, Russian and Spanish languages, the versions in all these languages being equally authentic.

(2)   An official text in any language other than those referred to in paragraph (1) shall be established by the Director General of WIPO on the request of an interested party, after consultation with all the interested parties. For the purposes of this paragraph, 'interested party' means any Member State of WIPO whose official language, or one of whose official languages, is involved and the European Community, and any other intergovernmental organization that may become party to this Treaty, if one of its official languages is involved.

Article 33
Depositary

The Director General of WIPO is the depositary of this Treaty.

Appendix 8

E-COMMERCE DIRECTIVE, Arts 12–15

(12) It is necessary to exclude certain activities from the scope of this Directive, on the grounds that the freedom to provide services in these fields cannot, at this stage, be guaranteed under the Treaty or existing secondary legislation; excluding these activities does not preclude any instruments which might prove necessary for the proper functioning of the internal market; taxation, particularly value added tax imposed on a large number of the services covered by this Directive, must be excluded from the scope of this Directive.

(13) This Directive does not aim to establish rules on fiscal obligations nor does it pre-empt the drawing up of Community instruments concerning fiscal aspects of electronic commerce.

(14) The protection of individuals with regard to the processing of personal data is solely governed by Directive 95/46/EC of the European Parliament and of the Council of 24 October 1995 on the protection of individuals with regard to the processing of personal data and on the free movement of such data[1] and Directive 97/66/EC of the European Parliament and of the Council of 15 December 1997 concerning the processing of personal data and the protection of privacy in the telecommunications sector[2] which are fully applicable to information society services; these Directives already establish a Community legal framework in the field of personal data and therefore it is not necessary to cover this issue in this Directive in order to ensure the smooth functioning of the internal market, in particular the free movement of personal data between Member States; the implementation and application of this Directive should be made in full compliance with the principles relating to the protection of personal data, in particular as regards unsolicited commercial communication and the liability of inter- mediaries; this Directive cannot prevent the anonymous use of open networks such as the Internet.

(15) The confidentiality of communications is guaranteed by Article 5 Directive 97/66/EC; in accordance with that Directive, Member States must prohibit any kind of interception or surveillance of such communications by others than the senders and receivers, except when legally authorised.

---

1   OJ L 281, 23.11.1995, p 31.

2   OJ L 24, 30.1.1998, p 1.

INDEX

References are to paragraph numbers.